Lessons from Fort Apache

Lessons from Fort Apache

Beyond Language Endangerment and Maintenance

New Edition

M. Eleanor Nevins

With a new foreword by the author,
Cline Griggs, and Mona Eleando

University of Nebraska Press
Lincoln

© 2013 by John Wiley & Sons, Inc.
Foreword © 2023 by the Board of Regents of the University of Nebraska

Acknowledgments for the use of copyrighted material appear on pages xiii–xv, which constitute an extension of the copyright page.

All rights reserved

The University of Nebraska Press is part of a land-grant institution with campuses and programs on the past, present, and future homelands of the Pawnee, Ponca, Otoe-Missouria, Omaha, Dakota, Lakota, Kaw, Cheyenne, and Arapaho Peoples, as well as those of the relocated Ho-Chunk, Sac and Fox, and Iowa Peoples.

First Nebraska paperback printing: 2023

Library of Congress Control Number: 2023946164

Cover image: *Four Directions, Land, Stars, White Mountains, Arizona* (Dustinn Craig, 2012).

The Americanist tradition, having begun as the study of languages of a fading past and far west, will find fruition as the study of the language of citizens.

Dell H. Hymes (1983, *Essays in the History of Linguistic Anthropology*. Amsterdam: John Benjamins, p. 121)

Dustinn Craig (White Mountain Apache) designed the cover art for this book. He grew up in White River on the Fort Apache reservation. He now lives in Mesa, Arizona, where he and his wife, writer Velma Kee Craig, are codirectors of the film and media design company White Springs Creative, LLC. He provides the following statement to help explain the meaning of the elements incorporated into the cover:

In this cover, the four crosses represent the four directions, but in my interpretation of them and the various philosophies behind them, they represent balance, harmony and clarity of thought, the foundation for developing language to convey thought, feeling, intellect. The stars represent the vastness of the universe, and also demonstrate the indigenous awareness of the magnitude of "creation." This awareness of how small we are instills in us humility and gratitude for the language that conveys and communicates our life way and historical experience. The trees are incorporated to emphasize being rooted into the land, being part of the landscape, not separate from it. In the same way we are just part of the vast universe, so how could we as tiny beings ever proclaim that we know what comes next, or the mind or minds of creation?

Contents

Foreword by M. Eleanor Nevins, Cline Griggs, and Mona Eleando		ix
Acknowledgments		xiii
1.	Introduction	1
2.	Indigenous Languages and the Mediation of Communities	12
3.	Learning to Listen: Coming to Terms with Conflicting Meanings of Language Loss	47
4.	They Live in Lonesome Dove: English in Indigenous Places	79
5.	Stories in the Moment of Encounter: Documentation Boundary Work	113
6.	What No Coyote Story Means: The Borderland Genre of Traditional Storytelling	152
7.	"Some 'No No' and Some 'Yes'": Silence, Agency, and Traditionalist Words	186
8.	Sustainability: Possible Socialities of Documentation and Maintenance	215
Appendix A:	Lawrence Mithlo	229
Appendix B:	Eva Lupe on Her Early Life	237
Index		250

Foreword

The Lessons Continue

M. Eleanor Nevins, Cline Griggs, and Mona Eleando

This foreword has three authors: two are members of the White Mountain Apache Tribe, and one is a linguistic anthropologist who can now be described as "ndaa' sáan" (white elder woman). Cline Griggs is a former tribal councilman, former school board member at the Theodore Roosevelt Boarding School at Fort Apache, and current director of the Family Enrichment Program at Rainbow Treatment Center. Mona Lisa Eleando teaches Apache language and culture at Seven Mile Elementary School in Eastfork and coordinates Apache language and culture classes across an additional three schools. Marybeth Eleanor Nevins is a linguistic anthropologist who has variously lived and worked with members of the White Mountain Apache Tribe since 1996. We are grateful to acquisitions editor Matt Bokovoy at the University of Nebraska Press for taking an interest in this book and for making it available as an affordable paperback. We hope that the book will now reach more readers, including members of Apache and other indigenous language communities.

The material in this book is based upon a long-standing practice in linguistic anthropology of studying everyday speech in particular communities. The researcher typically lives for an extended period of time with a family that has agreed to host her. From there, she participates in any aspect of their lives where she is permitted. Eva Lupe was Marybeth's primary host. This book includes everyday speech in the homes of her extended family. It also includes speech from workplaces, classrooms, churches, ceremonies, political gatherings, and more.

Most important for this reprint, another long-standing practice in the linguistic anthropology of Native North America is the maintenance of relationships between researchers and host families over the lifespan of both. Among Apache, life is defined according to four stages: birth, youth, maturity, and old age. In the 1990s when Marybeth Nevins conducted the most intensive part of the study for this book, she had the status of a youth. In fact, she was often referred to as "ndaa' it'een" (white girl). The author had the advantage of working closely with the wife of a former tribal chairman and with the wife of a then-chairman, each of whom held the status of "sáan" (elder woman).

From them she learned how to make bread and grind corn and acorns. She regularly helped prepare meals in homes of their extended families. She ate with their families, shared daily jokes and stories, helped with their Sunrise Ceremonies, and waited with them in hospital corridors for the births of grandchildren. She relied on the strength of their support over three years of working for the tribe, especially when she found herself in political trouble during an election season (see chapters 2 and 3).

This pattern, in which the most intensive research period in an ethnographer's life occurs when the researcher is a youth and her primary relations are to elders, has been common in anthropology. It is also morally consequential. While the university understands the student to be researching or studying the community in question, that same relation is most often described by elder members of host families as one of teaching. Teaching is a morally appropriate role for an elder to assume with respect to a young person (see Eva Lupe's speech in the appendix and in chapter 5). Our teaching and learning relationship is what we emphasize in the title of this book, *Lessons from Fort Apache*. For all young people, some of what elders teach them is understood and applied directly in the near term. However, some remains to be understood later. The author of the main text, no longer a youth, having matured to the status of ndaa' sáan, apologizes for ndaa' it'een's mistakes, including her overreliance on academic jargon.

From its first chapter, this book defines an interesting kind of trouble often shared by Apache language researchers and Apache language programs in schools. The trouble comes from the fact that both research and school lesson plans bring together different ways of knowing and caring about Apache language. One way to boil it down is to identify the difference between a bureaucratic approach and an understanding rooted in experiences of self, family, community, land, and beyond. The bureaucratic approach abstracts language from other parts of life, such as culture and environment. This can result in disharmony when it leads people to act as if such things really are separate. By contrast, when participating in family and community activities, language is not set aside in one corner, culture in another, and environment in yet another. Instead, these are all one. From this standpoint, isolating Apache language in a research paper, a book, school curricula, or an app has advantages, but it can also raise problems. When a bit of Apache language, like a song, is brought into a research project or school lesson plan, this brings in more than just the words that are included. Any bit of Apache language brings with it everything that goes with those words. A song can bring a ceremony. A story can bring a family history of tellers and listeners. There is an old saying among Apache people that language is alive. It has its own being. To an Apache person, Apache language is their language. It is an inalienable part of the universe of being.

It should not be isolated and placed in its own category. Because language is alive, it follows that one cannot just take something that is alive, bottle it, sell it, and put it on the shelf for the next year. For school language programs and language research, not to mention any commercial ventures to create Apache language apps and teaching materials, this is a concern that requires sustained dialogue to adequately address. Cooperation and conflicts described in the first two chapters are best understood as components of a long-term dialogue that continues to this day.

Another theme that runs throughout the book is the idea that Apache communities and the notion of Apache language are complexly mediated. This is because the notion of being Apache and knowing or caring about Apache language as such comes into awareness at the intersection of Apache communities and other communities and institutions in the surrounding society. The ways that Apache language may be discussed, researched, and institutionalized are full of paradoxes. A paradox is something that appears to be contradicting itself but is in fact founded upon those apparently contradictory aspects. Often paradoxes are formed in boundary zones between communities. Marybeth offers the example of herself as "ndaa'" (outsider) but also as a member of the late Eva Lupe's family at the same time. It was through this and other paradoxes that the work for this book was done.

Expanding on this idea from the other side of community and documentary research relations, Cline Griggs shared a story from his years as a tribal councilmember. The story is about how an opportunity provided by NAGPRA to repatriate Apache ancestral remains held at the Chicago Field Museum was answered in a remarkable way by Apache leadership across the federally recognized tribes. They formed a coalition among White Mountain Apache, San Carlos Apache, Yavapai Apache, and Tonto Apache tribes around a common strategy centered on the ethnolinguistic term "Western Apache." Together they devised a successful bid to assert their own leadership and cultural authority according to a deliberative process of their own design.

Leadership from these different Arizona Apache tribes anticipated that museums might use the diversity of possible claimants and discrepancies between ethnolinguistic identifiers in documentary collections and self-designations of Apache tribes to slow down repatriation. They were concerned that this had the potential to pit Apache tribes against one another—leaving museum leadership to reserve adjudication to themselves. Anticipating this challenge, the Arizona Apache tribes agreed to present a united front in their dealings with the museum. Tonto, San Carlos, Yavapai Apache, and White Mountain—all of them agreed to travel together to Chicago and together claim all remains that were identified as Western Apache. The coalition was successful, and once they brought the remains back within Apache lands, they worked together to determine where the remains came from so as to return them to their appropriate homes. Cline Griggs ended the story with the idea that if Apache people formed coalitions in response to opportunities for language restoration, they might come to a better understanding of the importance of preserving language and better ways of working together to do it. This possibility speaks directly to the problem of political sustainability of language documentation and maintenance defined in the final chapter of the book. In fact, it represents an explicitly deliberative political model of language maintenance built upon indigenous sovereignty and empowerment.

This book is designed for a range of audiences who may have many different reasons to read it. It presents a case study in the politics of language maintenance among White Mountain Apache people. However, it is also an ethnography of speaking that demonstrates linguistic and cultural creativity across domains of everyday life in Apache homes, churches, ceremonial grounds, radio programs, street signs, government offices, workplaces, and schools. It is an account of a politically dynamic community in which an indigenous language, Apache, is important to most everyone, including non-speakers. If you are a linguistic anthropologist, a teacher, a linguist, or a student of religion, or if you are interested in verbal play or indigenous and colonial history, you will find much interest in this book. If you simply want to learn more about Apache language, you will also find certain things that you can use. Just as the people described in this book have different ways of thinking and caring about Apache language, we expect the book's readers to bring new and different reasons still, and for the lessons to continue.

Acknowledgments

Funding for the research upon which this book is based was provided by grants from the Wenner Gren Foundation, the Phillips Fund of the American Philosophical Society, the Jacobs Research Fund of the Whatcom Museum, and two University of Virginia pre-field grants, as well as scholarly and creative activity grants and summer stipends from the College of Liberal Arts at the University of Nevada Reno. I am grateful to these organizations for their support.

This book would not have been possible without the generosity, care, and guidance of Eva Lupe. I owe a great debt of thanks to her and to members of her extended family, especially Vera Lupe, Leo Cruz, Annette Tenejieth, Gary Lupe, Everett Lupe, Arlene Natan, and Valerie Lupe. I also thank Paul Ethelbah and Genevieve Ethelbah, Genevie Chinche, Cline Griggs, Ramon Riley, Dustinn Craig, and many others who helped along the way, some of whom prefer to remain anonymous. Thanks also to Charles R. Kaut, whose more than fifty-year association with Nelson Lupe and with the communities of East Fork and Whiteriver helped make it plausible that admitting two "kids from Virginia" might be worth the risk. I am grateful for lessons learned from Nelson Lupe, Jerry Lupe, Carmen Lupe, and Rebekah Lupe: it is my intention to honor their memories here.

In the body of the monograph all names have been changed in order to protect the privacy of those who worked with me. My goal has been to portray the kinds of innovation at play at Fort Apache and to suggest parallels in other indigenous communities. There are many instances when the words of people who worked with me, and of the Apache interlocutors of prior researchers, are represented in this monograph. The former were parts of dialogues, recorded performances, and exchanges over the course of three years. My status as a researcher was part of the framing of these exchanges for all involved, and included the anticipation that publications on the model of those in circulation from Keith Basso's work would be the likely result. Most of the quotes from consultants were tape recorded in open-ended interview or storytelling sessions. Some were from untaped conversations that I have rendered from memory and doublechecked for accuracy and for permission to use with the persons involved. The status of ethnographic relations is ongoing and reciprocal. I take responsibility for having been given these words for use in this work of scholarship by my consultants, and I note that their receipt entails further obligations to maintain good faith relations with those consultants and their words. I also make use of speeches and stories given by Lawrence Mithlo to Harry Hoijer in Hoijer's 1938 text collection, *Chiricahua and Mescalero Apache with Ethnological Notes by Morris Opler* (Chicago: University of Chicago Publications in Anthropology, Linguistic Series). I thank the University of Chicago Press for permission to reprint extended excerpts of those texts and their translations in this work.

The chapters of this book were developed over more than ten years and have benefited from the critical contributions of many people. Of these it is Tom Nevins, my colleague and spouse, whose creative influence, shared experience, and support pervade every chapter, and without whose sacrifice of time and attention this book would never have been written. I also express here my enduring gratitude to Dell Hymes for his encouragement and critical engagement with this project from its very beginnings. The example he set in living and the wake he left in passing continue to channel and embolden my efforts. I owe debts of gratitude to Dick Bauman, Paul Kroskrity, and James Collins for having, at different junctures, provided needed encouragement, criticism, and theoretical tools, and filled gaps in my knowledge of disciplinary history. I warmly thank Jim Wilce for his editorial and practical acumen in moving this book project along and for inviting me to Northern Arizona University to air some of my arguments in front of an audience whose work and experience directly intertwined with my subject matter! Thanks also to the editorial board of the Wiley-Blackwell Discourse and Culture Series for their helpful critical responses to the book proposal and chapter samples. And I am especially grateful to two anonymous reviewers for reading the full manuscript and providing thorough assessments of the whole and its parts. Where I was able to incorporate suggested changes they have improved the manuscript. There were some suggested expansions that would have been well worth addressing, but which time and space constraints compel me to defer to future work.

I have benefited from engagement with a lively cohort of Southern Athabaskanists: Tony Webster, David Samuels, Margaret Field, Willem de Reuse, and Phillip Greenfeld. Many of the ethnographic and textual materials presented here took presentable form as they bounced out of dialogues with and among these colleagues, or were developed in conference sessions organized by them.

Individual chapters of this book benefit from critical readings given to them by Ilana Gershon, Paul Manning, Magnus Course, Matthew Engelke, Eve Danziger, Ellen Contini-Morava, Bonnie Urciuoli, Erin Stiles, and Sarah Cowie. Special thanks are due to Ilana Gershon, whose suggestions for a radical restructure of the second chapter prompted me to write something much better than what I started with, and had a happy spill-over effect on the book as a whole.

Thanks are also due to Debra Harry and Leonie Pihama for answering my questions concerning decolonization in research relations as this is being discussed among indigenous scholars and activists in global forums like the United Nations and in university indigenous studies programs in the Pacific.

I single out for salutation Nick Thieberger, Brook Lillehaugen, and Lise Dobrin, all of whom helped me to better understand how my arguments were likely to be received by documentary linguists and challenged me to refine and improve my presentation. Broadcasting an argument across disciplinary audiences is the most challenging aspect of this book, and I benefited immensely from our discussions. The "Phantom Linguist" cartoon in Chapter 5 is taken from Nick Thieberger's field linguistics course materials and reproduced here with his permission.

Dustinn Craig designed the book cover. He was my coworker fourteen years ago at Ndee Benadesh, when he was a high school student already making films and cartoons for youth media projects and I was a graduate student working on language materials. He is now an accomplished professional filmmaker, educator, and graphic artist. It is a real pleasure to find myself in a new relation to him, years later, both of us "grown up" now in our respective fields.

The author and publisher gratefully acknowledge the permission granted to reproduce the copyright material in this book:

Chapter 3 is a revised and expanded version of an article: Nevins, M. Eleanor. 2004. Learning to Listen: Coming to Terms with Conflicting Discourses of "Language Loss" among the White Mountain Apache Speech Community. *Journal of Linguistic Anthropology* 14(2):269–288. With permission to republish from the *Journal of Linguistic Anthropology*.

Chapter 4 is a revised and updated version of an article originally published as Nevins, M. Eleanor. 2008. "They Live in Lonesome Dove": Media and Contemporary Western Apache Place-naming Practices. *Language in Society* 37(2):191–215. Cambridge University Press.

1

Introduction

Every language reflects a unique world-view with its own value systems, philosophy and particular cultural features. The extinction of a language results in the irrecoverable loss of unique cultural knowledge embodied in it for centuries . . . (UNESCO 2011)

Native identities are traces, the *différance* of an unnameable presence, not mere statutes, inheritance, or documentation, however bright the blood and bone in the museums. (Vizenor 1998:35)

I begin with a consideration of the meanings attributed to indigenous languages and cultures by differently placed actors. For example, both quotes that appear as epigraphs for this introduction express affiliation with indigenous peoples, and both imply opposition to forces that would disempower them. Yet the two statements, one from UNESCO and the other from a prominent Anishinaabe author and literary critic, sit uncomfortably next to one another. The first is typical of funded documentation and maintenance projects and presents indigenous languages in relation to concepts like "worldview," "value system," "philosophy," and "cultural knowledge," all of which suggest broad commensurability with mainstream institutions. The quote reflects use of "endangerment" as a resource mobilization tactic for research and education program funding, and for influencing language policies. This is coupled implicitly with the notion of "language rights," which casts indigenous languages within a logic of multicultural inclusion, or fair representation, within participatory democracies. It also places indigenous languages, and by implication all attendant institutions of indigenous knowledge and cultural property, at the brink of extinction and requiring technocratic forms of intervention if they are to be saved.

Lessons from Fort Apache: Beyond Language Endangerment and Maintenance, First Edition. M. Eleanor Nevins.
© 2013 John Wiley & Sons, Inc. Published 2013 by John Wiley & Sons, Inc.

The second quote takes a different tack. Vizenor casts doubt upon mainstream terms of recognition: "not mere statutes, inheritance, or documentation," and locates Native voices elsewhere, in an "unnameable presence," or in "traces" that require radical acts of reinterpretation in order to be perceived. Importantly for problems of indigenous language advocacy, the two conflict in the role each attributes to documentation, and in the possibilities and limitations for recognition of indigenous voices therein. In the chapters that follow I present an ethnographic account of contrasts and conflicts in claims to Apache language among residents of the Fort Apache reservation in Arizona that reflect this kind of divide. Doing so reveals some of the covert politics of language documentation and maintenance, and provides a basis for bringing additional considerations into efforts to support indigenous languages and communities.

The past twenty years has seen copious scholarship devoted to language endangerment and maintenance: conferences, articles, edited volumes, books on documenting languages and developing language education materials, along with a few ethnographies of language shift and/or maintenance. A portion of this literature also addresses terms of collaboration between scholars of indigenous languages and community members. However, much of this is framed too narrowly, to the question of "how to make language revitalization work," rather than to larger questions of processes of social mediation entailed by language programs, and the often ambivalent uptake of programs within the communities they purport to serve. Many scholars and activists treat community ambivalence as if it can be attributed to an anti-heritage language camp whose members want to assimilate to mainstream norms and shift away from their heritage languages, pitched against a pro-heritage language camp whose members want to hold to tradition and accentuate ways the community is different from the surrounding society. With this book I open up another dimension of the problem: that heritage language programs, utilizing ideologies and textual models from the dominant society, assert notions of language, and authorize ways of knowing language, that compete with other forms of authority and other language practices in many indigenous communities. Therefore, in addition to "language documentation" ethnographic attention to social relations of speaking would be usefully added to efforts to engage with communities on language issues that concern them.

As the title suggests, the book tacks between a firsthand ethnographic account of language dynamics on the Fort Apache reservation, comparable work by other linguistic anthropologists in other indigenous communities, and broader questions about language maintenance as a site of engagement between indigenous communities and the sociopolitical orders that encompass them. While one point of the book is certainly to throw into relief ways in which language maintenance programs extend the discourses and institutions of encompassing polities, I also want to complicate any account that would reduce language programs to "internal colonialism." Rather, my purpose is to situate language maintenance efforts more accurately within the ongoing dialectics of which they are a part. I demonstrate that many of the empowering effects of indigenous language programs can occur outside the purview of the programs themselves. A signature quality of many, I might add, is that they are rarely described by anyone as truly accomplishing what they set out to do – so as ostensible instruments of power they are full of gaps and interpretive openings. Most importantly, by recontextualizing local speech as cultural heritage, language documentation and maintenance programs cast local languages as carriers of value and as key terms of recognition in national and global arenas. In turn, members of local leadership recontextualize the products of documentation that come to represent a "heritage language" in culture centers and schools to their own dynamic purposes, retaining traces of national and international significance but subsuming these to ongoing local practices and concerns.

Ultimately, what I hope this book contributes is a precedent and a set of interpretive tools that facilitate recognition of differences in orientation between the ostensibly cooperative, but sometimes clashing, parties to "saving" a language. The ethnographic accounts I present should be viewed with this in mind. They represent my best efforts to engage with residents of the Fort Apache reservation on language issues that concerned them. They bear all the partiality of my conditions of access and theoretical orientation. I do not claim to present in any comprehensive way a portrait of Apache language shift (cf. Adley Santa-Maria 1997, 1998) or how the "White Mountain Apache" interpret language maintenance. What I do claim is to provide an account of *the kinds of* innovation and social complexity at play at the intersection of university-trained language experts (of which I was one, as were some of my consultants who were members of the tribe and who worked as Apache language teachers) and differently positioned actors (for example, elders, parents, and religious leaders) within this indigenous community, and reasons why similar innovative and conflictual dynamics are likely in language efforts elsewhere. My goal is to provide a means by which to listen to diverse community voices by establishing a framework through which to anticipate processes of (creative) misrecognition in indigenous language advocacy.

Throughout the book I refer to the area in which my consultants lived as "the Fort Apache reservation" and I often refer to them as "reservation residents." This is in contrast to recent changes in terms of self-representation adopted by different offices of the tribe, who use the "White Mountain Apache Reservation" or "White Mountain Apache

Lands." I adopt "Fort Apache reservation" here because to do so specifies a history of colonial encounter that otherwise anchors my account. The use of "Fort Apache" also locates the representational claims of the present account in that ambivalent history and positions my voice differently from those of White Mountain Apache persons, who have their own.

Structure of the Book

In the next chapter, entitled "Indigenous Languages and the Mediation of Communities," I attempt to reset the frame from "languages" as objects of documentary knowledge to the symbolic role indigenous languages play in the mediation of communities within encompassing sociopolitical orders. In doing this, I adopt two strategies. First, I offer an ethnographic description of the ambivalent responses that my presence as a language researcher, and the language programs with which I was involved, provoked in persons whom I encountered in the Fort Apache speech community. I show that there is a quality of relativity to terms like "language loss," "heritage," "language maintenance," "cultural survival," such that meanings across different sectors of the Fort Apache community only apparently coincided with those imputed to the terms by researchers and educators.

And, second, I trace a history through which "saving endangered languages" has emerged as a point of global relevance for indigenous communities as well as for the language-oriented disciplines. Language maintenance, as an extension of notions of language rights, is identified as a liberal democratic discourse that bears similarly upon many indigenous communities due to parallels in histories of colonial disruption and engagement. I identify why language endangerment and maintenance represents an improvement over assimilationist policies in negotiated terms of political coordination. I propose reasons why, at the intersection of an encompassing national regime and an indigenous-identified community, there can be *both* political alliance *and* a challenge of fit between academic maintenance discourses and alternatives circulating within local communities. I make the case that ambivalence in community reception should be anticipated and recognized, because it is not at all trivial to the political role of research and maintenance programs. Chapter 2 establishes the broad argument that some ethnographic inquiry into local meanings is therefore necessary in order to attend to alternative community discourses otherwise obscured by the terms and practices of documentation and educational language programs.

In the third chapter, entitled: "Learning to Listen: Coming to Terms with Conflicting Meanings of Language Loss," I tell the story of how I gradually became aware of different understandings of language loss between home and school environments on the Fort Apache reservation and the role these differences played in controversies surrounding language programs. I elaborate the way different language ideologies found expression in the contrasting pedagogies and socialization practices of extended family homes, on the one hand, and school language programs, on the other. I describe how a language program with which I was involved became embroiled in controversy because it brought these contrasting language ideologies and pedagogies into conflict with one another. I suggest that other language programs described in the broader literature occasion similar controversies and can be understood in relationship to conflicting language ideologies, conflicting pedagogies and socialization practices across extended family-centered and school-centered social contexts.

My fourth chapter: "They Live in Lonesome Dove: English in Indigenous Places" describes the use of English language mass media place names on the Fort Apache reservation in order to illustrate one, often overlooked, dimension of language shift: the use of a colonial language of wider circulation to assert, among other things, the contemporary relevance of indigenous voices (e.g. Dobrin 2012). Just as language maintenance programs subsume indigenous languages within a nationalist framework by posing indigenous grammars and texts as items of cultural property; indigenous communities very often appropriate historically colonizing languages to their own purposes, seizing upon them to pursue their own ends in their own way precisely because they are strange and connote places at a remove from familiar everyday life. I illustrate this with an example from the Fort Apache reservation in which English language mass media discourse is used to coin playful names for newly constructed neighborhoods, which are then officialized on government maps and street signs. By using idioms from English language commercial discourse for official place names, and placing these on road signs and maps, reservation residents subvert dominant expectations as they also project their voices in ways that resonate beyond the local. These are strategic acts of community definition, which draw upon established naming practices to pose shared jokes as terms of community belonging. With these names reservation residents simultaneously communicate their difference from surrounding nonindigenous communities as well as their participation in a global, mass media-infused world.

Chapter 5, entitled "Stories in the Moment of Encounter: Documentation Boundary Work," examines language documentation as a form of cultural encounter to which linguists and the people they work with bring contrasting purposes and strategies. I trace a history of Apache documentary encounters from mission philology to salvage linguistics to contemporary documentary concerns with saving indigenous languages.

The documentation produced by linguists is often taken by language experts, and by the broader public interested in endangered languages, as the purpose of the interaction. In this chapter I attempt to make other purposes and voices audible. I compare two collected texts, which are also accounts of Apache lives: one spoken by Lawrence Mithlo to Harry Hoijer and published in a 1938 text collection, and another spoken by Rebekah Moody to me in 1996. First, I show that neither is cast by its speaker as neutral information. Rather, both are extensions of an oratorical strategy labeled *bá'hadziih*, through which the speaker presents a group with which s/he identifies to an audience that includes those figured as Other. Through *bá'hadziih* the speaker attempts to transform the relationship between her own group and the addressed Others by first invoking what the speaker anticipates to be the image held of her group from the Other's point of view and then posing terms for its transformation. The difference between the framing purposes of documentation and *bá'hadziih* defines language research as an encounter between persons engaged in contrasting regimes of meaning.

In the sixth chapter: "What No Coyote Story Means: The Borderland Genre of Traditional Storytelling," I treat Coyote stories, not as items of cultural knowledge, but as a voice at the edge of familiarity and otherness. I portray histories of storytelling (Kroskrity 2012) that span the colonial and documentary encounter with focus upon the transformative actions of "Coyote." I attend to the poetic devices of Apache language traditional storytelling and show that the same features that mark them as traditional stories for language and culture documentation serve a different function in family storytelling. In the latter, storytelling orients participants to persons and landscapes as agents whose continuing influences bear upon the lives of listeners. I draw attention to the difference in relations of authority when family storytelling is repackaged as items of cultural knowledge in a school curriculum or culture center. I qualify this, though, by noting that indigenous language and culture instruction in schools is domain-specific and not totalizing, existing alongside other domains of use and other ideological processes.

The seventh chapter, "'Some "No No" and Some "Yes"': Silence, Agency, and Traditionalist Words," addresses the fact that it is not at all uncommon for heritage language program developers in Native American communities to encounter restrictions posed by local religious leaders upon what can and cannot be included in school programs. For different reasons, both Traditionalists and Apache Independent Christians police school programs to insure the exclusion of words and idioms associated with Traditionalist ceremony. Some curriculum developers have lamented the silence of heritage language programs on religious tradition, noting that this excludes entire canons of oral literature and song, and reduces the teaching of the native language to prosaic matters, less likely to compete with English language use for the attention of young people. I propose an apparent paradox: that the silence of school programs on sacred language in fact indicates the continuing power of such language, and of local leadership who insist on its prohibition from the schools. On the Fort Apache reservation this power, linked to the continuing relevance of Apache language, is evident in the emergence of vibrant Apache language innovations outside of education programs. Two opposed religious identities: Traditionalists and Apache Independent Christians, utilize different elements of a loosely share repertoire of Apache language genres, rhetorical forms, and poetics to appropriate the Christian Bible to their own meanings and purposes. I propose that this and analogous local appropriations of symbolically global texts might be considered alongside language programs as alternate sites of production in which a heritage language is wielded by members of the community as they negotiate relations to one another and to wider exogenous national and global orders.

I conclude with a short chapter suggesting "Possible Socialities of Documentation and Maintenance," where I draw some of the implications of the preceding chapters for more politically symmetrical language documentation and advocacy work.

My Approach

A key argument of the book is that indigenous languages exist at the threshold between indigenous communities and surrounding social orders and figure importantly into community definition at that juncture (Merlan 2009). Therefore, concerns with saving or supporting indigenous languages are articulated at the same threshold, and have a complicated relationship with local communicative practices because they are often dually articulated through historically imposed institutions like schools, on the one hand, and across generations in extended families, on the other. My concern throughout this book is to set this as the frame within which to analyze not only the play of indigenous language issues in institutions (like schools) that clearly articulate with state, federal, and international discourses; but to also recognize how community members employ language in ways relevant to local notions of indigeneity to pose alternate definitions of community, centered in family, place, and often through explicitly religious discourse.

I focus my investigation upon sites of engagement with encompassing social orders such as schools, reception of mass media, and Christianity. I show how the imputed authentic indigeneity of one's speech is often at stake in self and community definitions, but figured differently across different social contexts. At all three "sites" it is plausible to trace extensions and transplants of institutions and discourses from outside the reservation. Within these transplanted institutions there are strong interpretive pressures to draw contrasts and comparisons between Apache and English languages through terms established in the institutions of the encompassing society. However, educational, mass media, and Christian discursive materials are also met with and recontextualized (Bauman and Briggs 1990; Silverstein and Urban 1996; Spitulnik 1997) within the discursive practices of extended families and clans, and are often transformed in their reception and use within the terms of precedents established therein (see Nevins 2008, 2010b). In this way, I elaborate a complex local-global social field in which indigenous languages and acts of language use have meaning.

Another aspect of this book that distinguishes it from other ethnographic treatments of indigenous language issues is the use of the notion (adapted from Hanks 1986; Hymes 1966; Keane 2007; Wagner 1981) that there are multiple modes of discursive action, or discursive regimes (also Gal 1998; Kroskrity 2000), at play in many communities, with different entailments for reflecting upon "language" and what it might mean to save or lose such a thing. Minimally, we can identify one pole of contrast with a discursive regime (premised on the a priori alienability of individual persons, languages, and goods) centered in historically imposed institutions like schools, missions, and businesses; and another (premised on temporally deep flows involving persons, language, and land) centered in extended family and quasi-familial contexts, including feasts, harvests, ceremonies, and religious revivalism (Nevins and Nevins forthcoming). To approach language and the ways people reflect upon it, I focus upon texts, and ideological processes of contextualization and recontextualization (following Hanks 1986; Keane 2007; Kroskrity 2004; Silverstein 1996), for the window these provide upon ways that members of indigenous communities orient to one another and to more extended global orders (also Nevins 2010a). The sorts of texts (following Hanks 1989) I discuss range from individual Apache words to place names, stories, songs, personal names, speeches/oratory, names of cosmological figures, but also English language phrases from church, school, and media discourse. Such items are circulated across multiple sites and their meaning and evaluation transformed through recontextualization (Bauman and Briggs 1990; Silverstein and Urban 1996).

To sum up for now, as the dueling statements with which I began this chapter illustrate, there is gap between indigeneity as a term in ethnonational discourses and the place that it holds as a link in a historical chain of events between a colonizing national entity and indigenous sociocultural practices based on other terms. Some kind of alterity, that "unnameable presence" described by Vizenor (1998), looms in the very premise of indigeneity, but, as he indicates, has a complicated relationship to documentation efforts. Therefore, the nature of my comment upon language endangerment and maintenance rhetoric is to place qualifications and limits upon it, limits drawn from recognizing alternate voices, pedagogies, and claims upon language in indigenous communities. For many language programs that have stood the test of time, this process of attending to community critique and accommodating community intervention is already familiar in practice, but not built into the explicit theories informing programs and planning. By defining indigenous languages as a "matter of concern" (Latour 2004), the rhetoric of endangerment directly supports linguistic documentation and school maintenance programs; but it also set new conditions for innovation that extend beyond the purview of linguistic experts.

Community critiques, controversies, and interventions into indigenous language programs tend to be both underreported and poorly understood in the indigenous language endangerment literature. In many accounts of language programs, such things are treated obliquely, as obstacles to be avoided to clear the way for the "real work" of documentation and maintenance. Given the embattled placement of most indigenous languages relative to majority languages, some linguists advocate avoiding community controversies on the rationale that one should not "air dirty laundry," or that muddying the advocacy narrative with social complications would only hamper public support for those fragile efforts that are underway. My intention is to open up the discussion of language maintenance to allow for the fact that language programs figure importantly in community empowerment, but not always in ways their designers anticipate or intend. The present effort is an attempt to enable recognition of community criticisms and interventions into maintenance programs, not as noise or obstacles to progress, but as relevant to indigenous community empowerment more broadly conceived.

Ethnography can help reframe the "noise" of community critique of language programs into alternate claims to authority and into alternate definitions of community that are themselves germane to the ongoing relevance of indigenous languages. On the Fort Apache reservation, as elsewhere, language programs are politically necessary and desired by many, but they do not exist in a vacuum. I will show how multiple ways of "doing language" coexist, interpenetrate, and sometimes conflict with one another in community language efforts. These alternatives have relevance to the political status of language programs, particularly in whether they are perceived as empowering or alienating. I elaborate an account of these processes on the Fort Apache reservation in order to make the broader suggestion that for indigenous communities in parallel historical circumstances elsewhere we can expect that diverse ways of objectifying and reflecting upon language are also to be found, and that they inflect the meaning and functioning of language efforts in parallel ways.

References

Adley-Santa Maria, Bernadette. 1997. White Mountain Apache Language Shift: A Perspective on Causes, Effects, and Avenues for Change. Master's thesis, University of Arizona.

Adley-Santa Maria, Bernadette. 1998. White Mountain Apache Language: Issues in Language Shift, Textbook Development, and Native Speaker–University Collaboration. Paper presented at the Annual Meeting of the American Indian Language Development Institute, University of Arizona, Tucson, Summer.

Bauman, Richard and Charles Briggs. 1990. Poetics and Performance as Critical Perspectives on Language and Social Life. *Annual Review of Anthropology* 19:59–88.

Dobrin, Lise. 2012. Reading the Encounter from between the Lines of the Text: Ethnopoetic Analysis as a Resource for Endangered Language Linguistics. *Anthropological Linguistics* 54(1):1–32.

Gal, Susan. 1998. Multiplicity and Contention among Language Ideologies: A Commentary. In *Language Ideologies: Practice and Theory*. Bambi Schieffelin, Kathryn A. Woolard and Paul V. Kroskrity, eds., pp. 317–332. New York: Oxford University Press.

Hanks, William. 1986. *Intertexts: Writings on Language, Utterance and Context*. Lanham: Rowman & Littlefield.

Hanks, William. 1989. Text and Textuality. *Annual Review of Anthropology* 18: 95–127.

Hymes, Dell H. 1966. Two Types of Linguistic Relativity. In *Sociolinguistics*. W. Bright, ed., pp. 114–157. The Hague: Mouton de Gruyter.

Keane, Webb. 2007. *Christian Moderns: Freedom and Fetish in the Mission Encounter*. Berkeley: University of California Press.

Kroskrity, Paul V. 2000. Regimenting Languages: Language Ideological Perspectives. In *Regimes of Language: Ideologies, Polities, and Identities*. Paul V. Kroskrity, ed., pp. 1–4. Santa Fe: School of American Research.

Kroskrity, Paul V. 2004. Language Ideologies. In *A Companion to Linguistic Anthropology*. Alessandro Duranti, ed., pp. 496–517. Oxford: Blackwell.

Kroskrity, Paul V. 2012. Introduction. In *Telling Stories in the Face of Danger: Language Renewal in Native American Communities*. Paul V. Kroskrity, ed., pp. 152–183. Tulsa: University of Oklahoma Press.

Latour, Bruno. 2004. "Why Has Critique Run out of Steam: From Matters of Fact to Matters of Concern. *Critical Inquiry* 30:225–248.

Merlan, Francesca. 2009. Indigeneity: Local and Global. *Current Anthropology* 50(3):303–333.

Nevins, M. Eleanor. 2008. "They Live in Lonesome Dove": Media and Contemporary Western Apache Place-Naming Practices. *Language in Society* 37: 191–215.

Nevins, M. Eleanor. 2010a. Editorial: Intertextuality and Misunderstanding. *Language and Communication* 30(1):1–6.

Nevins, M. Eleanor. 2010b. The Bible in Two Keys: Traditionalism and Apache Evangelical Christianity on the Fort Apache Reservation. *Language and Communication* 30(1):19–32.

Nevins, Thomas and M. Eleanor Nevins. forthcoming. Speaking in the Mirror of the Other: Dialectics of Intersubjectivity and Temporality in Western Apache Metapragmatics. Special issue of *Language and Communication*, "Intersubjectivity: Cultural Extensions and Construals." Alan Rumsey and Eve Danziger, eds.

Silverstein, Michael. 1996. The Secret Life of Texts. In *Natural Histories of Discourse*, Michael Silverstein and Greg Urban, eds., pp. 81–105. Chicago: University of Chicago Press.

Silverstein, Michael and Urban, Greg. 1996. The Natural History of Discourse. In *Natural Histories of Discourse*. Michael Silverstein and Greg Urban, eds., pp. 1–17. Chicago: University of Chicago Press.

Spitulnik, Debra. 1997. The Social Circulation of Media Discourse and the Mediation of Communities. *Journal of Linguistic Anthropology* 6:161–187.

UNESCO. 2011. Frequently Asked Questions, Endangered Languages. United Nations Educational, Scientific, and Cultural Organization. www.unesco.org/new/en/culture/themes/endangered-languages/faq-on-endangered-languages/ (accessed November 12, 2012).

Vizenor, Gerald, ed. 1998. *Fugitive Poses: Native American Scenes of Absence and Presence*. Lincoln: University of Nebraska Press.

Wagner, Roy. 1981. *The Invention of Culture, revised and expanded edition*. Chicago: University of Chicago Press.

2

Indigenous Languages and the Mediation of Communities

A Difficult Morning

It is 7:30 a.m. on a Monday morning in 1998, a year and a half into a nearly three-year ethnographic field term. The phone rings as I am having coffee and toast with Tom, my spouse (and a cultural anthropologist) at our rental in Pinetop-Lakeside, a reservation border town. We were preparing to make the twenty-minute drive to work in an office where we were both paid by the tribe's health authority to develop Apache language curricula for circulation in the reservation schools via the tribe's server. I pick up the phone and hear a loud, angry-sounding male voice: "This is Carl Collard, tribal attorney, and I am calling to tell you to *cease and desist* from all work on the language project. Call off your film crew and present the tribe with all your tapes. *Cease and desist.*" I had heard from members of the tribe's cultural advisory board that the tribe's legal office was currently pursuing several lawsuits against film companies, and against an international amusement park, all of whom had broken terms of permission for filming and commercially reproducing an Apache girl's coming of age ceremony called the Sunrise Dance. I was alarmed that our work was now being perceived in the same light. I tried to explain that I was not involved in any commercial venture but was a linguistic anthropologist hired by the tribe as a consultant to develop Apache language curricula. I noted that the project was run by an educational office of the tribe and directed by tribal members. I told him that I did not have a film crew, but did have an old 8 mm camera that I, along with several tribal members, including employees of the tribe's culture center, had used for filming a Sunrise Dance as part of a project jointly sponsored by that office and the Arizona Humanities Council. I was still in the process of producing copies of the tapes for

Lessons from Fort Apache: Beyond Language Endangerment and Maintenance, First Edition. M. Eleanor Nevins.
© 2013 John Wiley & Sons, Inc. Published 2013 by John Wiley & Sons, Inc.

all the families who participated as well as for the culture center, as stipulated in the Arizona Humanities Council grant award that he could find on file at the culture center. I also directed him to the dissertation research proposal I had submitted to the tribe and to the subsequent proposals submitted for language materials development projects through various tribal offices. I wanted him to know I was not trying to hide what I was doing, or to steal anything from the tribe, but this only provoked him to yet louder reiterations of *"cease and desist."*

A group of us at the health authority had been working for roughly nine months on the Ndee Biyati' Apache Language project, where our purpose was to create language materials that were to be hosted on the tribe's server and accessible through it to reservation schools. We had developed an interactive alphabet, narrative-based activities placed in a "typical" extended family household that was rendered with the drawings of a talented young Apache cartoonist, as well as a unit on clan names and kinship terms. We had just begun to present these in venues that included the tribe's culture center, several classrooms in schools on the reservation, and an intertribal education conference. In all venues they were received with apparent enthusiasm. However, with increased circulation came rumors, and, to add tension to the mix, this was an election year, with council seats and the tribal chairmanship at stake. Some candidates running for the council voiced criticism of the project's reliance upon computers, and cast doubt upon the motivations of the nontribal members involved (myself and my husband) at political meetings that were reported upon in the tribe's newspaper, the *Fort Apache Scout*. In the same week the computer lab at Alchesay high school was broken into and vandalized, leaving each monitor disabled. As I will explore in greater detail in the following chapter, the language project was singled out for criticism along several fronts, which rode atop a political dynamic in which affiliation against the project was part of ongoing election year politics. I thought (correctly) that the attorney's call was the end of the language project, and I also worried (needlessly, as it turned out) that it meant the end of my relations to many of my ethnographic consultants as well.

When the chairmanship is at stake, there are usually two candidates, and all the council candidates affiliate with one or the other of the chair candidates. Campaign events, accompanied by feasts and speeches, are held in the yards of extended families, with political affiliation to councilman and chair traced along relations of kinship. For any given family the effect is to talk about one's own group and candidates in first person plural and to refer to political opponents as "the other side." Like everyone else, we had friends and consultants on both sides of the election year political divide, but were closest with the extended family of Rebekah Moody, who had a brother running for tribal council and a brother-in-law running for the chairmanship. Consistent with the political nature of family alliance, I was one of the many women who were not Rebekah Moody's biological daughters, but who were conferred a sort of diplomatic kin status. I addressed and referred to her as *shimaa*, or 'my mother' and she addressed and introduced me as *shizhaazhé West Virginiayu*, or 'my daughter from West Virginia,' often playfully, or in ways that suggested that the term as applied to our relation was always a creative act. She and others also commonly referred to me in casual conversations among the family as *ndah it'één*, or 'White girl.' The ambivalence of our relation as both kin and *ndah*, or Other/White, was sometimes a source of tension in the broader family, but also a focus of interest, joking, and creativity. In our work with the language project it was the members of Rebekah Moody's extended family who had at times offered the most thoroughgoing criticisms of the project design (treated at length in Chapter 3), but who, even so, also devoted a good deal of their time as unpaid consultants helping develop the Apache language content.

Tom and I were concerned that association with two now controversial *ndah*/White researchers might prove to be a political liability for the people closest to us across the several offices and families with whom we were involved. We prepared ourselves for the possibility of losing friends, quasi-family, and consultants in this heated political climate, especially now that I had been identified a persona non grata by the tribal attorney's office. I knew of another linguist who had left the community after being asked to stop working with the tribe on language efforts because of parallel conflicts. So there was some basis for anticipating estrangement.

As it turns out, becoming the target of political and legal attacks did sever our relations with the particular language project, but it brought all our other consultants in Rebekah Moody's family and in other tribal education offices into closer dialogue, involvement, and empathy with us. Suddenly we were enmeshed in many of the same conflicts and paradoxes that they had to deal with. "Now you know what it's like," was something we heard many times, and comments like "everyone says they want to save the language but when you try something, they don't want it." By running up against acrimonious opposition and by publicly failing to complete a project, we had become involved in dynamics that were recognizable and a source of shared stories and troubles with many in the reservation community. We learned that language projects, and persons – including tribal members – associated with them, were often received ambivalently and often became the target of controversy, despite the fact that nearly everyone voices concern about keeping Apache language going in the face of apparent loss in fluency among young people. The ambivalence and volatility we encountered was widespread – experienced by outsiders and tribal members alike on the Fort Apache reservation.

One of the motivations for writing this book is that Fort Apache is not unique in this respect. Conflicts surrounding indigenous language projects are common, but with notable exceptions (Dauenhauer and Dauenhauer 1998; Hofling 1996; Wilkins 2000), remain underreported in the language maintenance literature. When I have presented papers about conflicts surrounding the Ndee Biyati' Apache Language Project to audiences that include those involved in indigenous language documentation and maintenance, I am inevitably approached by audience members who share similar stories from the communities in which they work. That is, other language projects in other indigenous communities occasion controversies despite apparently widespread interests in "saving" a language. With this book I suggest that ambivalence emerges from contrasting ways of reflecting upon language, and contrasting ways of contextualizing language in social relations. In the chapters that follow I will draw out paradoxes and conflicts surrounding Apache language, or *Ndee Bik'ehgo Biyatí'*, on the Fort Apache reservation and suggest that parallel dynamics can be found in other indigenous communities. I argue that such contrasts are implicit in the terms through which indigenous communities are related to surrounding sociopolitical orders and are germane to the meaning and political status of indigenous language maintenance efforts in ways that often go unrecognized by language planners.

Relevance of Endangerment and Maintenance

Language endangerment is a matter of concern (Latour 2004) voiced by linguists and by members of many indigenous communities, and this concern provides a vector of mutual relevance and therefore a basis for university-accredited language professionals to engage with issues that members of the broader public care about. It was certainly relevant to my engagement with residents of the Fort Apache reservation. And, in my position as a professor at University of Nevada Reno, language maintenance has been the focus of conversations initiated by Paiute, Washoe, and Shoshone language educators, all requesting forms of greater university involvement in their language efforts. Linguists and other language experts use the authority they have acquired through university accreditation to advocate for funding and institutional support for programs designed to save and maintain endangered indigenous languages.

Distinct from the local community discourses that will be the focus of the rest of this book, minority language advocacy is almost always advanced across another contentious political field: that of state and national politics. Here advocates for minority languages face opponents in the form of majoritarian, "English-Only," or other monoglot standard (Silverstein 1996), language movements. Becoming involved as both a researcher and an advocate for the development of community infrastructure is profoundly immersive. The struggle to build infrastructure in the face of institutional inertia in the schools and in the face of opposition in state governments provides terms of coordination and common cause between researchers and communities.

My research term, like that of other linguists and ethnographers on the Fort Apache and neighboring San Carlos reservation, occurred within a political climate in Arizona that, following similar developments in California, was perceived by many reservation residents as increasingly threatening for indigenous and other minority languages. Most of the legislation hostile to Native American languages that people were discussing during my field term was drafted in order to marginalize another linguistic minority with indigenous ancestry but whose colonial legacy afforded different terms of identification: Spanish-speaking immigrants from Mexico.[1] On the Fort Apache reservation political sympathies ran to the immigrants. Reflecting a history of raiding and trading with Mexican villages, one of the more common clan affiliation terms still in circulation is *Nakaiyéń*, which many translate as 'Mexican clan.' My consultants reported being mistaken for Mexican immigrants when they traveled to Phoenix or Tucson. Members of my extended family expressed appreciation for Mexican parents whom they heard speaking to their children in Spanish in public places, with remarks like "that reminded me of the way my Dad talked." For many, the anti-immigrant political discourse was also an assault upon Mexican families that, like their own families, they cast in morally valorized contrasts with White, majoritarian norms.

Just following my field term in 2000, an English-Only political movement was successful in passing proposition 203 (Crawford 2001), also known as the "Unz initiative," which not only withdrew state funding for bilingual education, but mandated exclusive instruction in English for state-funded schools, with exemptions for federally protected Native American language instruction. More recently, in 2010 Arizona passed SB2281, which "prohibits a school district or charter school from including in its program of instruction any courses or classes that . . . are designed primarily for pupils of a particular ethnic group." An aspect of this legislation required the retraining or removal of any teacher who speaks English with "a heavy accent" (Jourdan 2010), which one might have if one speaks a Native American language as a first language, or a Native American variety of English (Bartelt et al. 1982). Add to this a notorious piece of legislation passed in 2010, immigration law SB1070, which mandates police searches of those who might be suspected of being illegal immigrants, and requires people to carry and present papers documenting their residency status in order to avoid arrests. The law was designed to target Mexican immigrants, but drew opposition from the Inter Tribal Council of Arizona whose members refused to enforce it, and who described it as an assault on tribal sovereignty, anticipating that implementation would inevitably increase police harassment of Native Americans as well (Wyloge 2010).

Portrayals of minority languages and peoples in such a political climate by their opponents can be derogatory. More than one non-Indian[2] shopkeeper in the frontier town of Pinetop-Lakeside on the border of the Fort Apache reservation, upon learning that I was living there to study Apache language, expressed surprise that there was anything to learn from what they depicted as the "guttural babble" of their Apache customers. In the context of the conflictual political fields surrounding indigenous identities and languages linguists and other university-accredited language experts can be important public allies. My colleagues in reservation language programs drew upon scholarship, including linguistic and cultural documentation, as well as research establishing the cognitive benefits of bilingualism, to argue against English-Only legislation and to argue for the dedication of more resources to teaching indigenous and other minority heritage languages in schools throughout the state.

I draw this out here because while most of my attention in this book is upon demonstrating differences between the ostensibly cooperative parties to saving an indigenous language, there is nonetheless a sense in which the common cause between university-accredited language experts and other language advocates within a reservation community is undeniably real. My purpose here has been to locate that common cause with respect to a specific context of action. Common cause in saving a language is specific to a relation of mutual orientation to the same political opponents. In the chapters that follow I will show how equally real differences in perspective among the diversity of stakeholders in an indigenous language are often obscured in documentation and maintenance efforts. In the same vein, the rhetoric of language endangerment has been an effective resource mobilization tactic, and has justified a burgeoning network of linguistic documentation and maintenance efforts that cross-cut university, school, local government, and community contexts. However, as I will discuss in the next section, the terms in which indigenous languages are rendered in the rhetoric of endangerment obscures the complex role played by documentation and maintenance in the political articulation of indigenous communities within modern nation states.

Global Linguistic Ecology: What Endangerment and Maintenance Have in Common

The notion of "language endangerment" is rooted in a history of colonial encounter, which not only shapes the phenomena, but also shapes the way we see and respond to it. Popular books addressed to language endangerment typically begin by citing numbers of languages that have fallen out of use, and by predicting the number of languages that are likely to fall out of use, or go extinct, within the next fifty years (Harrison 2008; Krauss 1992; Nettle and Romaine 2000). While other minority languages are often included, the bulk of endangerment numbers come from languages of communities identified as indigenous by their placement in relation to European colonialism of the past several hundred years. A number of elements – colonialism, globalization, language decline, documentation, and maintenance – are brought together into a coherent narrative in which cause and effect seem to be straightforward. Colonialism and globalism lead to language loss, and documentation and maintenance programs are the urgently needed correctives that lead to the opposite process: language preservation. In this story endangerment and maintenance appear to be fundamentally opposed processes.

To complicate the endangerment and maintenance narrative I draw upon Mufwene's arguments concerning the linguistic ecology of indigenous language shift. Mufwene offers a treatment that is both finer grained with respect to variations in colonial histories and of greater temporal scope than what is provided in the language endangerment literature. Shifting our perspective from language structures to understanding language use by speakers within linguistic ecologies reveals a different set of cause–effect relations, within which endangerment and maintenance have quite a lot in common.

Mufwene (2002, 2008) shows that shift away from indigenous languages is not a uniform result of colonialism, but of particular colonial styles (Wolfe 1999 makes a similar argument). He draws the most consequential differences between "settler colonialism," and "exploitation colonialism." The latter describes much of Asia and Africa, where the primary interest of the colonizing party was resource extraction, with relatively little permanent settlement of persons to the colony from the colonizing nation or corporation. In exploitation colonies indigenous groups demographically swamp those functionaries who have relocated there. A small number of local elite learn scholastic versions of the language of colonial administration and business, but must also speak local languages in order to coordinate their workforce, and to move between city and countryside. Outside of cities, people living in the rural areas:

> have barely been affected by the economic and political transformations undergone by their territories, including the formation of nation-states. Most of them have not even had options other than to continue operating in their traditional world or, at best, to work in the low-cost colonial and post-colonial labour system that does not require a European language. (Mufwene 2002:15–16)

Contrary to the story of indigenous languages told in the endangerment literature, in exploitation colonies shift from indigenous vernaculars to a European colonial language was not common. Shift was more frequent among indigenous languages towards an indigenous regional lingua franca associated with cities. Mufwene cites Swahili, Malay, or Town Bemba (Spitulnik 1998) as exemplary cases.

Into the twenty-first century, the national infrastructures of former exploitation colonies have tended to weakly support universal obligatory schooling, as reflected in literacy rates under 60 percent in many countries, and declining from this in rural areas (Richmond et al. 2008:23–26). The majority population has had little incentive to abandon indigenous languages because they remain only loosely integrated into globalizing political-economic systems, and on broadly unfavorable terms, as reflected in comparative mortality rates. Language change in exploitation colonies, then, has not reflected in a straightforward way the global narrative of language loss told in the endangerment literature.

The colonization style that better fits the endangerment narrative is settlement colonialism, especially the more industrialized non-plantation settlement colonies. The difference is that "the colonists in non-plantation settlement colonies (the continental Americas, Australia and New Zealand) became the overwhelming majorities and instituted socio-economic systems that function totally in their own dominant language" (Mufwene 2002:15). The language shifts decried in the endangerment literature and addressed today with documentation and maintenance began late in the colonial encounter in the nineteenth century and occurred once indigenous groups were brought into more intimate articulation with national institutions. Mufwene describes as ironic the fact that the "language wars," or "language killings" of the endangerment literature predominantly occurred after the military wars were over, and through less violent, relatively more negotiated, forms of accommodation. Human deaths from colonial war and disease occurred, and were succeeded several generations later by the deaths of languages described in the literature. Accordingly, it is in peacetime, with increased integration into the political and economic institutions of the dominant society, that shifts away from indigenous vernaculars occur.

In Mufwene's account, shift to the language of the dominant political group is one of many adaptations members of indigenous communities make to changes in their socioeconomic ecology. My purpose in this section is to extend Mufwene's political integration argument concerning language shift to documentation and maintenance as well. Viewed in this light, rather than being opposed processes, indigenous language shift, documentation, and maintenance programs are facets of the same process of negotiated political integration within the institutions of the surrounding national order.

The precedents for contemporary English-Only and other monoglot standard movements can be traced to assimilationist ideologies that informed late nineteenth and early twentieth-century public policy. The non-plantation settler states, which Merlan (2009) describes as liberal democratic settler states (US, Canada, Australia, New Zealand),[3] all had parallel official assimilation policies. These policies were predicated on assumptions of unilineal cultural evolution and formulated to convert native peoples, and other racialized minorities, into ethnically unmarked modern citizens. In Pratt's (the architect of the residential school system in the United States) parlance, this meant: "Kill the Indian, save the man." Assimilationist policies were coercive and in hindsight widely interpreted to have been disempowering for indigenous communities (although see Reyner and Eder 2006). Applied to American Indian reservations, official assimilationism worked to dissolve collective treaty or title claims into individual rights. This resulted in loss of land through allotment and private sale, and loss of control over some of the means through which people were permitted to publicly form their communities. Indigenous languages and cultural practices were stigmatized and repressed. Occasions for enacting community, like public ceremonies and large-scale exchange events, were outlawed.[4] Perhaps most disempowering for indigenous peoples across the settler states was the forced dismantling of extended families as children were taken away from their families for adoption or to attend residential schools. Boarding schools, under the explicitly militaristic Protestantism of "muscular Christianity," were designed to remove children from the socializing effects of their families and communities (McCarty and Zepeda 1999; Reyner and Eder 2006). Traumas endured in boarding schools prior to the Collier reforms, or in some cases prior to civil rights reforms, included shaming and physical punishment for speaking an indigenous language. These experiences have become woven into the family stories of many persons in contemporary indigenous communities and inflect understandings of language loss and maintenance.

By contrast, the notion of indigenous rights is traceable to the emergence of a political discourse on human rights, formulated in the middle twentieth century in international politics following upon the two world wars. The plight of indigenous peoples was taken up within a more general discussion in which liberal democracies redefined themselves with respect to aspects of their own internal social diversity, and posed new legal provisions to accommodate social difference (Merlan 2009; Niezen 2003). Concerns about the treatment of indigenous peoples were voiced alongside discussions of the deplorable working conditions of the world's poor by global labor organizations. These converged in a global discourse of human rights – culminating in the 1948 United Nations Universal Declaration of Human Rights. The discourse of rights, as noted in Collins' treatment of Tolowa histories, has a complex relationship to indigenous empowerment:

> In the twentieth century they have increased population, gained some small parcels of land, and organized ongoing political struggles, but this has been done increasingly in terms of dominant, non-Indian definitions of identity and rights. . . . Tolowa possibilities of life – ways of getting a living, forms of spiritual expression, and categories of political identity – have been much more embedded in the matrix of Indian/white relations, and specifically in a framework of rights. (Collins 1998:53)

As Collins and Merlan both note, the institutional elaboration of rights enables and constrains strategies of self-determination available to indigenous communities and persons.

The mid-twentieth century saw the subsequent formulation of "language rights" (Paulson 1997) and the application of these in different ways to indigenous and other minority language communities (e.g. Collins 1998; Hornberger 1998). Linguistic documentation and its extensions in the form of literacy development play supporting roles in the institutional elaboration of language rights. Contemporary concerns about indigenous language endangerment as a crisis that requires intervention are reflexes of these fairly recent changes in available terms of political incorporation.

Indigenous rights and language rights are actively in play on the world stage today and still negotiated. A prominent recent example of this is the United Nations Declaration on the Rights of Indigenous Peoples, endorsed (with disclaimers and qualifications) by the United States and Canada in 2011 (IPS Arctic Council 2011). The recent shift in political discourse from the hegemony of assimilationism to the discourse of language and cultural rights (and the apparent diametric opposition entailed) obscures the fact that the latter is also a device of integration into national political discourses. It is not surprising that processes of shift have often intensified with the establishment of indigenous language documentation and maintenance alongside other ethnonationalist terms of political recognition and participation (more on this below).[5]

To summarize, I argue in this section that endangerment and maintenance only appear to be opposed processes. They are in fact two facets of the same process of political integration within surrounding national regimes. Settler colonialism led to shifts away from indigenous vernaculars. It did so through geographically marginalization of indigenous populations, and through posing terms for political and economic integration as individual persons, and as subnational aggregates, within national infrastructures. This latter process provides the precise social ecology in which language endangerment as well as documentation and maintenance programs take place as mutually implicated aspects of an emergent, specifically modernist total social fact. As Strathern puts it: "those who think they exemplify the new and those who think they exemplify the old may, in pursuing that very division, be radical agents of change" (1999:89). What linguists are actually doing with documentation is recasting local languages into "old" forms recognizable as such within the institutions of the dominant society. While, in the name of preserving the past, documentation and maintenance programs create new linguistic markets (Meek 2010; Moore et al. 2010) in which indigenous languages hold new kinds of value. Documentation and maintenance establish infrastructure (Star 1999) through which members of indigenous communities participate in national institutions. This is accomplished by recasting vernacular speech from local meanings and uses to the representational regime of the modern nation-state – as emblems of ethnic or cultural identity.

Alongside Political Integration: Indigenous Histories of Differentiation

Political integration of colonized peoples within nation-states is predicated on inequality, and the terms in which they are represented within the various media and knowledge practices of the nation state often perpetuate inequality, overtly or covertly. However, there is another dimension of community mediation in play: strategies of differentiation from encompassing regimes employed by members of indigenous communities in their relations with one another. While acknowledging significant variation across communities, parallels of colonial and postcolonial histories should prompt us to anticipate, and make a place in our accounts for, the likelihood that local, indigenous discourses of difference exist alongside colonial and national discourses of difference and may be couched in alternate terms. To provide an example of a history of locally constituted terms of difference on the Fort Apache reservation I rely upon the Western Apache ethnography of speaking conducted by Keith Basso over his more than fifty years (and counting) of engagement with members of the Fort Apache reservation community. His established body of work allows me to place Apache discursive innovation in relation to local precedents (Basso 1966, 1969, 1979, 1990, 1996). Basso's work is especially valuable to language maintenance because he establishes an account of how community members have reflected upon their own ways of speaking by defining these in oppositional contrast with what they present as the problematic ways in which *ndah*, or "White people," speak and behave (Basso 1979).

Reflections upon differences between *Ndee bik'ego yati'*, Apache ways of speaking, and *Ndah bik'egho yati'*, "White" (strange) ways of speaking, described by Basso, continued to be prominent in reservation discourse during my field term twenty years later. Portrayals of difference in the ways that White people speak, as opposed to Apache people, have emerged out of a history of colonial encounter. These are germane to language maintenance because they comprise a local exegetical tradition on Apache and English languages that inform concerns about Apache language loss as well as local reactions to language programs. Even earlier comments upon disjuncture between "Apache" and "White" ways of thinking and speaking can be found in records going back to the late 1800s and early 1900s. For example, Lawrence Mithlo, a Chiricahua Apache who had lived on the adjacent San Carlos reservation before being shipped away to Florida as a prisoner in the aftermath of the "Apache Wars," made the following statement to linguist Harry Hoijer in 1936.

> At that time long ago, they lived poorly.
> But Apache women taught their children well, they say.
> . . .
> "My child, one does not curse.
> One hates no one.
> One behaves foolishly to no one.
> One laughs at no one.
> One treats with respect those to whom one can do nothing.
> Pray to God [and] Child of the Water.
> We live because of those two.
> They made the earth [and] the sky," they said to them, they say.

> Even when the boys [and] girls were twenty five and over,
> > they listened well to their fathers [and] mothers.
>
> You who are white people, then, do not realize that
> > even though these people back then knew nothing,
> > they taught their children in a good way inside their poor camps.
> Though hardship, hunger, cold, heat, poverty all overmastered them,
> > they talked to their children about God [and] Child of the Water.
> Though their camps were everywhere poor,
> > they inside of them spoke by means of good words [and] good thoughts.
>
> They thought by means of them.
> They taught by means of them.
>
> All of this is true.
> It is true just as that which I told you [about] our eating wood rats [and]
> > burros is true.[6] (Hoijer 1938:47)

Like Basso's consultants in *Portraits of "the Whiteman"* (1979), Mr. Mithlo focuses upon ways of speaking as he asserts a distinction between Apache people and the ways they were understood by "White people." He spoke this in the mid-1930s on the Mescalero reservation, where he had opted to resettle with his family. Here he worked with cultural anthropologist Morris Opler, who introduced him to Hoijer for the purpose of documenting Chiricahua Apache language. Government policies at the time were assimilationist, and the act of linguistic documentation framed as "salvage." Mithlo had been invited to talk about the way Apaches had made their living prior to the reservations and imprisonment. Speaking into this space, after describing tools, shelter, and food; Mithlo counter-asserts a different definition of Apaches, one not so easily assimilated to the portrait of ethnological difference constructed by Hoijer and Opler. He couches his counter-representation of Apaches/*ndee* in terms of morally valorized ways of speaking, teaching, and thinking in homes and families. He presents this as a way of understanding what it means to live and speak as *ndee*, or Apache, that he presents as having gone unrecognized by *ndah*, or "White people."

Traces of local discourses of differentiation can be found in other records spanning the Apache colonial encounter (Goddard 1919, 1920; Goodwin 1938, 1942, 1994; Hoijer 1938; Opler 1938, 1996). Today these local ways of constituting difference stand alongside, and sometimes in dialogue with, representations of difference imputed to the community in mainstream public discourses (as having a distinctive language, culture: T. Nevins 2010), of being endangered (see Deloria 1998; Meek 2010:4–7); but are not reducible to them. Therefore, an adequate treatment of language issues on the reservation must reflect the historically situated and ongoing invention of such distinctions. It requires a provision for the multiple ways in which relations to surrounding non-Apache communities may be mediated in colonial and postcolonial social contexts.

What "Indigeneity" Affords: Equivocation Regarding "Imagined Communities"

I have argued that while apparently opposed to one another, assimilation and calls to save endangered languages share much in common. Both are modernist and nationalist devices of integration. However, each affords a different set of possibilities for the form that political integration might take. As a framework for local-national or local-global mediation, calls to "save endangered languages" are more amenable to the expression of political agency by indigenous persons than was the case for previous late nineteenth and early twentieth-century policies that suppressed indigenous languages and the practices associated with them. Similarly, linguistic documentation and school maintenance programs valorize indigenous languages as (in principal) equivalent national languages, and provide opportunities for expressions of political agency not afforded by the terms of contemporary English-Only majoritarian movements. However, as noted above, converting a local vernacular into an emblem of ethnonational identity is never a unitary, or monolithic, functional change. Authorship over the terms in which a local vernacular can be wielded as a national language is unevenly distributed within and across indigenous communities, and subject to negotiation and struggle. The notion of indigeneity, and its currency within nation and international politic discourses, allows for the introduction of alternative terms into that negotiation.

Indigeneity locates communities with respect to a history of colonial disruption and of partial encompassment within the colonizing society on terms that are widely recognized as having been unfavorable or unfair. What was disrupted can be imagined in terms of communication networks, established and different means of making a living, of enacting social relationships, and moral relations to land, among other things. The notion of indigeneity implies inclusion of that form of alterity from the colonial order that is locatable in the colonized community. So local practices and forms of authority that pose an alternative to the mainstream would by implication appear to be germane – even if they exist in uneasy tension with mainstream ways of recognizing difference.

However, inclusion in wider publics and in extensions of government and private funding require packaging indigenous ways of doing things in terms recognizable within mainstream institutions.[7] The result is a sort of necessary paradox in which, in order to be recognized as "indigenous," the alterity presented by indigenous ways of doing things must be objectified and made comprehensible within mainstream institutional terms. When a local language is recontextualized as an indigenous language within institutions like schools and culture centers, the manner in which it is re-presented can run counter to those ways of doing language that provide the alternative, Vizenor's "*différance*" (1998:35), that the notion of indigeneity would otherwise seem to privilege.

Merlan describes public discourse surrounding indigeneity as both enabling and constraining for empowerment efforts in indigenous communities:

> In bringing matters of recognition as well as social participation and economic support onto the terrain of the state, the liberal democracies extended their administrative and bureaucratic functions to regulate them. Many forms of regulation are, almost by definition, different from the range of usual community practices, and the resulting regulatory systems are both enabling and constraining, may stimulate opposition, and may bear the unmistakable stamp of the liberal political cultures that house them. (2009:316)

This statement applies readily to "language rights" and programs designed to "save endangered languages": Language endangerment rhetoric enables members of indigenous communities to mobilize support from various quarters of the mainstream public in order to bring wanted resources into their communities. Language documentation and maintenance programs are a means for combating the stigma that had been attached to indigenous vernaculars under the previous assimilationist regime (and which continue in English-Only and other monoglot standard movements), and for valorizing indigenous languages as heritage languages, and linking communities to particular land claims. However, after the grammar has been written, and curricula composed, teachers trained, assessment plans devised, the resultant "regulatory system" bears the stamp of a political culture (down to the micropolitics of classroom pedagogy, see Phillips 1992) that runs counter to other pedagogic practices across other community domains (e.g. elders, extended families, ceremonial leadership). The dissonance can be substantial, because elders in extended families and ceremonial leadership pose their own morally and symbolically weighted claims upon what it means to know an indigenous language. And, as I establish in the next section, accommodation to quasi-national forms of recognition does not exhaust the range of self-fashioning strategies available to members of indigenous (and other) communities.

Fort Apache Reservation – a Complexly Mediated Indigenous Speech Community

As indicated in my opening vignette, the ethnographic portions of this book are based upon continuous ethnographic study among the residents of the Fort Apache reservation from 1996 to 1999, and followed up in the decade and a half since with shorter visits and electronically mediated communications, such as social networking sites and phone conversations. There are somewhere between 12,000 and 14,000 persons living on the reservation, with a near majority under age twenty-five. Another roughly 9,000 persons live on the adjacent San Carlos Apache reservation. During my field term, it was my impression, and the impression of my consultants living on the reservation, that most adults, age thirty and older, were bilingual in Apache and English; but that Apache language fluency dropped off sharply with younger people. Apache language use figured prominently in political life, as tribal council meetings were required by law to be conducted primarily in Apache; and in ceremonial life, as Apache formed the primary language of both Traditionalist ceremony, some Lutheran services, and of the grassroots network of Apache Independent Christian churches. Apache language was also broadcast in a variety of innovative genres and styles through the tribe's radio station KNNB "Voice of the Apache Nation," in what older people characterized as the Apache-English "slang" of young people. New styles and registers of Apache could be heard in workplaces as well as in grocery and convenience stores. The Fort Apache reservation community in the late 1990s presented a situation of apparent language vitality, in which an indigenous language, alongside English, formed an important part of the communicative repertoire of the majority of influential persons in the community.[8]

I describe the reservation community as complexly mediated, and by this I mean that the local community's articulation with more extended communities occurred through multiple sets of social relationships corresponding to multiple contexts of language use. On the one hand there were necessary political relations established through the tribe's constitutional government, Indian health service, Christian missions, state department of education, through industries like timber, cattle, and tourism, and by consumption of consumer goods and mass media. But equally important were social relations expressed in intimate everyday talk amongst extended families, in the stories, songs, and gossip according to which members of the more influential extended families established claims to sources of wealth, including land, jobs, and cattle. Movement between domains – such as the daily movement of young people across school and family home environments, or the daily movement of adults between homes, workplaces, church or ceremonial ground, government offices, and dinners with their extended families – is both necessary and common. In the course of everyday life people applied ways of speaking associated with one domain to another in ongoing, creative ways. Apache and English languages were among those communicative resources that were used creatively across contrasting social domains in this way.

The complexity of community mediation on the Fort Apache reservation meant that language maintenance efforts in the tribe's various educational offices took place against a dynamic social backdrop in which government institutions (including schools) and participation in the wider economy were treated as important and obligatory, but existed alongside other local discourses and practices couched in alternate terms. Examining social dynamics surrounding language maintenance at Fort Apache throws into relief a contrast between language advocacy within state and national public institutions and what wanting to "save our language" means within alternate, especially familial, domains within an indigenous community.

Indigeneity, Complex Mediation, and Paradox

Communities defined as "indigenous" carry with that designation a history of colonial encounter, defined by terms of political integration with respect to encompassing polities as well as histories of political differentiation in alternate terms. Accordingly, there are multiple resources that people draw upon to politically mediate their communities. On the one hand, people appeal to wider publics using symbols through which the community, as an indigenous one, is represented in dominant discourses. However, alongside these, are local political discourses framed in other terms, and articulated with the power of families and ceremonial leadership. In this sense, members of indigenous communities are engaged in dual or multiple communicative regimes, which have been and continue to be related to one another on unequal terms. For language planning and advocacy, because the communicative regime of the encompassing society is taken for granted, particularly in the institutional contexts through which planners and advocates work, it is easy to overlook alternative voices emerging from other, local community domains. Because of this, my tactic with this book is to draw an ethnographic portrait of contrasting claims upon indigeneity and language that were made within the particular community with which I am most familiar, and to suggest terms of comparison and contrast with other indigenous community language efforts.

What I attempt to establish with this book is an understanding of documentation and maintenance as inventive actions (Wagner 1981) that are directly involved in articulating the modern nation-state through inventing indigenous communities as distinct ethnic entities. Documentation reinvents local speech as dictionaries, grammars, and oral literatures. These new traditional forms are politically charged because they serve as points of recognition within the standardizing practices of the surrounding national order, and, more ambivalently, because their production and circulation are largely controlled by those conferred with authority by means of that order (see Dobrin et al. 2009).

Therefore, common cause against English-Only movements and majoritarian nativism does not necessarily translate to straightforward cooperation and harmony in community language programs between university-credentialed experts and those who derive their authority from other sources. This is because "endangerment" and "maintenance," viewed from the standpoints of participants in indigenous communities, are riddled with apparent contradictions (cf. Richland 2007). In the section that follows I elaborate upon three dimensions of paradox that indigenous community members engaged with language endangerment and maintenance confront. One concerns the temporal framing of the language in question, another concerns who is credited with having expertise and authority with respect to the language, and a third concerns the meaning of language, or what it is that people are concerned about losing or saving in the first place.

Temporal Paradox: Endangerment in Modern Times

Language endangerment and maintenance are obviously about a great deal more than language. As a public discourse, language endangerment is a persuasive tactic valuable for its capacity to mobilize public support. And while the implied analogy between endangered languages and endangered species makes for an effective resource mobilization tactic (in winning grants and building programs), it also carries strategic disadvantages. Specifically, it places indigenous languages in a temporal paradox in which, embedded in the motivation to support indigenous languages, is the assumption of their inevitable demise. That is, endangerment elicits for some an interpretation of indigenous languages as fossils or museum pieces, as remnants of an obsolete way of life (Fabian 1983; Moore 2006).

A good deal of the drama and appeal of language endangerment, as well as its strategic drawbacks, are derived from the ways it plays upon notions of the modern and the traditional. The literature on modernity is immense and I cannot do it justice here, but draw upon it selectively to contextualize the notion of "tradition" as a product of a particular social history. Tradition emerged with the formation of nationalism as both an emblem of national belonging and a necessary antipode in the assertion of a modern orientation (Anderson 1991; Bauman and Briggs 2003; Latour 1993). What I present here is a minimal working sketch of modernity as a sociohistorically specific mode of interpretation and action, for the purposes of setting a coherent framework for discussing some of the marginalizing entailments of endangerment and maintenance for indigenous languages. In specifying nationalism and modernity, my purpose is not limited to critique, but is towards opening up a space for anticipating that historically colonized people, in this case those identified as indigenous, might very well formulate themselves in alternate terms.

Modernity is defined as a temporal orientation predicated on rupture, in which the present moment is separated out as different in kind from a traditional past, and in which the future is imagined to follow upon the present as effect to cause, and therefore is expected to also be different in kind from the traditional past (Gell 1992). Although its applications are myriad and sometimes contradictory, a modernist temporal frame is one of the most pervasive orienting tropes circulating in the articulation of polities on a global scale (Keane 2007). One of modernity's most obvious interpretive consequences in conjunction with colonialism has been that the colonized are framed in terms of an implicitly static traditional, or primitive, past (see Bauman and Briggs 2003; Fabian 1983) in contrastive relation to the modern, dynamic, colonizing West, which is expected to instigate the future.

Endangerment as a tactical rhetoric is effective because it mobilizes an established modernist narrative and in this way makes the situation of indigenous communities readily meaningful to a broad public. For example, here is a list of recent book titles:

Dying Words: Endangered Languages and What They Have to Tell Us (Evans 2009)
When Languages Die: The Extinction of the World's Languages and the Erosion of Human Knowledge (Harrison 2008)

Vanishing Voices: The Extinction of the World's Languages (Nettle and Romaine 2000)

The Last Speakers: the Quest to Save the World's Most Endangered Languages (Harrison 2010)

As emblems of that which was disrupted with colonialism and globalization, indigenous languages are figured in these accounts at the threshold of extinction and death (Perley 2012). Some of these titles identify indigenous languages with traditional knowledge and in this way harmonize, through analogy with species extinction, their current marginalized status with their expected demise. In this way the temporal frame implied by "endangerment" plays a role in clearing the way for presentations of English as the modern native language of America. As Vizenor (1998:35) intimates with "not mere statutes, inheritance, or documentation, however bright the blood and bone in the museums," the project of salvage documentation (Gruber 1970) figures Native American languages as museum pieces; and in so doing indirectly cast the "first White person" or "first English-speaking person" in a territory in a role more relevant to its imagined future than indigenous persons and voices.

Paradox of Expertise

In the books devoted to language endangerment listed above, it is documentary linguists who stand as intermediaries through which the wider public might learn from, save, or hear the voices of, indigenous languages. When applied to community maintenance, the products of linguistic documentation circulate alongside other locally salient ways of objectifying and reflecting upon language, for example through narrative, song, verbal wit, and oratory, that are also locally in play. This produces paradoxes of expertise and authority, in which persons recognized among community members as "good speakers" draw authority from domains of community life that are different from the quasi-national forms of political integration, via language standardization or "language development," that motivate language programs. Those accorded status as good speakers stand in contrast with those university-accredited experts (Hill 2002; Samuels 2006) who are empowered to discover the language through documentation and who define the ongoing terms of government support for programs designed to save it. The status of elders, parents, and grandparents as authorities with respect to an indigenous language, as opposed to researchers, translators, and teachers, poses paradoxes that people grapple with in various ways.

Paradox of Object(ives)

Returning again to the terms of the modern nation-state and its implications for social participation. Latour (1993) argues that the temporal rupture that serves as the touchstone for modernity is enacted and reflected upon in terms of discovery. He identifies in scientific discovery practices[9] carefully delineated procedures for separating out an aspect of the phenomenal world from its contingent surrounds. Acts of isolating phenomena, in Latour's loaded terminology, "purification," create their status as consequential objects, or facts. Researchers establish reliable and enduring facts by replicating parallel conditions, discovery procedures in a controlled environment, within which objects of study are delimited from their surrounds. In this way the objects of research are produced by scientists, and the regularities of their production establish the identity of objects of science across acts of discovery and across time (Gershon 2010). Like other sciences, linguistics constitutes its object, language, through methodologically replicable acts of bounding off an aspect of the phenomenal world from its contextual surround. In this case field elicitation identifies and bounds off grammar and lexicon from their contingency in the spoken life of the community. A language is documented, or discovered, by being objectified in this way.

Scientific practice is accompanied by, and precipitates, an ideological and aperceptual orientation in which the mediating procedures through which the objects of research were isolated recede into the background as the objects emerge into the foreground. The objects are cast as having been "discovered," that is, they are taken to preexist the act of bounding off through which they were defined. As things which preexisted discovery but which are brought to light by means of scientific methodology, they are taken to be aspects of an already given world, or "nature." Endangerment rhetoric places indigenous languages in the role of revealed natural object with respect to the discovery procedures of linguistic documentation. Saving endangered languages has been the rallying cry of documentary linguistics in a way that conflates "saving" with "discovering." Funding agencies, including national governments in the United States, Mexico, New Zealand, Canada, Brazil, Australia; international organizations like UNESCO; and independent foundations such as the Hans Rausing Endangered Languages Project, Terralingua, the Endangered Language Fund, and the Max Planck Institutes, all sponsor documentation projects addressed to language endangerment. Within linguistics the past twenty years has seen an explosion of scholarship devoted to language endangerment, documentation, and maintenance: conferences, articles, edited volumes, books (Bradley and Bradley 2002; Evans 2009; Grenoble and Whaley 2005; Harrison 2008; Nettle and Romaine 2000; Thieberger 2012; Tsunoda 2006). Grant programs designed to respond to language endangerment are first directed to linguists so that they may conduct professional documentation. The rationale for prioritizing documentation is that if languages fall out of use without documentation they will be doubly lost, in the sense that not only will no one speak them in the community with which they are associated, but that they will have also disappeared without ever having been discovered through documentation and accorded a place of memory within the public institutions of modern society.[10]

In the making of modern society, discovered facts become a basis upon which to introduce difference, as technocratic improvement, into social relations. In this way temporal rupture and knowledge creation are mutually implicated, and the social present and future are enacted as different in kind from the past. Documentation stands as the primary science that provides the basis, alongside second language acquisition research and established literacy pedagogies, for technocratic solutions to the problem of language endangerment. Language maintenance puts the products of documentation to use in building new infrastructure (Star 1999), in the form of indigenous language and culture education programs. Where sufficient resources are allocated (and there are rarely sufficient resources), indigenous education programs involve other technocratic actors, such as language acquisition teachers, language materials developers and curriculum developers, and language maintenance specialists.

The temporal assumptions entailed in "maintenance" and "preservation" as labels for what language programs are doing depends upon holding languages, as objects isolated through documentation, in the foreground. It is these objects, not their interpersonal or institutional context, that are identified with the past. Language programs are posed as if they reproduce the past in the present through the imputed continuity of that object, defined as grammar and lexicon, across successive social contexts. This poses paradoxes in just what is meant by "saving our language" for many community members. The items introduced in language programs under the mantle of preservation: alphabets, word lists, grammar drills, etcetera, are in fact quite different from, and not always an apt fit with, other contemporaneous meanings expressed in calls to save what community members describe as "our language." Language programs often reproduce the assumption that words, and other bits of language, can be alienated from social relations and retain continuity with prior speech. This can contrast with other rhetorics through which members of indigenous communities express desires to save a language, which more often cast language in terms inalienable (see Ball 2011) from moral qualities of social relations extending within and across families, through deep time and embodied in land (e.g. Rumsey 2001).

Indigenous Languages as Matter of Concern – a Postcritical Approach

One of the strengths of the Latourian approach to modernity (as opposed to post-structural treatments of Foucault), and to the linkages he draws between knowledge production and governance in democratic nation-states, is the explanatory weight given to acts and processes of mediation. Interpreting modernism as a mode of action underscores the fact that we are not dealing with a monolith, but with a heterogeneous field in which research and national technocratic governance operate across myriad social domains and carry inherent instabilities and contradictions. Because "purification," or "discovery" is always an act of bounding off against a field of contingency, the resulting objects – for our purposes "languages," "individuals," "cultures," etcetera, can never attain the final and absolute qualities ascribed to them. Add to this the fact that science and other academic knowledge productions are internally diverse, with multiple ways of bounding off the objects of knowledge across different communities of scientists and scholars, and there is no guarantee at all that the objects of knowledge will coordinate well with one another (Star and Griesemer 1989). This means that the work of purification, and the separation between an ostensibly already given nature and socially mediated culture, is never total or complete. The effect, to modern minds (who are resting upon the inherent separation of nature from culture as a working assumption), is of a proliferation of unsettling nature/culture hybrids, which goad us to further acts of boundary-making to put right. A consequence is that much of what is of interest and concern impresses itself upon public life as nature/culture hybrids.

For example, like other macro-narratives of our time, such as global warming, language endangerment figures as an impingement upon what is assumed to be an established natural state (here of linguistic diversity and rates of shift) by the excesses of a global social process (King et al. 2008; Mufwene 2002:2). And, like global warming, language endangerment is an encompassing crisis with vague causal links to what the average person may intend or control. It captures our attention, and requires us to think about intervention strategies in terms of coordinated, technocratic efforts. Advocacy for such efforts provokes political affiliations and disaffiliations in which the boundary between nature and culture is salient, though drawn differently by different actors. Proponents of language maintenance advocate for technocratic intervention to reinstate and stabilize a natural equilibrium of diversity (King et al. 2008; Nettle and Romaine 2000); while opponents decry the impingement of technocratic efforts upon a natural process of change and shift already underway (McWhorter 2009; arguably Mufwene 2002). One of the arguments of this book is that these internal dynamics and the heterogeneity of positions within the workings of modernity and the nation-state often take the entire field of our vision, obscuring concerns cast, for example, by some members of indigenous communities, in other terms. In the chapters that follow I propose widening the field of vision through which we address matters of concern that follow upon colonialism, to allow for alternative ways of rendering those concerns by those who are affected.

Pointing out the nationalist, or modernist, underpinnings of endangerment and maintenance appears to undercut some of the justifications for "saving languages" in the first place. But that is only true if we continue to hold to the idea that indigenous languages are really about tradition, or really about a time before colonialism. Instead, if we understand linguistic documentation and maintenance projects as acts within the broader discursive mediation of communities, this sets the stage for a "postcritical" approach to knowledge production and forms of technocratic intervention (Latour 2004) in the sense that the objects produced and critiques launched from the vantage point of various disciplinary domains are taken to be germane to "matters of concern" around which the attention and stakes of multiple actors, including the subjects of linguistic and ethnographic study, converge.

Indigenous languages then figure as matters of concern addressed by persons situated across contrasting disciplines and across different social domains and positions in an indigenous community. What inevitably emerges are hybrid social networks across which indigenous languages are emphatically not stable objects, but are rendered and understood in different, sometimes conflictual, ways. "Language" and the cause of "saving languages" operates as what linguistic anthropologists term "strategically deployable shifters" (Urciuoli 2010) in that the meanings attributed to the terms shift with situation of use and positions of persons. Shifters like "saving languages" have a special role in the political articulation of communities in that they allow for expressions of mutual affiliation around what are ostensibly common, but in fact nonidentical, goals. So strategically deployable shifters can enable the various parties who share a matter of concern to loosely work together (everyone can agree "save the language") but can also prevent them from recognizing their differences from one another. So is it not surprising that paradox, or the appearance of contradiction in a common effort, or the appearance of commonality in contradictory efforts, also proliferates in the matters of concern through which diversely positioned actors mediate communities. When networks extend across contrasting, mutually differentiated, social domains, as is true for academic–community engagements aimed at "saving languages," it is necessary to add a consideration of dialogue and encounter across those domains into the account.

Language Research and Development as Cultural Encounter

While "outside experts" are almost always involved in language documentation and maintenance in some capacity, processes of indigenous community mediation around indigenous language issues are more complex than can be captured with a dichotomy between "outsider linguists, language planners" and "insider community members." This is because members of indigenous communities often undertake university training in order to qualify for funded positions in heritage language research and program development (as advocated by Smith 1999). Language rights and language endangerment rhetorics provide the rationale for programs through which members of indigenous communities obtain accreditation for themselves and their efforts, including linguistic documentation and school-based indigenous language education efforts.[11] Even in the absence of "outside experts" language programs are still complexly articulated, in that they involve community members with university accreditation working alongside other community members who derive their authority from other sources.

In language programs differences in pedagogical practice, ways of speaking, and what it means to "know" a heritage language can be a source of both conflict and creativity between diverse people identified as indigenous. Family households and school language programs pose contrasting models of authoritative language use; and, in the course of everyday life, people move across and participate in both social domains, bringing them to bear upon one another in ways that are alternately complementary and conflictual. I want to make it clear that I am not claiming that schools and culture centers make a sort of false claim upon an indigeneity that is properly attributed to homes and families; only that they pose one site of mediation among others. I devote more ethnographic attention to alternate, extended familial and ceremonial sites of discourse because schools and culture centers are already more likely to be recognized and supported since they articulate most closely with government regulating functions. The "taken for granted" quality of knowledge as embodied in state formal education settings tends to obscure articulations of indigenous languages and communities in other contexts and terms.

A key argument of this book is that indigenous languages exist at the threshold between indigenous communities and surrounding social orders and that they figure importantly in community definition at that juncture. Therefore, concerns with saving or supporting indigenous languages are articulated at the same threshold, and have a complicated relationship with local communicative practices because they are often dually articulated through historically imposed institutions like schools, on the one hand, and across generations in extended families, on the other. My concern is to set this as the frame within which to analyze not only the play of indigenous language issues in institutions (like schools) that clearly articulate with state, federal, and international discourses, but to also recognize ways in which community members employ language in ways relevant to other notions of indigeneity to pose alternate definitions of community, centered in family, place, and, often, in religious discourse.

For example, as *ndah*/stranger/White person, and as a researcher interested in changes in ways of using Apache and English, a threshold of sorts surrounded me as I moved through the community – a threshold that differently positioned people interpreted and addressed in different ways. Within the politically prominent family with whom I worked most closely, senior family members responded to my request to learn to speak Apache by directing me to learn how to make bread (which in political families is more than a performance of domesticity, but a perpetual readiness for visitors), and to become an aware participant in the life of the extended family. This involved being attentive enough to (hopefully) get the jokes in conversational banter, to infer and perform necessary actions, and to realize when I was being teased or being invited to help tease someone else. By contrast, my supervisors in educational offices of the tribe paired me with fluent speakers and paid me to create written curricular materials for the schools. Their overriding concern was that we make a product that would foster student pride in their indigenous heritage by presenting their language in terms that compared favorably with materials students were using for their English classes. In both home and school contexts, discourses about *Ndee bik'ehgo yatiʼ*, 'Apache way of speaking,' were prominent but cast in different, sometimes conflicting, terms. My work in the school language program elicited both assistance and criticism within my quasi-familial relations. By paying attention to the terms of these, I was able to trace the differences between pedagogies and notions of what it means to speak Apache, addressed to me, as a language researcher, between these two different contexts. As I will demonstrate in the chapter that follows, attending to these differences helped me understand the political controversies that emerged concerning the language program with which I was involved, and helped me understand some of the reasons for the success of other, more longstanding programs.

The Generativity of Otherness across Mutually Implicated Boundaries

Language programs provide community members with representations of a local language infused with national and international connotations that can be taken up and used to figure local events in terms of wider significances. Put into play at the threshold of indigenous communities and their global surrounds, alongside other language practices, documentation and maintenance comprise one pole in what Weiner and Glaskin term a "conjunctural field" (2007:12) in which:

> The Indigenous and the 'Western' are . . . defined against each other, and the articulation of each includes the other in its foundation. The struggle for recognition . . . is as much a moment in the development of Western social economy as it is an historical trope for indigenous peoples of the world. (Weiner and Glaskin 2007:12)

Skimming through the popular language endangerment literature, it does not take long to become convinced that the prospect of encountering, discovering, and documenting indigenous languages energizes the development of certain sectors, including linguistics, ethnography, tourism, multicultural education, green politics consumers (Moore 2006) of a Western social economy. Similarly, advocacy for equality and representation energizes the enactment of democratic governance. At the same time, and from the standpoint of members of indigenous communities like Fort Apache, engagement with *ndah*, or White people, is one of the ways in which people define what it means to speak and behave as *ndee*, or Apache. The products of documentation and maintenance might be stamped in a nationalist mode in one context but their meaning in subsequent acts of contextualization as they circulate through the community is underdetermined. Dictionaries, Bibles, and stock phrases from language classes can serve as fodder for alternate contextualizations as they are circulated across contrasting social domains. As the notion of "conjunctural field" implies, the association of a language form with one set of modern national political contexts motivates recontextualization in others framed through local processes of differentiation, and vice versa. So while I do argue that language maintenance programs are rife with misrecognition, interpretive gaps, and paradox, I also cast the indeterminacy of community response to them as productive and conducive to further, distributive acts of political mediation. Products of documentation and maintenance add to the store of resources that community participants intercept and recontextualize in alternate ways as they navigate their futures.

Conclusion

In sum, the discourse of language endangerment and related forms of indigenous language promotion takes place in complicated local social environments that neither the disciplinary tools of linguistics nor language acquisition training in education explicitly prepare their bearers to address. Nearly anyone who has worked on community language maintenance programs can attest to the fact that many programs provoke local controversy and are often modified to accommodate community interventions (see Florey 1993; Hofling 1996; Morgan 2009; Nevins 2004; Samuels 2006; Wilkins 2000). This book provides a set of principles, illustrated with ethnography, through which to anticipate forms of complexity and plurality built into indigenous communities through their history of colonial encounter and through the contemporary terms in which they articulate with the polities that encompass them. I complement efforts to save endangered indigenous languages by revealing the contextualizing processes otherwise obscured in the focus upon "language" as an object of documentation and transmission. This is offered in the hope that placing endangerment and maintenance within a more reflexive understanding of the complex social field in which they operate will further the open-ended collaborations and conversations between community members, researchers, and language program developers which are already well underway.

Community ambivalence in response to language programs is often overridden by language experts, disregarded on the rationale that the problem of endangerment is too urgent to allow for distractions from the programmatic goals of documentation and maintenance (Loether 2010; Walsh 2002). Failure to recognize the nature of such struggles in the rush to "save endangered languages" serves to reinforce political asymmetry in the relation between schools and museums as sites of knowledge and learning over other authorities and learning practices in indigenous communities. By contrast, building into language work attention to the relativity of social perspectives can offer an alternative to the naturalization of mainstream discourses and educational practices they entail. If indigenous community empowerment is the goal, then, community critique and intervention are valuable opportunities to modify and reinterpret language programs in their relation to voices authorized from other sources and for recognizing multiple ways in which language is very much at stake in the mediation of a local community within wider polities. In fact, it is often in expressions of ambivalence and controversy that the stake community members have in indigenous or heritage languages can be found.

In the following chapter I provide an ethnographic illustration of what there is to be learned from conflicts that arise from differences in perspective on language loss from the interrupted language project with which I was involved on the Fort Apache reservation. By attending to differences in understandings of language loss, described as different language ideologies (Kroskrity 2000; Silverstein 1985; Woolard 1998), across school and extended family (as well as other) environments, I try to show why the various parties clashed in how they defined the problem and in what they took to be desirable ways of addressing it.

Notes

1 Moore (2007) notes the different ideological framing of indigenous languages as precious, "endangered" remnants of the past as opposed to immigrant languages, which are cast in national political discourse as a "dangerous" part of the present sociolinguistic landscape.
2 My usage often varies to reflect the voices of my consultants and the politics of representing them to an audience that includes critical indigenous readers. "Indian" tends to be a term that is used by insiders and for describing themselves among themselves.
3 Selecting liberal democratic settler states from the broader range of places where endangerment and maintenance are matters of concern allows for finer grained precision, and arguably illuminates precedents and models that are exported elsewhere. However, this does leave gaping questions about that "elsewhere" that I do not pretend to adequately address here.
4 Assimilation, while posing severe constraints, also can be approached as a framework of mediation that has been actively negotiated by Native Americans and other indigenous or minority persons. For examples, see Bartelt (1992).
5 See Morgan (2009), for example, on the language shift effects of the Collier administration's 1934 Indian Reorganization Act, or the "Indian New Deal," at Fort Belknap.
6 This is Hoijer's English translation of a speech Lawrence Mithlo dictated for him in Chiricahua Apache. The Apache language portion of this speech is presented in Chapter 5. (Hoijer, Harry. 1938. *Chiricahua and Mescalero Apache Texts with Ethnological Notes by Morris Opler*. Chicago: University of Chicago Press. With kind permission from University of Chicago Press.)

7   That indigenous community members do not author these terms, but are subjected to them is a point argued by Povinelli (2002).
8   Other languages, such as Navajo (which many report to be mutually intelligible with Western Apache), and other Native American languages, as well as Spanish and German were spoken in enclaves according to marriage histories, but were not as prominent in public life.
9   Bauman and Briggs (2003) trace an intellectual genealogy through which language has been disciplinarily bounded off an object (and instrument) of knowledge in parallel terms.
10 This meaning of "lost" noted by Moore (2006).
11 In North America, good examples are: the American Indian Language Development Institute (AILDI) http://aildi.arizona.edu/; Northwest Indian Language Institute (NILI) http://pages.uoregon.edu/nwili/.

References

Anderson, Benedict R. 1991. *Imagined Communities: Reflections on the Origin and Spread of Nationalism.* London: Verso.
Ball, Christopher. 2011. Inalienability in Social Relations: Language, Possession and Exchange in Amazonia. *Language in Society* 40(3):307–341.
Bartelt, Guillermo. 1992. American Indian Discourses of Assimiliationism. *Language and Literature* 17:59–75.
Bartelt, Guillermo, Susan Penfield-Jasper, and Bates Hoffer, eds. 1982. *Essays in Native American English.* San Antonio: Trinity University Press.
Basso, Keith. 1966. The Gift of Changing Woman. *Bureau of American Ethnology Bulletin 196.* Washington DC: Smithsonian Institution.
Basso, Keith. 1969. *Western Apache Witchcraft.* Tucson: University of Arizona Press.
Basso, Keith. 1979. *Portraits of "the Whiteman": Linguistic Play and Cultural Symbols among the Western Apache.* New York: Cambridge University Press.
Basso, Keith. 1990. *Western Apache Language and Culture: Essays in Linguistic Anthropology.* Tucson: University of Arizona Press.
Basso, Keith. 1996. *Wisdom Sits in Places: Language and Landscape among the Western Apache.* Albuquerque: University of New Mexico Press.
Bauman, Richard and Charles Briggs. 2003. *Voices of Modernity: Language Ideologies and the Politics of Inequality.* Cambridge: Cambridge University Press.
Blommaert, Jan. 2010. *The Sociolinguistics of Globalization.* Cambridge: Cambridge University Press.
Bradley, David and Maya Bradley. 2002. *Language Endangerment and Language Maintenance: An Active Approach.* New York: Routledge.
Collins, James.1998. *Understanding Tolowa Histories: Western Hegemonies and Native American Responses.* New York: Routledge.
Crawford, James. 2001. Proposition 203: Anti-Bilingual Initiative in Arizona. www.languagepolicy.net/archives/az-unz.htm (accessed October 31, 2012).

Dauenhauer, Nora Marks and Richard Dauenhauer. 1998. Technical, Emotional and Ideological Issues in Reversing Language Shift: Examples from Southeast Alaska. In *Endangered Languages: Current Issues and Future Prospects*. Lenore A. Grenoble and Lindsay J. Whaley, eds., pp. 57–98. Cambridge: Cambridge University Press.

Deloria, Phillip. 1998. *Playing Indian*. New Haven: Yale University Press.

Dobrin, Lise, Peter K. Austin, and David Nathan. 2009. Dying to Be Counted: The Commodification of Endangered Languages in Documentary Linguistics. In *Proceedings of Conference on Language Documentation and Linguistic Theory*. Peter K. Austin, Oliver Bond, and David Nathan, eds., pp. 59–68. London: SOAS.

Evans, Nicholas. 2009. *Dying Words: Endangered Languages and What They Have to Tell Us*. Oxford: Wiley-Blackwell.

Fabian, Johannes. 1983. *Time and The Other: How Anthropology Makes Its Object*. New York: Columbia University Press.

Florey, Margaret J. 1993. The Reinterpretation of Knowledge and Its Role in the Process of Language Obsolescence. *Oceanic Linguistics* 32(2):295–309.

Gell, Alfred. 1992. *The Anthropology of Time: Cultural Constructions of Temporal Maps and Images*. Oxford: Berg.

Gershon, Illana. 2010. Bruno Latour. In *Agamben to Zizek: Contemporary Critical Theorists*. Jon Simons, ed., pp. 167–176. Edinburgh: Edinburgh University Press.

Goddard, Pliny. 1919. San Carlos Apache Texts. *Anthropological Papers of the American Museum of Natural History* 24(3):141–367.

Goddard, Pliny. 1920. White Mountain Apache Texts. *Anthropological Papers of the American Museum of Natural History* (24)4:369–527.

Goodwin, Grenville. 1938. White Mountain Apache Religion. *American Anthropologist* 40(1):24–37.

Goodwin, Grenville. 1942. The Social Organization of the Western Apache. *Memoirs of the American Folklore Society* 33.

Goodwin, Grenville. 1994. *Myths and Tales of the White Mountain Apache*. Tucson: University of Arizona Press. (Original work published 1939.)

Grenoble, Lenore and Lindsay Whaley. 2005. *Saving Languages: An Introduction to Language Revitalization*. Cambridge: Cambridge University Press.

Gruber, Jacob. 1970. Ethnographic Salvage and the Shaping of Anthropology. *American Anthropologist*, New Series 72(6):1289–1299.

Harrison, K. David. 2008. *When Languages Die: The Extinction of the World's Languages and the Erosion of Human Knowledge*. Oxford: Oxford University Press.

Harrison, K. David. 2010. *The Last Speakers: The Quest to Save the World's Most Endangered Languages*. Washington DC: National Geographic.

Hill, Jane H. 2002. "Expert Rhetorics" in Advocacy for Endangered Languages: Who Is Listening and What Do They Hear? *Journal of Linguistic Anthropology* 12(2):119–133.

Hofling, Charles Andrew. 1996. Indigenous Linguistic Revitalization and Outsider Interaction: The Itzaj Maya Case. *Human Organization* 55(1):108–116.

Hoijer, Harry. 1938. *Chiricahua and Mescalero Apache Texts with Ethnological Notes by Morris Opler*. Chicago: University of Chicago Publications in Anthropology, Linguistic Series.

Hornberger, Nancy. 1998. Language Policy, Language Education, Language Rights: Indigenous, Immigrant, And International Perspectives. *Language in Society* 27:439–458.

IPS Arctic Council Indigenous Peoples Secretariat. 2011. Qualified UNDRI Support. February 21. www.arcticpeoples.org/index.php?option=com_k2&view=item&id=367:qualified-undrip-support&Itemid=2 (accessed October 31, 2012).

Jourdan, Miriam. 2010. Arizona Grades Teachers on Fluency: State Pushes School Districts to Reassign Instructors with Heavy Accents or Other Shortcomings in Their English. *Wall Street Journal*, April 30.

Keane, Webb. 2007. *Christian Moderns: Freedom and Fetish in the Mission Encounter*. Berkeley: University of California Press.

King, Kendall A., Natalie Schilling-Estes, Lyn Fogle, Jia Jackie Lou, and Barbara Soukup, eds. 2008. *Sustaining Linguistic Diversity: Endangered and Minority Languages and Language Varieties*. Washington, DC: Georgetown University Press.

Krauss, Michael. 1992. The World's Languages in Crisis. *Language* 68:4–10.

Kroskrity, Paul V. 2000. Regimenting Languages: Language Ideological Perspectives. In *Regimes of Language: Ideologies, Polities, and Identities*, Paul V. Kroskrity, ed., pp. 1–34. Santa Fe: School of American Research.

Latour, Bruno. 1993. *We Have Never Been Modern*. Cambridge, MA: Harvard University Press.

Latour, Bruno. 2004. Why Has Critique Run out of Steam: From Matters of Fact to Matters of Concern. *Critical Inquiry* 30:225–248.

Loether, Christopher. 2010. Language Revitalization and the Manipulation of Language Ideologies: A Shoshoni Case Study. In *Native American Language Ideologies: Beliefs, Practices, and Struggles in Indian Country*. Paul V. Kroskrity and Margaret C. Field, eds., pp. 238–255. Tucson: University of Arizona Press.

McCarty, Teresa and Ofelia Zepeda. Amerindians. In *Handbook of Language and Ethnic Identity*. Joshua Fishman, ed., pp. 197–210. Oxford: Oxford University Press.

McWhorter, James. 2009. English: The Cosmopolitan Tongue. *World Affairs*, Fall.

Meek, Barbara. 2010 *We Are Our Language: An Ethnography of Language Revitalization in a Northern Athabascan Community*. Tucson: University of Arizona Press.

Merlan, Francesca. 2009. Indigeneity: Local and Global. *Current Anthropology* 50(3):303–333.

Moore, Robert E. 2006. Disappearing, Inc.: Glimpsing the Sublime in the Politics of Access to Endangered Languages. *Language and Communication* 26: 296–315.

Moore, Robert E. 2007. From Endangered to Dangerous: Two Types of Sociolinguistic Inequality (with Examples from Ireland and the US). *Working Papers in Urban Language and Literacies*, 45.

Moore, Robert E., S. Pietikäinen, and J. Blommaert. 2010. Counting the Losses: Numbers as the Language of Language Endangerment. *Studies in Sociolinguistics* 4(1):1–26.

Morgan, Mindy J. 2009. *The Bearer of This Letter: Language Ideologies, Literacy Practices, and the Fort Belknap Indian Community*. Lincoln: University of Nebraska Press.

Mufwene, Salikoko S. 2002. Colonisation, Globalisation, and the Future of Languages in the Twenty-First Century. *MOST Journal on Multicultural Societies* 4(2). www.unesco.org/most/vl4n2mufwene.pdf (accessed October 31, 2012).

Mufwene, Salikoko S. 2008. *Language Evolution: Contact, Competition, Change*. London: Continuum.

Nettle, Daniel and Suzanne Romaine. 2000. *Vanishing Voices: The Extinction of the World's Languages*. Oxford: Oxford University Press.

Nevins, M. Eleanor. 2004. Learning to Listen: Confronting Two Meanings of Language Loss in the Contemporary White Mountain Apache Speech Community. *Journal of Linguistic Anthropology* 14:269–288.

Nevins, Thomas J. 2010. Between Love and Culture: Misunderstanding, Textuality and the Dialectics of Ethnographic Knowledge. *Language and Communication* 30(1):58–68.

Niezen, Ronald. 2003. *The Origins of Indigenism: Human Rights and the Politics of Identity*. Berkeley: University of California Press.

Opler, Morris. 1938. A Chiricahua Apache's Account of the Geronimo Campaign of 1886. Narrated by Samuel E. Kenoi. *New Mexico Historical Review* 13(4):360–386. http://etext.virginia.edu/toc/modeng/public/OplKeno.html (accessed November 6, 2012).

Opler, Morris. 1996. *An Apache Life-way*. Lincoln: University of Nebraska Press. (Original work published 1941.)

Paulson, Christina Bratt. 1997. Language Policies and Language Rights. *Annual Review of Anthropology* 27:73–87.

Perley, Bernard. 2012. Zombie Linguistics: Experts, Endangered Languages and the Curse of Undead Voices. *Anthropological Forum* 22(2):133–149.

Phillips, Susan. 1992. *The Invisible Culture: Communication in Classroom and Community on the Warm Springs Indian Reservation*. Long Grove: Waveland Press.

Povinelli, Elizabeth A. 2002. *The Cunning of Recognition: Indigenous Alterities and the Making of Australian Multiculturalism*. Durham: Duke University Press.

Reyner, Jon and Jeanne Eder. 2006. *American Indian Education: A History*. Tulsa: University of Oklahoma Press.

Richland, Justin B. 2007. Pragmatic Paradoxes and Ironies of Indigeneity at the "Edge" of Hopi Sovereignty. *American Ethnologist* 34(3):540–557.

Richmond, Mark, Clinton Robinson, and Margarete Sachs-Israel. 2008. *The Global Literacy Challenge: A Profile of Youth and Adult Literacy at the Mid-point of the United Nations Literacy Debate 2003–2012*. Paris: UNESCO.

Rumsey, Alan. 2001. Tracks, Traces and Links to Land in Aboriginal Australia and Beyond. In *Emplaced Myth: Space, Narrative and Knowledge in Aboriginal Australia and Papua New Guinea*. Alan Rumsey and James Weiner, eds., pp. 19–42. Manoa: University of Hawai'i Press.

Samuels, David. 2006. Bible Translation and Medicine Man Talk: Missionaries, Indexicality, and the "Language Expert" on the San Carlos Apache Reservation. *Language in Society* 35(4):529–557.

Silverstein, Michael. 1985. Language and the Culture of Gender. In *Semiotic Mediation*. Elizabeth Mertz and R. Parmentier, eds., pp. 219–259. New York: Academic Press.

Silverstein, Michael. 1996. Monoglot "Standard" in America: Standardization and Metaphors of Linguistic Hegemony. In *The Matrix Of Language: Contemporary Linguistic Anthropology*. Don Brenneis and R. Macauley, eds., pp. 284–306. Boulder: Westview.

Smith, Linda Tuhiwai. 1999. *Decolonizing Methodologies: Research and Indigenous Peoples*. London: Zed Books.

Spitulnik, Debra. 1998. The Language of the City: Town Bemba as Urban Hybridity. *Journal of Linguistic Anthropology* 8(1):30–59.

Star, Susan Leigh. 1999. The Ethnography of Infrastructure *American Behavioral Scientist* 43(3):377–391.

Star, Susan Leigh and James R. Griesemer. 1989. Institutional Ecology, "Translations" and Boundary Objects: Amateurs and Professionals in Berkeley's Museum of Vertebrate Zoology, 1907–39. *Social Studies of Science* 19(3): 387–420.

Strathern, M. 1999. *Property, Substance and Effect: Anthropological Essays on Persons and Things*. London: Athlone.

Thieberger, Nicholas, ed. 2012. *The Oxford Handbook of Linguistic Fieldwork*. Oxford: Oxford University Press.

Tsunoda, Tasaku. 2006. *Language Endangerment and Language Revitalization: An Introduction*. Berlin: Mouton de Gruyter.

Urciuoli, Bonnie. 2010. Entextualizing *Diversity*: Semiotic Incoherence in Institutional Discourse. *Language and Communication* 30(1):48–57.

Vizenor, Gerald, ed.1998. *Fugitive Poses: Native American Scenes of Absence and Presence*. Lincoln: University of Nebraska Press.

Wagner, Roy. 1981. *The Invention of Culture, revised and expanded edition*. Chicago: University of Chicago Press.

Walsh, Michael. 2002. Teaching NSW's Indigenous Languages: Lessons from Elsewhere. Report for the Aboriginal Curriculum Unit of the New South Wales Board of Studies. University of Sydney.

Weiner, James F. and Kate Glaskin. 2007. Customary Land Tenure and Registration in Australia and Papua New Guinea: Anthropological Perspectives. In *Customary Land Tenure and Registration in Australia and Papua New Guinea: Anthropological Perspectives. Asia Pacific Environment Monograph 3*. James F. Weiner and Kate Glaskin, eds., pp. 1–14. Canberra: Australian National University E Press.

Wilkins, David P. 2000. Even with the best of intentions...: Some Pitfalls in the Fight for Linguistic and Cultural Survival (One View of the Australian Experience). In *As Línguas Amazônicas Hoje / Les Langues d'Amazonie Aujourd'hui*. Francisco Queixalos and O. Renault-Lescure, eds. São Paulo: Institut de Recherche pour le Développement, Instituto Socioambiental, and Museu Paraense Emílio Goeldi.

Wolfe, Patrick. 1999. *Settler Colonialism: The Politics and Poetics of an Ethnographic Event*. New York: Cassell.

Woolard, Kathryn. 1998. Introduction: Language Ideology as a Field of Inquiry In *Language Ideologies: Practice and Theory*. Bambi B. Schieffelin, Kathryn A. Woolard, and Paul V. Kroskrity, eds., pp. 3–49. Oxford: Oxford University Press.

Wyloge, Evan. 2010. Native American Tribes Say They Won't Enforce Immigration Law. Arizona Capitol Times, June 14. http://azcapitoltimes.com/news/2010/06/14/indian-tribes-oppose-new-immigration-law/ (accessed October 31, 2012).

3

Learning to Listen
Coming to Terms with Conflicting Meanings of Language Loss

They might be using some Apache-sounding words, but what they are really teaching the kids is English. They think they are teaching the kids the Apache word *nakih*; but they don't teach the kids *nakih*. Instead they are teaching: "*nakih* means two." Nick Hosay

"A is for *aasitini*, B is for *bįįh*, Ch is for *chaa*"; is this what is really what it means to know Apache? Robert Moody

This chapter is based on my engagement as a language materials developer and ethnographer in a diverse network of residents of the Fort Apache reservation speech community about language matters that concern them. I found that not only was the threat of Apache language loss cause for concern (see also Adley Santa-Maria 1997, 1998), but also that people were concerned about challenges to what many posed to me as an enabling condition for speaking "good Apache": mutual involvement across generations within extended families. Young people's distractions with television and other media, and the dangers posed to them as they became older from drug and alcohol use, were part of the discussion, but also institutional education, including, somewhat ironically, Apache language programs in the schools. I learned that many Apache parents and grandparents responded to such programs with ambivalence. On the one hand, people voiced support for putting Apache on equal footing with English in the schools. On the other, language education programs were perceived by some as posing a threat to other Apache pedagogical practices and to

Lessons from Fort Apache: Beyond Language Endangerment and Maintenance, First Edition. M. Eleanor Nevins.
© 2013 John Wiley & Sons, Inc. Published 2013 by John Wiley & Sons, Inc.

relations of authority between young and old. I argue that the expression of ambivalence or opposition toward these programs by some reservation residents was not the result of emotional or ideological confusion,[1] but more often involved incisive critique of challenges to the authority and legitimacy of elders (or rather, more general relations of seniority, *báyáń*) within extended families by a contrasting model of what it means to know Apache language and culture located in schools. I argue further that attending to such critiques, rather than dismissing them as obstacles to progress, is an important step toward more politically symmetrical community language programs.

In the previous chapter I argued that controversy and conflict are almost inevitable in indigenous language advocacy, and that attending to conflict and to differences of purpose should by no means undermine that work. Put another way: if indigenous languages did not matter very much to people, no one would be fighting over them. So here I hope to provoke a reconsideration of the object of documentation and maintenance in order to clarify forms of community negotiation already underway in many language programs, but often misrecognized. As I will demonstrate by elaborating upon conflicts and critiques that emerged around language programs with which I was involved on the Fort Apache reservation, a key source of misrecognition is the assumption that the "language" documented by linguists as grammar and lexicon, and reproduced in school lessons as vocabulary and grammar, is what people in the community who are not linguists mean when they express concern about language loss.

The majority of literature on language endangerment stresses its status as a world problem, involving macro-processes that encompass and transform local speech communities from outside inward (e.g. Bradley and Bradley 2002; Evans 2009; Fase et al. 1992; Fishman 1989; Harrison 2008; Nettle and Romaine 2000; Tsunoda 2006). It is linguists and university-credentialed researchers and educators, stepping into the scene of a community affected by colonialism and globalization, who are cast in the role of problem-solving mediators of the crisis. In a 2002 special issue of the *Journal of Linguistic Anthropology*, contributions from Jane Hill, Nancy Dorian, Joshua Fishman, and Nora England draw attention to the need for ethnographic investigation into how threatened local language communities engage with linguists and other language experts interested in saving endangered languages. Hill (2002) examines the rhetoric employed by endangered language advocates as they attempt to raise support for the cause with general audiences (i.e. people who are not members of threatened language communities). She points to several features of this rhetoric that have the potential to inadvertently run counter to ideas and values concerning a threatened language held by those who speak it or otherwise have claim to it. In this chapter I provide an ethnographic treatment of just such a conflict.

Similarly, Dorian (2002) advocates expanding the range of studies deemed essential to preserving threatened languages from narrowly defined accounts of linguistic structure to ethnographic treatments of communicative competence. Communicative competence is inclusive of grammatical and lexical documentation, but extends the range of concerns to the speaker's knowledge of how to use language and understand others' uses of language across social contexts (Hymes 1972). It directs our attention to ways that language is embedded in interpersonal, ethical, aesthetic, political, and temporal relations. Language maintenance programs operate at the nexus of a minority community and institutions of state. Hymes (1996) points out that the social embeddedness of language is directly to the point when we are tasked with addressing social concerns like language loss or considerations of the role of language use in educational settings involving minority communities (Heath 1983). Expanding the project of language documentation, maintenance, and advocacy to include considerations of communicative competence better prepares us to address the manner in which maintenance programs recontextualize the products of documentation within specific institutional contexts (especially schools), and to investigate relations between this social context and others within an indigenous community. Here I describe a case in which conflicts between the social and political relationships entailed by standards of communicative competence associated with school maintenance efforts on the one hand, and alternative standards emerging from other local contexts, on the other, are key to understanding controversies surrounding a local Apache language program. Political controversies arise, not only due to "factionalism" within the community, but because language programs, as institutional educational programs, are themselves a particular, intimate politic nexus with the institutions of surrounding state and national orders.

As noted in the previous chapter, during my stay there, the White Mountain Apache reservation speech community was in some ways similar to other indigenous speech communities within liberal democratic settler states. The late nineteenth to early twentieth century was a period of relative isolation from English speaking settlers. Apache people were increasingly integrated into the labor force, but often in groups of people who already knew one another and who spoke Apache with one another. Many Apache men worked with cattle, or moved with their families as small mobile camps travelling to mining, logging, and construction sites throughout the southwestern United States (Watt 2004). Experience of residential, or boarding, schools under assimilationist policies was uneven. Many of the students who attended Saint John's residential school went on to fill key leadership positions in the tribe and to extol the virtues of bilingualism and biculturalism (Watt 2004). However, some left boarding school at San Carlos with harrowing stories of humiliation and cruelty, with lasting trauma and resentment towards school efforts to "civilize" Indians (Greenfeld 2001; Watt 2004). The Collier administration reforms ushered in a period in which tribal leaders utilized legal mechanisms of state to claim back lands from timber and mining companies, and to start tribal businesses in their stead. Along with these forms of relative empowerment came increased integration into the surrounding political-economic regime, in the context of which tribal leaders placed a high value upon Apache–English bilingualism. Chairman Benjamin Moody, reflecting upon his father's experience as chairman in the years following the establishment of the tribe's constitution, said that speaking good English and good Apache had been necessary to leadership throughout the twentieth century. A tribal chairman needs to be able to broker relations with settler institutions on the one hand, and with local institutions in which speaking Apache was crucial to leadership and participation on the other, as in family feasts and gift exchanges, religious ceremonies, harvests, etcetera.

This pattern persisted into my research period except that there were by then more young people on the reservation than old people, and not enough jobs on the reservation to provide work and sustenance for all of them. At the end of the twentieth century the language that had served as a local vernacular, Western Apache, was perceived to be in decline among the young and to be threatened with replacement by the language of mass media, most job opportunities, commerce, national government, and of the majority population in the non-Indian towns adjacent to the reservation. As in other such communities, many expressed concern that they, as a people, were losing their heritage language. There was a widespread perception that, in unprecedented numbers, young children had not been learning to speak the language (Adley-Santa Maria 1997, 1998). Children were perceived to be speaking mostly English, the language they encountered through watching television, going to movies, and listening to music, and the one language that they absolutely had to know for school.

In response, various branches of the tribal government had mounted efforts, many of them grant-funded educational programs, to "do something" about it. The tribal council had passed resolutions to encourage the teaching of Apache in public schools on the reservation, and required Apache language fluency of any person elected to the council or to tribal chairmanship. Apache was one of the tribe's two official languages for use in tribal government and service programs. Speaking and understanding Apache was not only required by law of those running for tribal council; it was also necessary in practice, since many council sessions are conducted primarily in Apache. The chairman and council members also predominantly spoke Apache for their radio broadcast speeches. Apache language emerged as a focus for negotiation and coordination with researchers and state educational institutions. As a language researcher, I was to learn immediately, in my first conversations with most of the Apache people that I met, that this apparent decline was alarming to them. These expressed concerns, together with the need to supplement my research grants for a longer than expected field term, drew me into work for the tribe on Apache language education projects. It would take me longer to realize that the problem of language loss and the desired survival of the Apache language were understood differently from different positions within the contemporary speech community.

My Intersection with Changing Researcher–Community Relationships

At White Mountain and elsewhere, the development of institutional language and culture preservation programs has informed the relationship between researchers and the communities in which they work. In fact, concern about Apache language loss partly framed the way people interpreted and discussed my research. Upon learning that I was interested in ways that Apache and English languages are used in everyday life, many people would be prompted to discuss how kids "nowadays" are not learning Apache. Many also gave personal accounts of failed attempts to get their own children to speak Apache. Doing research on the Apache language and on the dynamics of change in language use implicitly involved me in what for many people were larger overriding moral concerns, not only about language loss, but also about researchers. In many Native American reservation communities, researchers have been criticized for using their research to make their own living, which to many tribal members appears to be a very good one, without giving anything back to the tribe. In this environment, it can be difficult to secure permission to do research, and once in the field it can be difficult to avoid becoming the object of controversy. In my own case, working for a tribal office developing language resources for the schools won me important friends and supporters who came to my defense on many occasions. I was defensible as a researcher because I could be described as giving something back to the tribe. Likewise, many field linguists and sociolinguists studying Western Apache have produced materials to be used in Apache language literacy programs (Adley-Santa Maria 1998; Bray 1998; de Reuse 1997; Liebe-Harkort 1980) or acted as consultants and materials developers for tribal programs. My spouse, Thomas Nevins, a cultural anthropologist, and I became involved with three different but interrelated language maintenance efforts during three years of ethnographic research.

This situation reflects a general trend in field linguistics in minority language communities (Thieberger 2012). The politics of access as well as disciplinary critique in cultural anthropology of the political ethics surrounding knowledge production about politically marginalized communities (e.g. Marcus and Fischer 1999) make it increasingly untenable to assume the role of neutral observer in conducting field research in such communities. This has led ethnographers as well as documentary linguists to become more involved in issues of interest to the community's members. Increasingly, contributions to language development programs have been written into grant proposals as collateral benefits of research or stipulated by political representatives of minority language communities as a precondition to permission to conduct research.

Many scholars as well as local language educators view this trend toward increasing involvement in maintenance efforts as an improvement upon the older colonial relationship. It can be interpreted as the replacement of an expropriative relationship between researcher and language community with a reciprocal one. However, as I was to learn through participating in several failed or controversial language programs, the relationship between such programs and members of the local language community is often quite a bit more complicated and problematic than reciprocity would seem to imply. Institutional Apache language preservation programs were described by many on the reservation as arousing strong feelings and moral judgments from both supporters and opponents. Because Apache language programs promote the Apache language within a state and national school system that has been historically intolerant and denigratory, they have inspired strong commitment and support in many quarters (Fort Apache Scout 2000a, 2000b). However, as I learned through participation in several failed language projects, programs also elicited critique from community members, many of whom were themselves deeply concerned about Apache language loss. It was difficult at first for me to understand why, if all parties were genuinely concerned with saving the language, language programs so frequently became targets of controversy.

As an entry point I describe here the rise and fall of one Apache language education program in which I participated. I treat this example in some detail in order to explore what it reveals about the meanings of language loss and language survival within the contemporary White Mountain Apache reservation speech community. What is interesting about this program is the controversy that it elicited, which eventually led to its termination.

As the controversy developed it became clear that the way educators envisioned the problem of language loss and language survival differed significantly from how these were envisioned from the perspective of Apache families and family-related activities.[2] I argue that these differently situated representations came into conflict because what was offered as language maintenance solutions by the schools were construed by some to exacerbate the problem of language loss as understood within extended family-centered contexts.

Ndee Biyati' Project: Its Rise and Fall

In this section I first give an account of the language program from the perspective of its developers in a tribal education office. I then describe some of the early critical responses I received from friends and consultants who were not directly involved with the project, but who were supportive and helpful in the project's development. Following this, I describe the controversy that led to the project's termination, noting that other projects have become similarly embroiled. In succeeding sections I explore some of the differences between the contrasting meanings of language loss that contributed to this controversy.

When I first arrived at the White Mountain Apache reservation, articles appeared in the *Fort Apache Scout* (2000a, 2000b) newspaper announcing that the tribe had just successfully established Internet connections for all the schools and libraries on the reservation. After living there for a year and becoming colleagues and friends with several Apache people involved in Apache language education (and after running out of my own grant money), I started to work as a language materials developer for Healthy Nations Ndee Benadesh: The People's Vision, one of the tribe's more youth-oriented and technologically innovative educational programs. Linda Goody, a tribal member who grew up on the reservation and returned to it after earning a master's degree in sociology and social work, initiated Ndee Benadesh. The organization had enjoyed a good deal of public acclaim for its town hall-style public meeting series, which solicited concerns from community members (language loss was always first on the list) and for its youth-oriented video composition programs. In the latter, Apache youths learned how to compose and edit videos and utilized this skill to address issues that concerned them. These videos focused on issues as diverse as drug abuse, alcoholism, child–parent relationships, skateboarding competitions, the land, and the meaning of Apache identity. Students would compose five-minute segments on these and other topics and play them one after another on television monitors set up in various prominent public venues on the reservation. Longer compositions were viewed in the Whiteriver movie theater, with generally enthusiastic audience responses from young and old alike. The Ndee Benadesh offices were an exciting atmosphere in which to work.

My job brought me into direct collaboration with Apache language teachers in several of the reservation schools. A common complaint among teachers was that they were expected to teach Apache but lacked established teaching materials. They said that it was difficult to coordinate efforts because each school had its own Apache language program, often developed by an individual teacher, and there was no established way of publishing the materials or sharing them among the various programs scattered throughout the school system. Additionally, many of the materials were handmade in a sometimes ad hoc manner, and some teachers worried that the appearance of the Apache photocopies and mimeographs in contrast to glossy English language textbooks contributed to an impression among students that Apache was less valued than English. In answer to this, my colleagues and I at Ndee Benadesh developed a proposal to utilize the tribe's new Internet facilities, along with Ndee Benadesh's already established emphasis on audiovisual media, to develop a set of cutting-edge interactive audiovisual language materials that we thought would be exciting to young people. In this way, the Ndee Biyatí' Apache Language Web Project began. The materials we developed incorporated images, sounds, activities, and stories from the local community. It was hoped that this would be a relatively inexpensive way to reach all the reservation's schools in a form that could be continuously expanded and developed.

The project involved four principal people: the director, Linda Goody, a tribal member, who provided content oversight, community outreach, and institutional support; Patricia Nash, an educator with experience teaching the Apache language, also a tribal member, who provided content and offered her own classroom as a venue for trying out our language teaching materials; me (at that time I was going by the name Marybeth Culley), not a tribal member, hired as a linguist and anthropologist to develop culturally appropriate language materials; and Tom Nevins, a cultural anthropologist (and my spouse), also not a tribal member, who designed the Web presentation and created a unit on Apache clans.

Also involved in the project but not on the payroll were several teachers and teacher's aides and other employees at one of the reservation's schools who contributed content or tried out materials in their classrooms and helped in many other ways. The project also involved coordination with the tribe's information technology office, which had just finished outfitting all the schools and libraries on the reservation with Internet connections and which would have handled publication of the pages on the tribe's server, had the project reached that stage.

In an attempt to create continuity with already established Apache language programs, we often attempted to consolidate existing written materials, but within a more interactive audiovisual format. For example, several teachers had developed alphabet lessons with sets of word lists to illustrate particular sounds and letters of the practical Apache alphabet. Other teachers had developed sentence drills, requiring, as English grammar lessons do, that students use "full sentences," with separate words for subjects, objects, and verbs.[3] I would often ask for help from friends I knew from family contexts outside the office to help me rework the existing materials, check for idiomatic fitness, and to help establish an audio component to accompany the texts. Although I did not recognize it at the time, while helping me, many times my friends were also offering gentle criticisms or suggesting alternatives to what I was doing that made more sense from their perspective. The criticisms they offered were hard to recognize because they were not directed to issues that I, as a materials developer, was prepared to address. I was prepared, as a matter of course, to recognize criticism concerning the proper way to say this or that, the appropriateness of certain words or content, whether or not a statement was grammatical or idiomatic, or how to decide between two different dialectal varieties of the same word. But, instead, the criticisms pertained to the whole set of assumptions I was using to frame the project.

For example, after working with me to establish sound files of a long list of words to accompany a lesson on reading and writing Apache consonants, Robert Moody, a close consultant and the father of school-age children, as quoted in the epigraph to this chapter, recited them back to me incredulously: "bįįh, chizh, ch'ah, dį́į́'í, dlǫ, dził, góchi ('deer, firewood, hat, the number four, bird, mountain, pig'). . . . Is this really what it's supposed to mean to know the Apache language?" I replied that the exercise was specifically tailored for teaching the use of the alphabet and was not intended to represent the kind of linguistic knowledge that a fluent speaker would have. This answered a smaller question but left his larger question unanswered.

Another time Nick Hosay, a consultant and friend and the father of a school-age child, was helping me with a narrative exercise for the project. I was trying to develop short vignettes set in everyday life in order to target vocabulary for items and events around homes and neighborhoods. Mr. Hosay had just told me a story that took place when he was fishing in the mountains with his three younger brothers. Returning to their trucks before the rest of the group, he found he had left his headlights on. He was so embarrassed at the oversight that he waited until everyone else had driven away before trying to start his truck, preferring to be stranded alone on the mountain to the prospect of revealing his lapse to his younger brothers. Not wanting to use his personally embarrassing story but hoping to create a vignette involving similar themes for the language project, I asked Mr. Hosay to help me write a script that involved a man arriving at his brother Dan's house and noticing that Dan's unoccupied truck is in the driveway with the headlights on. I asked Mr. Hosay how to say, in this situation, "Dan, your headlights are on." He obliged me, saying, "*Dan, ninałbił bikǫ daadiłtł'i*" ('Dan, your automobile, its light is lighted'). But then he added, "You know, somebody who is a really good speaker would not say it like that – with every single thing included. More likely he would come in the door, gesture from the person to the open door behind him, and say '*kǫ*' ('light'). That person will know just what he means from that, because he has just come in from outside where he would have passed that truck." Mr. Hosay went on to say his son's Apache language homework is similar to the language I first proposed for use in the vignette in that it does not reflect the way that a good speaker uses Apache in actual situations. Again, I did not respond to this criticism and others like it except to delimit the confines of the project. As a materials developer, my job of building up explicit vocabulary and examples of sentence structure was defined in almost antithetical terms to those of Apache pedagogical practices and ways of speaking. The question of what to means to be a good speaker in his terms was left unanswered. There were many other such incidents when I solicited the help of people outside of institutional contexts. And despite unanswered concerns, many people, like Robert Moody and Nick Hosay, continued to help me and other project members and offer insight and support where possible.

Before the project's termination we had completed an interactive alphabet, which incorporated photographs from the local community, along with words that illustrated the sounds associated with individual letters, available at the click of a mouse as both text and sound files. We tried the materials out in several classrooms with positive responses from students and teachers. We had also developed a language and culture teaching unit on family and clans, which drew the interest of older people as well as students. And we were in the beginning stages of developing interactive narrative and image-based language lessons, designed with additional input from an Apache artist and film-maker, Justinn Begay, to reflect local contexts and practices. The project's design received favorable responses in a general southwestern intertribal education meeting, in which educators from several other tribes approached us to say that they were interested in starting similar programs. It was, from the perspective of those involved with it in the schools and other institutional contexts, an exciting project.

Our plan was to develop the pages to the point where we felt we could provide a convincing demonstration in front of the tribal council. If the council approved, we had already involved the tribe's information technology office in plans to publish the pages on the tribe's server, with the tribe holding copyright. However, before the project could get a hearing in the tribal council, I received the phone call that began the previous chapter, followed by a certified letter from the tribe's legal office instructing us to stop all activity on the project. People were beginning to become aware of the project and it elicited considerable controversy. A different tribal education office held an Apache language symposium where the primary speaker strongly criticized the idea of using computers to teach the Apache language to children (Baeza 1998). The tribal council and cultural advisory board passed resolutions against publishing Apache language materials on the Internet and cast suspicion on the motives of the nontribal members involved in the project. Reservation school boards were divided on the subject. To make matters much worse, this was an election year, and the project, as it turned out, had become a political hot potato. Consequently, it was canceled.

At that time there were many different Apache language educators, working independently of one another, scattered throughout the various educational offices of the tribe. The salience of Apache language as a matter of concern on the reservation is reflected in the fact that there were language education components built into the education department, the culture center, the cultural heritage foundation, the health authority's public education program – that is, in every educational sector of the tribe.

Some of these educators commiserated with us, saying, "Now you know what it is like. It is hard to get anything done. Everyone says they want the kids to learn Apache, but if you try to do something, then people don't want it." I knew of one linguist, not a member of the tribe, who was asked to leave the reservation as a result of a controversial language maintenance project with which she was involved. Tribal members who ran Apache language education programs were also the focus of gossip, negative evaluation, and controversy. One of my consultants described her own refusal to take the job of Apache language education director when it was offered to her by saying that she did not want to subject herself or her family to the many unsympathetic eyes upon her that such a position would entail. Thus the controversy surrounding this program was apparently not unique – others had become similarly embattled despite the fact that concern about Apache language loss and a desire to do something to get young people to speak Apache were widespread throughout the speech community.

Contrasting Language Ideologies Brought into Conflict

Despite a common interest in language preservation, then, controversy often follows the creation of such programs. The reason, I argue, is because of conflicts between understandings of what it means to know and speak Apache within the social environment of schools and other institutionalized educational settings as opposed to those environments defined by extended familial forms of relationship, whether this be through kin relations, ceremonial relations, or established familiarity as neighbors and friends. The conflict was based on differences between ideological reflections upon Apache language emerging through the schools and shaped by federal and state education, and their counterparts emerging from contexts where ways of speaking and knowing language associated with extended families were most salient (cf. Basso 1979; Hymes 1966, 1972, 1996). Differences in the language ideologies emerging from extended familial as opposed to school environments inflect the meaning and entailments of "Apache language" or *Ndee bik'ehgo biyati*. This quite directly produces ambivalence, or multiple valences and meanings attached to Apache language as a matter of concern across divergent social contexts.

Every reservation resident has experience with extended familial environments and with government institutions as well as schools. Young people receive implicit messages about the relative importance of schooling and of English to their future ability to get jobs and to make a living. They also encounter portraits of Apache language and culture presented as analogs to their English studies. The White Mountain Apache tribal government, like other tribal governments, had a political interest in defining itself and the Apache language in nationalist terms in relation to other identities within national and international political structures (Anderson 1991; Handler 1988; Silverstein 1998). Apache people who were not otherwise involved in tribal government or politics would encounter this language ideology through radio, newspapers, magazines, the Internet, and from other state, national, and international media outlets, and within educational institutions.

School-Oriented Language Ideology: Apache as a National Language

The discourse on Apache as a national language, and its institutionalization in schools and the tribe's culture center is necessary to the tribe's political interest and is predicated on the same ideas that inform the tribe's institutional relationships with the national government and with educational institutions. This ideology also provides the more obvious and necessary terms for defining language loss for an Apache person who is working to negotiate these institutional relations in order to secure support for language programs and by necessity for a language researcher who wishes to contribute to them. So it often happens that language programs involve recasting the local language community's imagining of itself in terms of institutions and ideas associated with national governance.

A corollary of this process is that language preservation programs place the linguist in the ambiguous position of being the recognized expert on the local language, often amid many people around her whose knowledge of how to employ the language is much more extensive but who are not afforded the same kind of expert standing. The structure of grant funding, the role of standardization in defining terms of national language recognition, and the Apache language's status as both an ethnic minority language and the language of the Apache nation all prejudice funding in favor of language preservation programs that are legitimized within state educational institutions. The products of linguistic analysis are privileged over locally derived standards of communicative competence in this context because they can be applied to fulfill standard requirements of Western language pedagogy: grammars, dictionaries, and other components of literacy education (Collins 1998a, 1998b). Moreover, the fact that schooling is compulsory forces institutional language programs into the consideration of nearly every family on the reservation.

This creates an asymmetrical political relationship, one that privileges linguists and educators (including those who are tribal members) above those, usually elders, who hold authority within homes and within other local pedagogical contexts.[4] Many controversies that arise concerning language programs are traceable to the asymmetry of this relationship. Because written Apache is a relatively recent addition to reservation school programs, language programs often seek out the services of language specialists, which is how I became involved in the Ndee Biyati' project. I was approached because I was doing research on Apache ways of speaking and it was thought that my skills as a linguist and experience with computer media would be useful to the project. In retrospect it is clear that my efforts and the efforts of those with whom I worked represent the application of certain ideas and values about language that differed from, and could conflict with those of many in the local speech community. Being an "expert" was doubly ambivalent for me as a researcher interested in ways of speaking, and discursive practices, because the relations of authority implicit in institutional programs threaten to overshadow (Irvine and Gal 2000; Kuipers

1998)[5] exactly those forms of language use defined by extended family relationships – the very practices that I set out to learn about in the first place.

My own dual engagement, working within tribal education programs while also conducting ethnographic research in settings such as homes and ceremonial events, afforded a valuable perspective. It paralleled the complex engagements of many tribal members working in education who must also move between pedagogy in the schools and pedagogy as defined in their own homes and extended families (cf. Gershon 2006). I learned that people are not mute on these topics, nor are they are blind to the paradox and ironies of institutional language preservation programs – one such irony being that programs change, through institutional recontextualization, the meaning and use of the language they purport to preserve. This has led me to realize that neither the problem of language loss nor the projections of desirable Apache language survival are simple and straightforward for anyone attuned to both discourses, or for anyone implicated, as all contemporary Apache people are, in both sets of concerns and commitments.

Let me clarify that my purpose is not to condemn language programs as neocolonial impositions. The fact that many Apache people repeatedly seek out such programs and work very hard to support them in the face of controversy and limited resources should be taken very seriously. On the White Mountain Apache reservation language programs and the Apache people who support them have emerged as necessary sites of mediation "between the encompassing polity's view of 'minority' languages" (Silverstein 1998:415) and the local language community's necessarily complex construal of itself. It is a mediation in which the community's own political interests and self-definition locally and within national and international arenas are very much at stake. I attempt here to contribute to the symmetry of that mediation by attending to the placement of language research and language maintenance in a space of encounter (T. Nevins 2010) between people, who in the course of everyday life orient to sets of different, but mutually implicated, sociocultural regimes.

Apache language educators, because they teach Apache language within a community in which schools are not the only environment in which young people encounter Apache language, are inevitably engaged in brokering between extended familial language practices and language practices associated with government educational institutions like schools and the culture center, in which Apache language is conceived as a national language in relation to other national languages. In order to place Apache on more equal footing with English, most of the programs concentrate on developing literacy-based language curricula for the schools, using principles of pedagogy adopted from those used for English. Here I want to be clear that it is not "literacy" that presents the contrast with extended family-oriented practices. Families employ literacy across multiple practices from reading magazines and other commercial print media, reading the Bible, to use of calendars, lists, and planning charts for everyday activities as well as ceremonies (compare with Heath 1983). Because of the prominence of English in the global media environment, many home uses of literacy involve English, but Apache print circulates in the form of signage, bumper stickers, informal lists, some versions of the Bible, and occasional *Fort Apache Scout* newspaper columns (see Samuels 2004).

The contrast between home and school environments is not captured with the absence or presence of literacy, but in the political and pedagogical relations between persons that the two kinds of social environments represent. Alongside English, Apache language was cast within the quasi-national concerns of standardization and assessment. The contextualization of Apache language in the classroom as one subject of knowledge among others is taken for granted in school pedagogy but contrasts sharply with concepts of language as represented in familial discourse.[6] Importantly, the concerns about language loss, as the loss of a discrete resource that can be reproduced through classroom transmission, contrasts with concerns about language loss articulated from the perspective of positions within homes and families.

Family-Oriented Language Ideology: Listening and Awareness

By contrast with the educational model of learning, family-centered pedagogy teaches language by cultivating a child's awareness of the social world in which speaking is possible. One method for doing so, especially with small children, is a form of teasing. While babies are praised, coddled, humored, and generally celebrated, in many ways this early indulgence sets them up for important lessons in humility and modesty of self-representation. One of the forms this takes is a kind of language play mainly addressed to children between the ages of two and four who are just learning how to speak. Through teasing, children are tricked out of their accustomed position at the center of attention in the family and led to appreciate the feelings of others. Perhaps this is best explained with an anecdote. I worked most closely with the family of Rebekah Moody. One of her maternal grandsons, Berto (age three), loved to talk about himself, and his grandmother would play into this preoccupation. While pointing at a picture of him on the wall she would ask him, "Who's that handsome boy?" and

Berto would ask the same question of virtually anyone he encountered. People would respond by exclaiming, "Wow! Berto, you're so handsome!" These moments would often elicit sidelong glances and muted chuckles. This and similar routines continued for several months. As Berto became more competent as a speaker, he became increasingly aware of the two-sided nature of this dialogue and became embarrassed by his grandmother's prompting and by others' perceptions of his own naive self-interest.

In another example, Robert Moody, Rebekah Moody's son, called my attention to the way that he teased his daughter, Darlene, saying, "This is how the old people teach their kids." Darlene at the time was a very lively two-year-old, much celebrated by the family and an obvious favorite at family get-togethers. He would ask her the question *"chąąz'es chįh?,"* knowing that Darlene did not know the meaning of the phrase, and taught her to point at her own rear end in response to the question. As it turns out, the phrase can be loosely translated as 'What smells like poop?' Robert would ask the question from time to time, especially when there were many family members around. When she pointed at her own rear end everyone would laugh, and Darlene, accustomed to being celebrated, assumed this was more of the same and basked in the attention. This routine went on for a couple of months, until her accustomed response to the question became more hesitant as she began to detect something else in the laughter of those around her. Eventually she began to realize the meaning of the question for others and either refused to respond or said, "No!" or "You!" in response to her father. Everyone, including her father, laughed – this time because she had figured out the joke that had been played on her. After this realization her father persisted in teasing her with this and other routines, challenging her understanding of what it said and what it means to others around her. Her responses progressed from unwitting compliance to embarrassed refusals, to attempts to tease him in return. Similar teasing takes places between older and younger siblings.

This routinized teasing is a form of language socialization (Schieffelin and Ochs 1986) that teaches children important values of respecting others by not egotistically setting themselves apart from other members of their family, as well as important skills of social awareness. This is accomplished not by directly intercepting and correcting the child's errors, but by getting the child to correct herself. It corresponds to what ethnographers in Athabaskan communities have observed as respect for individual autonomy (Greenfeld 1996; Lamphere 1977; Rushforth and Chisholm 1991; Scollon and Scollon 1979b, 1990; Witherspoon 1975, 1977). Through teasing routines the child is not taught a set of rules for what to do or say. Instead, she is encouraged to follow her own responses until these bring her into a self-conscious awareness of relations to others.

Teasing teaches children the value of such awareness, expressed in discourse as "listening." Babies, young people, and adults perceived to be headstrong or foolish are discussed as those who "don't listen" (*doo ídíts'ag dah*). The particle *doo...dah* forms the negative of *ídíts'ag* ('he or she listens'). In babies this is the expected way of things. They can be indulged because "They don't know anything, they are just babies." Ideally, children learn to "listen" (*ídíts'ag*) by being in the home, participating in what is happening there in everyday life, and being aware of and involved with family members. Awareness, or listening, is not forced but cultivated in ways like those discussed above as well as encouraged by other indirect techniques. Basso describes several of these in his many ethnographic descriptions of Apache moral and aesthetic values of speaking. In contrast with what is characterized by Apache as *Ndah bik'ehgo yatí'* ('speaking like a Whiteman') an Apache way of speaking or teaching is accomplished not didactically but through cultivating the learner's engagement in some aspect of the common immediate environment of meaning, whether this is a metaphor, a story, or the fact of being together in silence (Basso 1970, 1976, 1984, 1988). Claire Farrer (1991) has noted a similar emphasis on the cultivation of awareness for Mescalero Apache. As I found in other observations during my fieldwork, this is a model of learning and appropriate speech that extends throughout a person's life.

The discourse on listening is a way in which Apache people talk about the expected moral development that takes place from youthful unawareness and self-preoccupation to maturity and greater "knowledge," or *bígoñłzih* (lit. 'awareness of others'), within the intimate moral environment of family life (T. Nevins 2010; Nevins and Nevins 2012). One's moral development is expected to continue throughout one's life and is evidenced in one's speech. By listening one shows *dayiłsįh* ('respect') for older people in one's environment and ultimately for the ancestors as encountered through elders, stories, and the land itself (see Basso 1996:10–11).

In an interesting way this concept of listening has become important for what it means to know and speak Apache. It has also become important to understandings of language loss through the ways in which it relates language to knowledge of familial relations. A person's speaking proficiency ultimately reflects how attentively and to whom that person has been listening. Knowing how to speak "good Apache" reflects involvement with and awareness of family. Many older people perceive younger people as lacking proficiency in Apache, and this coincides with another common complaint: "Nowadays kids don't listen." In fact, a common, often playful, Apache-English idiomatic phrase used throughout the reservation community is *ts'adah-boy* or *ts'adah-girl* ('naughty boy/girl,' 'boy/girl who doesn't listen'). This prevalent idiom underscores the salience of the idea of listening to contemporary Apache understandings of intergenerational relationships and extends the meaning of the idea of "not listening" to the lack of Apache fluency among young people.

The Apache discourse on listening identifies speaking good Apache language with participation and fluency in practices constitutive of the family. Studies of Southern Athabaskan family life generally have stressed the importance of cooperation, sustenance, and sharing as constitutive of familial relations (Lamphere 1977; Witherspoon 1975). Participation or its lapse in key acts of sustenance, such as preparing and sharing food, is identified with participation or its lapse in understanding and speaking with others in the family environment. Both are indications of cooperative acts constitutive of family.

That this set of concepts is central within Apache discourse to what it means to know and learn the Apache language is borne out by how Rebekah Moody and her family approached teaching me to speak Apache. When I first arrived at Rebekah Moody's house during my first full day of ethnographic fieldwork, I sat at her kitchen table with her daughters Amy Gossay and Bernadette Moody and asked if they would help me to learn to speak Apache. Their immediate response was that I had better start by learning how to make bread, and they began what was to be a year-long process of teaching me to make the four different kinds of Apache bread, beginning with fry bread for that evening's meal. Similarly, Robert Moody, one night after working with my husband and me on transcribing and analyzing Apache words for the language project, sat silent for a long while. Then he said, "I think that . . . if a girl makes bread every day and if a boy chops wood . . . everyday, I think that boy and that girl would be speaking Apache." He proposed that we include this idea in the closing lesson of an Apache reading primer, in a statement that has the feel of a benediction:

> Kįhyóó nádołkáho ('Go home'),
> Chizh nik'é ('chop wood'),
> Kǫ' dé'įnjéh ('build a fire'),
> A'iłé ('cook'),
> Nahǫǫní ('may it be good/beautiful')

Again and again, in every family with which I was intimately acquainted, I encountered this discourse, which emphasizes awareness and participation in activities sustaining of family life as central to knowing the Apache language.

The view of language loss, then, within the Apache discourse of the family identifies it with a crisis in cooperative participation and awareness of others in family life. For example, in an interview with Rebekah Moody about differences in Apache fluency between older and younger people, when I asked if there were things that older people say that younger people do not seem to understand, she responded emphatically:

Everybody. I hear *everybody*, all over.
Sunday after church, after twelve, I put on a barbecue corn, beans.
That's how we used to do it long time ago.
And I bought some short ribs.
I put short ribs in there and I boiled it outside.
And it's been goin' on all afternoon!
Then, seems like when it's done, I make some bread.
And here the kids, they didn't eat that, they didn't touch it! <emphatic>.
They just went in here [her house].
There were two big pies that they sell at the store, two for five dollars,
    they warmed that up.
And nobody eats my barbecue corn! Just me, Nick, and Leander.
And I make a whole bunch of *bán dit'ááne* ('bubble/thick bread').
And then, ah, Robert came.
And I said, "Just help yourself. Eat some barbecue corn right there and I got
    some bread."
They ate some.
Then Levy came.
And I said "Go eat."<emphatic, laughing>
The kids didn't even touch it.
And I said: "Those White people!" <laughing>
M: Their pizza's in there.
E: *yééah.* <emphatic>
They never did touch it.
And all my kids, you know, *my* kids, they like it.

By *my kids* Mrs. Moody is referring to her sons, Nick, Robert, and Levy, who were all in their thirties and were perceived to be fluent in Apache. In her narrative they are represented as different from her grandchildren in that they are aware of the efforts of others in the home environment, and they willingly prefer to eat food prepared by their mother in a way that has come to signify care and attention, and thus they participate in the sustaining activities of the family. By contrast, the grandchildren do not pay attention to what their grandmother has been preparing all afternoon; rather they have been inside watching television and warming up frozen pizzas. This discrepancy in listening and participation is emblematic of changes in knowledge of Apache between younger and older generations. Young people were characterized similarly in other households I visited, especially when the issue of language was salient. Parents would laugh, looking at the kids eating pizza or hotdogs and watching television, and say with a mixture of good humor and exasperation, "I live with a bunch of White people here!"

In the family of one of Rebekah Moody's sons there was one girl, however, who was described by adults as the only one of the children in the family who listened. She was also talked about as the only of the grandchildren who always helped with cleaning the house. This was attributed to the fact that "she was raised by her grandmother in the old way." In the same breath it would be noted that when she was living with her grandmother, she, unlike her cousins, really knew how to speak Apache.

The discourse on "listening" does two things: it describes a moral and appropriate form for relations within the family, and it presents listening as the precondition for any appropriate and effective use of language. It is a precondition to *dińts'į* ('respect'), another important idea in Apache discourse on learning and knowing language. From the perspective of the home, language has its basis in understandings attained by the edifying practice of listening. This and related pedagogical practices focus attention on cultivating children's awareness of others. Knowing how to speak Apache is an index of the child's involvement in the intimate moral universe of family life. The authority that listening within the family ideally confers on the elder and more knowledgeable generation is exactly what is being threatened in language loss. Listening as a process constitutive of both family relations and the acquisition of the ability to speak Apache is threatened by the participation of young people in an English language-dominant regime of meaning. The young people are listening, but their listening does not take place within the family. Because of this the expectation that young people will learn Apache by listening and participating in the practices constitutive of family life is thwarted by the lure of a social world that is constituted in other terms.

The Basis of Conflict between Language Ideologies in the Fort Apache Context

I now explore the interplay of these two different language ideologies and discuss how it factors into the interpretation of Apache language programs in the schools. The fact that there are multiple language ideologies on the Fort Apache reservation is expectable and inevitable. In this section I establish why these differences are often brought into conflict with Apache language programs. Following this, I explore how language ideological differences are constituted by Apache people in terms of *Ndee bik'ehgo* ('Apache way') and *Ndah bik'ehgo* ('White way') and note the importance of this construal for definitions of Apache language. Finally, I discuss the often paradoxical nature of language programs, how this has been addressed in language programs that have survived, and the perceptive, informed, and reasonable nature of this critique.

Toward Understanding Community Critiques of Apache Language Programs

Unlike school definitions of language, language loss in familial discourse is envisioned not only as the loss of Apache grammar and vocabulary, but more saliently as a weakening of the relationships from which being able to speak Apache springs. It is therefore interpreted as an indication of problems within and among families. I have argued that language education programs have become controversial despite widespread concern about language loss because of the conflict between two different representations of language in the reservation speech community: one that identifies language with knowledge of vocabulary and grammar and another that subordinates processes of normative language acquisition to the pedagogical relations founded in listening and respect between different generations in the family. Apache language education programs bring these into conflict *by equating them with each other* and so, in effect, threatening to replace one set of concerns with the other. The schools therefore can be interpreted as contributing to the problem of language loss by shifting children's attention away from the family as a primary site of learning, and by redefining learning within a political ethic that not only contrasts with, but threatens to disrupt and marginalize, extended family relations.

Efforts that foreground the use of technologies, such as the one I participated in, can be particularly threatening. Educators identify these technologies with learning, but they can also be seen to violate the dialogic principles of listening so valued in the family, especially when elder members of families do not use them or have access to them. During my fieldwork, very few families had a computer or access to the Internet at home. In that environment, computers were perceived to remove children from the expected pedagogical relations, to set them apart from the dialogic nature of direct human contact and in a manner out of reach for elder family members. The tremendous power attributed to computer technology introduces new uncertainties into a situation that is already perceived to be unstable. A public objection to our program, aired in the tribe's newspaper, was that computers in the schools should not be allowed to take the place of parents and grandparents. Therefore, although the glamour attached to computers may have been one of the initial reasons why the program enjoyed initial support, the possibility that computer programs might capture children's attention and become the preferred way to teach and learn Apache was perceived to have the potential to further destabilize pedagogical relations in the family.[7]

This possibility is reflected in another concern: that the older generation may lose the language not by virtue of its disappearance, but by being dispossessed of the authority to teach it and by losing the pedagogical relationship to successive generations that makes meaningful continuity and sharing of the language possible. This is sometimes voiced in terms such as, "They are trying to steal our kids" or "They are trying to steal our language," familiar phrases to anyone working on language programs in Native American or other indigenous contexts, but which acquire their full meaning in this case only when viewed in relation to the Apache discourse on listening within the home.

It is also important to take into account inequalities of power between school and family, particularly in matters of language, established by the obligatory nature of schooling. Children come home with criticisms of their parents' English from their teachers, who are often non-Apache. In this context the prospect of the schools becoming a similar arbitrating authority on the Apache language becomes an additional impediment to getting children to listen within the family. Add to this the historical complicity of the schools with government-sponsored efforts to suppress the use of Apache, and it becomes especially important to address problems on this front. For example, it might help if school programs were to valorize homes and families as legitimate sites of learning.

Other critiques are also more understandable once it is realized that what is taken as important about language in familial language ideology is very different from the way language is viewed in the schools. When asked for the translation for "Apache language," many Apache people of my acquaintance answered, *"Ndee bik'ehgo yatí'"* ('speech according to the way of the [Apache] People'). When asked for the translation of "English language," they replied, *"Ndah bik'ehgo yatí'"* ('speech according to the way of non-Apache/strangers/White people'). Forms of pedagogy, aesthetics, and morality in the schools are associated in extended familial discourse with *Ndah bik'ehgo*, the 'White way' and by extension with *Ndah bik'ehgo yatí'* ('alien/White people's way of speaking'), which, as we have learned from Basso (1979), can be cast as unwise, unsettling, and un-Apache. Therefore, the Apache language, presented as Apache literacy in the schools, more closely resembles ways of using language that are associated with

English and with non-Apache, "White," identity (see Scollon and Scollon 1979a, 1990 for a parallel Northern Athabaskan case).

Mr. Hosay raised an important criticism when he let me know that a fluent Apache speaker would generally not make explicit reference to things that would already be in their awareness. School programs can be paradoxical in that they teach the sounds and some of the spoken patterns of Apache but in a strikingly un-Apache way. In another conversation, Mr. Hosay, talking about his son's Apache language homework, noted, "They might be using some Apache-sounding words, but what they are really teaching the kids is English. They think they are teaching the kids the Apache word *nakih*; but they don't teach the kids *nakih*. Instead, they are teaching '*nakih* means two.'"

Another Apache consultant, educator, and parent, Benjamin Benally, noted that to most fluent Apaches the meaning of Apache words is altered and reduced in the focus on spelling and "sounding out the letters." He had just attended the Athabaskan Languages Conference and had been unsettled by some of the linguistic presentations. Reminiscent of the explanations offered to Basso by his consultants, Mr. Benally had this comment to make: "In spelling you [i.e. linguists, teachers] think of *shash* as S-H-A-S-H, but when a fluent Apache speaker thinks *shash* he sees a vital presence moving up there in the mountains." School-based pedagogical practices are criticized by some as severing the utterance (spoken or thought) from its creative power – its existence with and participation in relations with what and who it evokes.

Finally, older people worry that younger people are not learning many of the interpersonal subtleties of appropriate language use. Robert Moody noticed that many people in their twenties were not making a set of important distinctions between terms that describe qualities independent of individual intentions or agency and terms that describe qualities with particular reference to the agency of persons. The example that he offered was that in describing someone as doing a good job, for example, in fixing a car; an older, fluent speaker would use the term *nłt'éégo* to characterize the job he was performing as being done well. But if that older speaker were talking about the mechanic as a man, to say that he was a good, knowledgeable mechanic, he would use the word *nzisgo* to signify that it was the man himself and his ability that were good. Younger people, Mr. Moody said, used only *nłt'éégo* for any positive evaluation, and thus do not make what for older Apaches is an important distinction, that hinges upon establishing interpersonal relations of awareness of and respect accorded to the difference made by the agency of others. It should not be a surprise that similar concerns on the part of many older Apache speakers to maintain subtle, but ethically and politically important, distinctions in the use of language have not yet begun to be addressed within existing Apache language programs.

Alternative Models Suggested

As described above, concerned Apache parents of school-age children often responded to the language program we were working on together by redefining its objectives in terms of home-based, family-sustaining practices in a manner similar to Mr. Moody's: "If boys would just chop wood for their families every day and girls would make bread, they would know Apache." Another father, an educator, said, "I teach my son Apache by building a *tałt'oh* ('shade/ramada') with him." Apache language and culture classes that survive with less controversy from the local community incorporate a good deal of these sorts of activities into their lesson plans. However, these kinds of programs are more vulnerable to being deemed superfluous within the school's own terms because standard tools of accountability and control do not apply.

So am I saying that Apache should not be taught in the schools, or am I claiming that Apache people, by and large, are against it? The answer on both counts is "No." There were many Apache language education programs running during my research period and still running at the time of writing this book. Further, the "failed" project with which I was involved enjoyed support from many Apache people who were disappointed when it was canceled. What I *am* saying is that scholars who are concerned about endangered or threatened indigenous languages should try to understand how the communities themselves perceive and represent these problems. There are likely to be more multiple language ideologies at play within any indigenous speech community, and what it means to know and learn the language may be defined differently in home as opposed to school environments, among others. The imposition of programs without listening and responding to criticisms from the communities they are intended to benefit runs the risk of being interpreted as yet another form of oppression.

One of my hopes for this chapter is that it helps demonstrate that the view of generational language shift from the perspective of Apache homes and families is perceptive, rational, compelling, and certainly worth listening to. It also suggests that steps to strengthen extended families – in terms that they themselves find appropriate – would not be out of place in language maintenance efforts. Let me also say that I do not intend this as an argument for cultural conservatism. As is evident in tribal radio-station discourse, in some of the Apache Independent Christian churches, and in the frequent, often ironic use of images, characters, and stories from mass media within local narrative practices, Apache people are fully capable of appropriating new media, technologies, genres, and styles into Apache discursive practices (Nevins 2004, 2008, 2010). What is lacking in language maintenance attempts so far is recognition of the importance of local language ideologies, ways of speaking, and pedagogical practices, and the creation of realistic possibilities for persons conferred with authority within Apache communicative practices to author or otherwise exert control over language programs.

In order for this to happen, there is a need for the educational language programs to locate language within ways of speaking and social relations of speaking:

> Through awareness of and sensitivity to the socioexpressive dimension of speaking, and to intergroup differences in ways of speaking within heterogeneous communities, ethnographic investigators are particularly well equipped to clarify those problem situations which stem from covert conflicts between different ways of speaking, conflicts which may be obscured by a failure to see beyond the referential functions of speech and abstract grammatical patterns. Understanding of such problem situations is a major step toward their solution, laying the groundwork for planning and change. (Bauman and Sherzer 1975:115)

The listening that an ethnographic approach affords an additional source of creativity in pedagogy. A dialogic ethnographic approach to local language values and definitions of communicative competence is an indispensable step toward developing the ability to accurately understand criticisms and recognize potential opportunities.

Many concerned linguists have drawn critical attention to the political asymmetries entailed in the treatment of minority languages within educational institutions (Collins 1998b; Dorian 1998; Hofling 1996). In a chapter entitled "Report from an Underdeveloped Country," Hymes (1996) criticizes educators in the United States for failing to make use of what has been learned in fields such as sociolinguistics, the ethnography of speaking, and ethnopoetics to address issues of diversity in communicative competencies, particularly for students coming to the school system from backgrounds in minority speech communities (Heath 1983). He suggests that it is our own models of language in relation to society and culture that need to be developed if educators are to recognize and cultivate the competencies that exist in minority language communities, but which are difficult to anticipate from models of language predominant in education today. A growing chorus of linguistic anthropologists (Collins 1998a, 1998b; Hill 2002;

Hofling 1996; Moore 2006; Silverstein 1998) have called for researchers who apply linguistic products to socially derived problems such as language loss to also bring a certain "social-scientific reflexivity" to their efforts, in order to be cognizant of the effect of the political relationships entailed in their activities upon the local speech community. This is necessary, notes Silverstein, "to avoid – or at least to face – the ironies of being more an agent of essentially colonial cultural change in local communities, the more one merely desires to play a role in sustaining or fixing a local language structure within the institutional assumptions of the surrounding society" (1998:408). There is a growing ethnographic literature addressing these issues (Collins 1998a, 1998b; Hill 1998; Hill and Hill 1986; Kulick 1997; Meek 2010; Moore 1999, 2006; Suslak 2011).

I would add that the reflexivity called for by such scholars involves an anticipation of alternative language ideologies. Indigenous language support should take into account the complex articulation of indigenous communities. As demonstrated here, on the Fort Apache reservation "language loss" is a widespread concern. However, the terms in which it is understood as a problem, and the terms in which desirable solutions are entertained, differs significantly depending upon one's position within the social life of the community.

The problem for language program developers is that their access to indigenous communities is often through state educational and other government institutions and the terms in which efforts are reported assessed are derived from that same institutional locus. Alternative discourses of language loss and desired survival are often invisible from such a perspective (Phillips 1992), or at least difficult to access and render with fidelity. The purpose of this chapter has been to make an alternative understanding of language loss visible in this way and to indicate the importance of paying attention to it. This chapter also establishes that it is not the fact of difference between school and home understandings that poses the problem, it is the political relationship between them such that one threatens to occlude or supplant the other in legitimacy. Therefore the answer is not necessarily to mimic a home "culture of language" within the school, but to allow for the legitimacy of alternate voices, alternate claims to authority, alternate sites for learning and teaching, alternate definitions of an indigenous language as a matter of community concern.

In the previous chapter I characterized language programs in indigenous communities as institutional loci of political integration. They involve "difference" in the specific sense of different languages, cultures, and bodies of traditional knowledge. This is a translation strategy in which indigenous social practices and symbols are recognized as analogues for familiar institutions of national public life. This serves an integrating function because the terms in which difference is recognized are predicated on a way of imagining community that is based upon the nation-state, on notions of the modern, and through technocratic interventions that apply the products of linguistic discovery procedures to social problems. The multicultural and multiethnic model of contemporary democratic nation-states represents an improvement, in that it allows for greater expression of agency by indigenous actors over what was the case under the previous assimilationist regime. However, the terms of multilingual, multicultural integration in the current regime also carry what to many are covert strategic disadvantages. Children, schools, and education are often described in terms of anticipating and preparing for "the future." This, combined with the manner in which indigenous cultures and languages are framed in endangerment (and other modernist) discourses as aspects of a disrupted, superseded traditional past, threatens to make indigenous parents and grandparents seem less relevant than schools to the future of their own children. When schools come to redefine more widely recognized symbols of indigeneity like "language" and "culture," this can be interpreted as eroding a source of authority that elders in the community also have claim to. This is a source of controversies surrounding language programs, and recognizing this is a condition for needed dialogue.

However, there is another sense in which indigeneity, and concern for indigenous language, makes a space for supporting alternatives arising from histories of differentiation with respect to surrounding communities. The difference marked by *ndee* and *ndah* is not reducible to ethnonationalism, and requires a different strategy of interpretation to follow. The next chapter attends to alternate, unexpected, and intentionally humorous acts of community mediation and also shows ways that the very strangeness attributed to English is put to work within an indigenous discourse genre.

Notes

1 For a parallel case in the Tlingit community of Southeast Alaska, see Dauenhauer and Dauenhauer (1998).
2 While this chapter focuses upon a contrast between homes and schools, this is not intended to reflect a public/private distinction. Familial politics are inextricable from public leadership. A more apt frame would be public/counter-public (Gal and Woolard 2001).
3 Western Apache is a "pronominal argument" (Jelinek 1989) language in which subject and object relations are established by person prefixes within the verb form. Nouns can be added to Apache sentences to approximate the form of English sentences, but these play a different role in Apache syntax (Hale 2003).

4 Although see Meek (2010) for an account of the complexity of expert and indigenous statuses in the context of Canadian First Nation language programs.
5 In Chapter 5 I provide an elaboration of "erasure" as a language ideological process.
6 For a more elaborate treatment of indigenous language pedagogy in a school program, and for a parallel exploration of disjunctures with indigenous speech outside of school, see Meek (2010).
7 At the time of writing this book, nearly fifteen years later, I stay in touch with friends, quasi-family, and consultants on the Fort Apache reservation with social networking sites. With home access to the Internet increasing on the reservation, it is likely that the basis for these complaints may have shifted.

References

Adley-Santa Maria, Bernadette. 1997. White Mountain Apache Language Shift: a Perspective on Causes, Effects, and Avenues for Change. Masters thesis, University of Arizona.

Adley-Santa Maria, Bernadette. 1998. White Mountain Apache Language: Issues in Language Shift, Textbook Development, and Native Speaker–University Collaboration. Paper presented at the Annual Meeting of the American Indian Language Development Institute. University of Arizona, Tucson, Summer.

Anderson, Benedict R. 1991. *Imagined Communities: Reflections on the Origin and Spread of Nationalism.* London: Verso.

Baeza, Jo. 1998. First Apache Language Symposium Explores Ways to Keep Language Viable. *Fort Apache Scout*, February 13.

Basso, Keith. 1970. "To Give up on Words": Silence in Western Apache Culture. *Southwestern Journal of Anthropology* 26(3):213–230.

Basso, Keith. 1976. "Wise Words" of the Western Apache: Metaphor and Semantic Theory. In *Meaning in Anthropology*. Keith H. Basso and H.A. Selby, eds., pp. 93–122. Albuquerque: University of New Mexico Press.

Basso, Keith. 1979. *Portraits of "the Whiteman": Linguistic Play and Cultural Symbols among the Western Apache.* New York: Cambridge University Press.

Basso, Keith. 1984. "Stalking with Stories": Names, Places, and Moral Narratives among the Western Apache. In *Text, Play, and Story: The Construction and Reconstruction of Self and Society.* Edward M. Bruner, ed., pp. 19–55. Washington DC: American Anthropological Society.

Basso, Keith. 1988. "Speaking with Names": Language and Landscape among the Western Apache. *Cultural Anthropology* 3(2):99–130.

Basso, Keith. 1996. *Wisdom Sits in Places: Language and Landscape among the Western Apache.* Albuquerque: University of New Mexico Press.

Bauman, Richard and Joel Sherzer. 1975. The Ethnography of Speaking. *Annual Review of Anthropology* 4:95–119.

Bradley, David and Maya Bradley. 2002. *Language Endangerment and Language Maintenance: An Active Approach.* New York: Routledge.

Bray, Dorothy, ed. 1998. *Western Apache–English Dictionary: A Community-Generated Bilingual Dictionary*. Tempe: Bilingual Press/Editorial Bilingue.

Collins, James. 1998a. *Understanding Tolowa Histories: Western Hegemonies and Native American Responses*. New York: Routledge

Collins, James. 1998b. Our Ideologies and Theirs. In *Language Ideologies: Practice and Theory*. Bambi B. Schieffelin, Kathryn A. Woolard, and Paul V. Kroskrity, eds., pp. 256–270. New York: Oxford University Press.

Dauenhauer, Nora Marks and Richard Dauenhauer. 1998. Technical, Emotional and Ideological Issues in Reversing Language Shift: Examples from Southeast Alaska. In *Endangered Languages: Current Issues and Future Prospects*. Lenore A. Grenoble and Lindsay J. Whaley, eds., pp. 57–98. Cambridge: Cambridge University Press.

de Reuse, Willem J. 1997. Issues in Language Textbook Development: The Case of Western Apache. *In Teaching Indigenous Languages*. Jon Reyhner, ed., pp. 116–128. Flagstaff: Northern Arizona University.

Dorian, Nancy C. 1998. Western Language Ideologies and Small-Language Prospects. In *Endangered Languages: Language Loss and Community Response*. Lenore Grenoble and Lindsay Whaley, eds., pp. 3–21. New York: Cambridge University Press.

Dorian, Nancy C. 2002. Commentary: Broadening the Rhetorical and Descriptive Horizons in Endangered-Language Linguistics. *Journal of Linguistic Anthropology* (12)2:134–140.

Evans, Nicholas. 2009. *Dying Words: Endangered Languages and What They Have to Tell Us*. Oxford: Wiley-Blackwell.

Farrer, Claire. 1991. *Living Life's Circle: Mescalero Apache Cosmovision*. Albuquerque: University of New Mexico Press.

Fase, Willem, Koen Jaspaert, and Sjaak Kroon, eds. 1992. *Maintenance and Loss of Minority Languages*. Amsterdam: John Benjamins.

Fishman, Joshua. 1989. *Language and Ethnicity in Minority Sociolinguistic Perspective*. Philadelphia: Multilingual Matters.

Fort Apache Scout. 2000a. Issues on White Mountain Apache Language. *Fort Apache Scout*, August 25:1.

Fort Apache Scout. 2000b. Threats to Native Languages: Issues That Could Affect Dzil Ligai Si'an Ndee Biyati' (White Mountain Apache Language). *Fort Apache Scout*, July 28:1.

Gal, Susan and Kathryn Woolard. 2001. *Language and Publics: The Making of Authority*. Wichita: St. Jerome Press.

Gershon, Ilana. 2006. When Culture Is Not a System: Why Samoan Cultural Brokers Cannot Do Their Job. *Ethnos* 71(4):533–558.

Greenfeld, Phillip J. 1996. Self, Family, and Community in White Mountain Apache Society. *Ethos* 24(3):491–509.

Greenfeld, Phillip J. 2001. Escape from Albuquerque: An Apache Memorate. *American Indian Culture and Research Journal* 25(3):47–71.

Hale, Kenneth. 2003. On the Significance of Elouise Jelinek's Pronominal Argument Hypothesis. In *Formal Approaches to Function in Grammar: In Honor of*

Eloise Jelinek Andrew Carnie, Heidi Harley, MaryAnn Willie, Eloise Jelinek, eds., pp. 11–43. Amsterdam: John Benjamins.

Handler, Richard. 1988. *Nationalism and the Politics of Culture in Quebec.* Madison: University of Wisconsin Press.

Harrison, K. David. 2008. *When Languages Die: The Extinction of the World's Languages and the Erosion of Human Knowledge.* Oxford: Oxford University Press.

Heath, Shirley Brice. 1983. *Ways with Words: Language, Life and Work in Classrooms and Communities.* Cambridge: Cambridge University Press.

Hill, Jane H. 1998. "Today There Is No Respect": Nostalgia, Respect, and Oppositional Discourse in Mexicano (Nahuatl) Language Ideology. In *Language Ideologies: Practice and Theory.* Bambi B. Schieffelin, Kathryn A. Woolard, and Paul V. Kroskrity, eds., pp. 68–86. Oxford: Oxford University Press.

Hill, Jane H. 2002. "Expert Rhetorics' in Advocacy for Endangered Languages: Who Is Listening and What Do They Hear? *Journal of Linguistic Anthropology* 12(2):119–133.

Hill, Jane H. and Kenneth C. Hill. 1986. *Speaking Mexicano: Dynamics of Syncretic Language in Central New Mexico.* Tucson: University of Arizona Press.

Hofling, Charles Andrew. 1996. Indigenous Linguistic Revitalization and Outsider Interaction: The Itzaj Maya Case. *Human Organization* 55(1):108–116.

Hymes, Dell H. 1966. Two Types of Linguistic Relativity. In *Sociolinguistics.* W. Bright, ed., pp. 114–157. The Hague: Mouton de Gruyter.

Hymes, Dell H. 1972. Editorial Introduction. *Language in Society* 1(1):1–14.

Hymes, Dell H. 1996. *Ethnography, Linguistics, Narrative Inequality: Toward an Understanding of Voice.* London: Taylor & Francis.

Irvine, Judith and Susan Gal. 2000. Language Ideology and Linguistic Differentiation. In *Regimes of Language: Ideologies, Polities, and Identities.* Paul V. Kroskrity, ed., pp. 35–84. Santa Fe: School of American Research.

Jelinek, Eloise. 1989. The Bi-Construction and Pronominal Arguments in Apachean. In *Athabaskan Linguistics. Current Perspectives on a Language Family vol. 17.* Karen Rice and E. Cook, with Merton Sandoval, eds., pp. 335–378. The Hague: Mouton de Gruyter.

Kuipers, Joel C. 1998. *Language, Identity and Marginality in Indonesia: The Changing Nature of Ritual Speech on the Island of Sumba.* New York: Cambridge University Press.

Kulick, Dan. 1997. *Language Shift and Cultural Reproduction: Socialization, Self and Syncretism in a Papua New Guinea Village.* New York: Cambridge University Press.

Lamphere, Louise. 1977. *To Run after Them: Cultural and Social Bases of Cooperation in Navajo Community.* Tucson: University of Arizona Press.

Liebe-Harkort, Marie-Louise. 1980. Recent Developments in Apachean Language Maintenance. *International Journal of American Linguistics* 46(2):85–91.

Marcus, George E. and Michael M. Fischer. 1999. *Anthropology as Cultural Critique: An Experimental Moment in the Human Sciences.* Chicago: University of Chicago Press.

Meek, Barbara. 2010 *We Are Our Language: An Ethnography of Language Revitalization in a Northern Athabascan Community*. Tucson: University of Arizona Press.

Moore, Robert, E. 1999. Endangered. *Journal of Linguistic Anthropology* 9(1–2):65–8.

Moore, Robert, E. 2006. Disappearing, Inc.: Glimpsing the Sublime in The Politics of Access to Endangered Languages. *Language and Communication* 26: 296–315.

Nettle, Daniel and Suzanne Romaine. 2000. *Vanishing Voices: The Extinction of the World's Languages*. Oxford: Oxford University Press.

Nevins, M. Eleanor. 2004. Learning to Listen: Confronting Two Meanings of Language Loss in the Contemporary White Mountain Apache Speech Community. *Journal of Linguistic Anthropology* 14:269–288.

Nevins, M. Eleanor. 2008. "They Live in Lonesome Dove": Media and Contemporary Western Apache Place-naming Practices. *Language in Society* 37: 191–215.

Nevins, M. Eleanor. 2010. The Bible in Two Keys: Traditionalism and Apache Evangelical Christianity on the Fort Apache Reservation. *Language and Communication* 30(1):19–32.

Nevins, M. Eleanor and Thomas J. Nevins. 2012. "They Do Not Know How to Ask": Pedagogy, Storytelling and the Ironies of Languages Endangerment on the Fort Apache Reservation. In *Telling Stories In the Face of Danger*. Paul Kroskrity, ed., pp. 129–150. Norman: University of Oklahoma Press.

Nevins, Thomas J. 2010. Between Love and Culture: Misunderstanding, Textuality and the Dialectics of Ethnographic Knowledge. *Language and Communication* 30(1):58–68.

Phillips, Susan. 1992. *The Invisible Culture: Communication in Classroom and Community on the Warm Springs Indian Reservation*. Long Grove: Waveland Press.

Rushforth, Scott and James S. Chisholm. 1991. *Cultural Persistence: Continuity in Meaning and Moral Responsibility among the Bearlake Athapaskans*. Tucson: University of Arizona Press.

Samuels, David. 2004. *Putting a Song on Top of It: Expression and Identity on the San Carlos Apache Reservation*. Tucson: University of Arizona Press.

Schieffelin, Bambi B. and Elinor Ochs. 1986. *Language Socialization across Cultures*. New York: Cambridge University Press.

Scollon, Ronald and Suzanne B.K. Scollon. 1979a. *Literacy as Interethnic Communication: An Athabaskan Case*. Working Papers in Sociolinguistics 59. Austin: Southwest Educational Development Laboratory.

Scollon, Ronald and Suzanne B.K. Scollon. 1979b. *Linguistic Convergence: An Ethnography of Speaking at Fort Chipewyan*. Berkeley: University of California Press.

Scollon, Ronald and Suzanne B.K. Scollon. 1990. Athapaskan-English Interethnic Communication. In *Cultural Communication and Intercultural Contact*. Donal Carbaugh, ed., pp. 259–286. Hillsdale: Lawrence Erlbaum Associates.

Silverstein, Michael. 1998. Contemporary Transformations of Local Linguistic Communities. *Annual Review of Anthropology* 27:401–426.

Suslak, Dan. 2011. Ayapan Echos: Linguistic Persistence and Loss in Tabasco Mexico. *American Anthropologist* 113(4):569–581.

Thieberger, Nicholas, ed. 2012. *The Oxford Handbook of Linguistic Fieldwork.* Oxford: Oxford University Press.

Tsunoda, Tasaku. 2006. *Language Endangerment and Language Revitalization: An Introduction.* Mouton de Gruyter.

Watt, Eva Tulene, with assistance from Keith Basso. 2004. *Don't Let the Sun Step Over You: A White Mountain Apache Family Life, 1860–1975.* Tucson: University of Arizona Press.

Witherspoon, Gary. 1975. *Navajo Kinship and Marriage.* Chicago: University of Chicago Press.

Witherspoon, Gary. 1977. *Language and Art in the Navajo Universe.* Ann Arbor: University of Michigan Press.

4

They Live in Lonesome Dove

English in Indigenous Places

> Native identities are more chance than the inheritance of an organic culture; the pronouns that bear a persona, a trace, a name, and native stories, are a chance convergence in language. (Vizenor 1998:36)

In an essay that ranges from the linguistics of Leonard Bloomfield to the cultural anthropology of Roy Wagner, Vizenor poses the question of how Native identities might be recognized. He steers his readership away from expecting "inheritance of an organic culture" and towards "chance convergence in language" which he locates in obviative pronouns. In his usage the latter are voices not immediately accessible but whose implicit, lingering traces invite acts of imagination. This chapter addresses just this sort of chance convergence in language by attending to relations between two ways of naming places on the Fort Apache reservation. Following Vizenor, I trace names and stories that, as they are used in everyday life, establish track records of mutual involvement, grounded in parallel acts of getting the same jokes. I present this because it illustrates an everyday enactment of community that is otherwise not anticipated if one's working assumptions are taken from notions of Apache language and culture as a bounded, organic system in which English plays no proper part (except as a despoiler).

In Chapter 2 I proposed the idea that indigenous communities are complexly mediated with respect to the surrounding social orders in which they are placed. On the one hand, recognition as "indigenous" engages reservation residents in processes of political integration with respect to national governance and, within these, language documentation and maintenance provide terms through which a community is recognized as a quasi-national entity. The means by which languages and cultures are objectified as systems,

Lessons from Fort Apache: Beyond Language Endangerment and Maintenance,
First Edition. M. Eleanor Nevins.
© 2013 John Wiley & Sons, Inc. Published 2013 by John Wiley & Sons, Inc.

as organic wholes, requires professional documentation. It is also technocratic forms of expertise that are relied upon to provide standardizing tools for the transmission of language and culture through schools and culture centers.

One the other hand, the notion of indigeneity also holds open the possibility of considering alternate means of constituting community, grounded in alternative, emergent histories of colonial and postcolonial differentiation. One example of this in the Western Apache literature is the joking genre Basso describes as "portraits of 'the Whiteman'" (1979). When people joke with each other this way, they switch to English in order to portray and inhabit the way "White people" are perceived to speak. Participants performatively mark and measure contrasts between *ndah* and *ndee* and make clear their evaluative preference for the latter. The introduction of a joking portrayal of the intrusive and unsettling speech of White people into the ongoing flow of a conversation is funny rather than insulting only among participants who have a long track record of familiarity with one another. English is appropriated as a symbolic resource in these jokes, and its use objectifies and invites comment from participants upon *ndah bik'ehgo*, or 'White ways of doing things.' Marking that boundary implicitly shifts the parties into mutual alliance with a felt, uncommented upon sense of *ndee bik'ehgo*, 'our/Apache way of doing things.' As a genre these jokes establish their own track records of reflection up what it means to be *ndee* on a reservation, where every *ndee* occasionally encounters *ndah* at close quarters, and often in politically asymmetrical circumstances, like doctor visits, trading posts, or schoolrooms. Liebe-Harkort (1979) and Samuels (2001) note similar performative dynamics in Apache–English bilingualism more broadly (cf. Stasch 2007).

This chapter traces additional contours of that ongoing history of differentiation, one in which the concern with boundaries drawn between English and Apache languages are germane, but are taken up and obviated as they are put to use in yet another joking genre. This is place-naming practice, in which people use English language discourse drawn from television, movies, advertisements, and other forms of commercial media to name newly constructed neighborhoods on the Fort Apache reservation. I show that these names do not represent simple assimilation to English or to mainstream discursive norms. Instead, they represent the deployment of media discourse to comment upon disjunctures posed by the new housing developments. Reflecting an expansive, outward orientation, these names are a means of positioning with respect to social contexts that extend well beyond reservation borders. As a strategy for engaging with the surrounding society, these names are acts of community self-definition that confound mainstream expectations for place names generally, and for Native

American place names in particular. Use of these names on street signs and in everyday conversation celebrates participation in media discourse but in terms that privilege reservation insiders. These names create a sense of the reservation as an interpretive community in which participation is not defined along nationalistic models of citizenship, but upon getting the same jokes about their lives.

The names, like Bengay, Smurfville, and Jurassic Park, are a form of wordplay that usually involves metaphor or punning, and many residents consider these names to be both funny and clever. Each name requires familiarity with local precedents as well as commercial media discourse in order to "get the joke." Some have acquired quasi-official status and appear on street signs and BIA maps, on local radio stations, and in local newspapers. Basso, in his well-known treatment of Apache language place names, makes passing reference to these English language names:

> A visitor to Cibecue today would discover that all of its housing complexes have been given English place-names – fanciful names like Rainbow City, Too Far Away, Desert Storm, and Hollywood – and that each name has a story behind it, amusing and light-hearted, which provides an account of its origin. (Basso 1996:151)

In this chapter I discuss a corpus of such names that I encountered during field research in the communities of Whiteriver and East Fork from 1996 to 1999. I am posing two related questions about these names. One concerns how we are to understand the use of English language media discourse within this Western Apache naming practice. In order to provide an adequate answer for this, I find it necessary to address the question of the relationship between these recently coined names and their more "traditional" counterparts as they have been described in the work of Basso (1990, 1996).

Basso says of the new English language place names:

> understandably, the visitor might suppose that the business of naming places is no longer taken seriously by Apaches, that it has fallen by the cultural and linguistic wayside, a casualty of modern times and accelerated exposure to non-Apache ways. (Basso 1996:152)

He then goes on to protest that this is not the case because traditionally styled Apache language place names continue to be coined.

I am making a different sort of argument, one that does not rely upon the notion that English and Apache forms necessarily belong to different cultural worlds. I argue that while these English language names appear to reflect a dramatic departure from the "traditional" Apache names described by Basso, a comparison of the two reveals that they are in fact informed by a common language ideology (Kroskrity 2000; Woolard 1998) concerning indexical contrasts between Apache and English languages, similar criteria for what makes a good place name and similar patterns of use. I further argue that it would be inadequate to interpret the exclusive reliance upon English idioms as a simple reflection of the "glamour of English" as the dominant language encountered in mass media, or of language shift from Apache to English. Rather, it represents a symbolic deployment of English media discourse in marked contrast to Apache language place names in order to highlight and comment upon the difference between the isolated single family residential patterns mandated by government housing developments versus the extended family multiple dwellings characteristic of more longstanding settlements. The "joke" in each name is often a comment upon the anomalous nature of the new residence patterns and the changes in lifestyle that attend them. I argue that these playful English language place names represent a recently emergent discourse genre (Bauman 2004; Hanks 1986) which draws upon some of the expectations at play in traditional Apache place-naming and other established genres of verbal play (for example Basso 1979) in its deployment of English language idioms to comment upon ongoing changes in reservation life.

The second question I address with this study concerns the definition of the local reservation community and its relationship to the surrounding dominant society as constituted by these place names. An analysis of intertextual relations along two axes: (1) decontextualization from the source discourse in mass media and (2) recontextualization in terms of prior texts and prior precedents in the local community (Spitulnik 1993), reveals these playful place names to be strategic acts of community definition in political engagement with the dominant society. Neighborhood names like Jurassic Park, Bengay, and Life Savers help to create a local experience of community on the reservation that is self-consciously different from that of surrounding nonreservation communities. At the same time, use of these names on road signs and in local media subvert dominant notions of what proper place names should look like even as their self-consciously innovative quality subverts dominant discourses of what it means to be an authentic (thus implicitly "traditional") Native American community.

Media, Discourse, and Communities

The literature on Apache place names is particularly rich (see Basso 1990, 1996; Bourke 1890; Goodwin 1942; Samuels 2001). The place names treated here differ from those discussed in previous studies in their exclusive reliance on English idioms and in the fact that they are predominantly drawn from commercial media. This fact raises the question of the nature of the role that mass media plays in contemporary definitions of the reservation community.

Early studies of the effects of mass media stressed the power of the culture industry to penetrate the everyday lives of people in diverse localities, indoctrinating them into prevailing hegemonic norms and assumptions (e.g. Powdermaker 1950). This has sometimes been termed the *hypodermic model* (Spitulnik 1993) because influence is taken to flow downwards from media producers into passive audiences. In this way mass media serves as a tool of established power. Put this in the context of colonialism, and mass media can be described as extending Western hegemony to indigenous peoples around the world. This assumption about the effects of mass media is reflected in much of the literature on language endangerment in which television and movies, because they extend the hegemony of world languages, are described as having an important role to play in the decline of indigenous languages and cultures (see Crystal 2002, 2003; Fishman 2001; Phillipson 1992).

An emergent field of scholarship in the anthropology of media draws on the strengths of the ethnographic method to complicate the "hypodermic model." This literature attends to the role played by audiences in determining the local reception and uptake of mass media, particularly in the context of postcolonialism (Abu-Lughod 1995; Askew and Wilk 2002; Mankekar 1999). Within this broader trend, a number of works in the ethnography of communication lend insight into how local audiences reconfigure the media discourse that they encounter to suit their own discursive practices and concerns (e.g. Hahn 1994; Kulick and Wilson 1994; Samuels 2004; Spitulnik 1997). The present study approaches the use of media discourse on the White Mountain Apache reservation through the rubric of intertextuality (Bakhtin 1981; Bauman 2004; Bauman and Briggs 1990; Silverstein and Urban 1996). In this respect it builds upon the work of Debra Spitulnik (1993, 1997) who examines intertextual relationships established by the recycling of pieces of media discourse in everyday talk in Zambia:

> While linguistic anthropology has tended to focus on the analysis of narrative, oratory, ritual speech, and other very well bounded and easily identifiable speech genres, little has been said about the smaller, scattered pieces of formulaic language, for example the public words of street signs, graffiti, and political parties, or the popular extracts from radio, film, and the world of advertising. I argue here that tuning into these smaller genres or "minor media" . . . is one productive avenue for beginning an analysis of the linguistic intertextuality of contemporary societies. (Spitulnik 1997:166)

In Spitulnik's treatment she argues that people in this new and internally diverse nation use media discourse as a reservoir of common reference points that can be readily recontextualized in the ongoing discourse of daily interactions. She suggests that recirculating words and catchphrases from radio shows is a means by which people create an imagined community, a national identity that extends beyond localities. The present study extends this model by examining a practice in which the recycling of mass media discourse by a local community is self-consciously different from that of surrounding communities. Thus, while using media discourse does index participation in the wider society, the (often sardonic) way in which that discourse is applied to local scenes and people simultaneously creates a sense of the reservation as an interpretive community distinct from its neighbors. It does so, not by using a distinctly different code, as would be the case in using an Apache language place name rather than an English language one, but by posing a difference through divergent interpretive positioning with regards to what are ostensibly "the same" mass media discourse reference points, and, through them, to reflect upon a history of changes in homes and families in reservation life brought about through political relations with the surrounding society.

Place, Discourse, Community

Place and land are especially salient to ways in which indigenous communities constitute themselves with respect to encompassing sociopolitical orders. Scholarship in the linguistic anthropology of place draws attention to the fact that places are not mere backdrops for the activities of culture, but are socially constructed, and that this construction takes place in large part through language. Established work on the anthropology of place focused upon the terms in which place is made meaningful by a particular social group (Basso and Feld 1996; Johnstone 1990; Weiner 1991). More recent scholarship focuses on the dialectic interplay between the constitution of place and the definition (often multiple or contested) of community. Places are subject to the defining acts of everyday discourse, and as such serve as resources in the constitution of community and individual identities. This scholarship stresses the contested nature of place and investigates the terms in which differently positioned actors struggle to define the nature of their communities, including who belongs and who does not (Gupta and Ferguson 1992; Modan 2006; Roth-Gordan 2002). This work brings our attention to the fact that any given place is likely to be constituted in multiple ways from different positions and according to different strategies (see also Samuels 2001).

The present study brings that literature to bear upon considerations of the terms in which indigenous voices are recognized by language researchers. I treat a previously unexplored place-naming strategy that exists alongside two others that have already been treated in Western Apache ethnography (Basso 1996 and Samuels 2001, respectively). As Samuels (2001) points out, Apache place names, whether they evoke the idea of an authentic indigenous practice still robust in the face of encroachment (as is the case for Basso 1996) or whether they take officially imposed names and subvert them with Apache reinterpretations (as in Samuels 2001), are inevitably a strategic engagement with the problem of domination by the surrounding society. The place names considered here are yet a third strategy. In this case playful, often media-derived, place names are applied to newly constructed government housing developments. New housing developments are constructed by the tribe every couple of years to provide housing for the reservation's growing population. The housing developments are built outside of the more established residential areas and are characterized by denser concentrations of houses where families unrelated through kinship or previous co-residence are packed together side by side. The place names described here are one means by which reservation residents make these new neighborhoods meaningful and, in so doing, define the contemporary reservation as a community and an alternately enacted public space.

The imagined community (Anderson 1991) these names evoke is one that is self-consciously engaged with while also remaining interpretively distinct from the dominant society. They do this by appropriating media discourse for the naming of neighborhoods according to criteria established through local genres of naming, joking, and wordplay. This practice creates a sense of community that is modeled on preferences for establishing sociality through personal knowledge and familiarity (see Nevins 2005). That is, the place names evoke an image of the reservation community, not as a group of people bound by a social contract, commonly adhering to a set of rules and precepts, but as people with overlapping experiences of place, who can know and empathize with one another by getting the same joke.

In the next two sections I describe two other place-naming strategies that have been identified in the existing literature: Apache language place names described primarily by Basso, and subversive bilingual Apache English place-naming described by Samuels. I do this to situate the media-derived names considered here within other related discourses of place and place names on the reservation.

Apache Language Place Names

Basso's (1996) account of Apache language place names establishes some of the expectations members of the White Mountain Apache speech community hold for the creation and use of a self-consciously "traditional Apache" sort of place name. Below I will argue that in coining, interpreting, and using the English language media place names treated here, reservation residents draw upon precedents established in the reservation community, especially the Apache language names described by Basso. Below I outline three qualities expected of Apache language place names that are salient to understanding the English language commercial media-derived place names.

Place Names Are Associated with Narratives

Each place name is associated with a well-known narrative about past (distant and recent) events that happened at that place. For example, a place named *Tséé Hadigaiyé*, which Basso translates as 'Line of White Rocks Extends Up and Out,' is associated with a story about a girl who failed to heed her grandmother's warnings and suffered frightening consequences. In the story, a young girl was collecting firewood and, against her maternal grandmother's admonitions, took a short cut home through a rocky canyon. She slipped on the rocks and fell, dispersing firewood all around. As she picked up the firewood, a snake bit her hand. She returned to her grandmother frightened and contrite with a painfully swollen arm. A curing ceremony was performed over her and she recovered. She realized her mistake, became determined to respect what her grandmother told her, and as a result knew better how to live. Basso reports that stories such as this, and the place names associated with them, are told repeatedly, particularly to young people (Basso 1996:94).

Many Names Describe Physical Attributes of a Place

Most of the place names discussed by Basso contain a physical description of the place that they designate. Examples of such place names include *Tuzhį' Yaahighaiyé*, which Basso translates as 'Whiteness Spreads Out Descending to Water,' and the example above: *Tséé Hadigaiyé*, 'Line of White Rocks Extends Up and Out' (Basso 1996:93–96). Of course, not every place is named. It is important to note that although most of the names he treats describe points on the landscape, the impetus for naming a particular place is not motivated by the physical qualities of place alone, but by the fact that something of note happened there. In this way, naming and storying are part of the same speech act. Some names in Basso's corpus do not describe physical aspects of spaces but refer to aspects of a narrative said to have taken place in that space. Examples include *Kolah Dahch'ewoołé* ('She Carries Her Brother on Her Back'), *Sá Silį́į́ Sidáhá* ('She Became Old Sitting'), *Naagosch'id Tóó Hayigeedé* ('Badger Scoops up Water') (Basso 1996:141). However, most of the names in Basso's accounts do describe some aspect of the physical space and so there seems to be a preference for names that evoke pictures of the places they designate.

Names Are Applied to People and Used as Interpretive Frames

Basso describes a practice he calls *speaking with names* in which place names are spoken to indirectly suggest how to interpret behaviors or events as they unfold. To illustrate this he recounts how the place name *Tséé Hadigaiyé* was used in a conversation in which a woman shared her worries with her friends about a nephew who had breached a traditionally mandated boundary and was now suffering a severe physical malady. By speaking the name *Tséé Hadigaiyé* her interlocutors applied the story of the girl who disregarded her grandmother to the woman's nephew's situation. Thus they were able to suggest, without stating it explicitly, that her nephew's current pains were a result of his disrespectful actions, and were, like the girl's snake bite in the story, frightening but reparable. Basso also describes how places and their associated stories can become identified with particular individuals, stalking them, and causing them to view their own actions through the associated story. Thus, part of the conventional expectations of the place-naming genre described by Basso involves a productive juxtaposition of stories, places, and people in which people creatively apply names in order to suggest metaphorical links with the behaviors of those around them and to events as these unfold.

A related use of Apache language place names has been described in the earlier literature on the White Mountain Apache by Goodwin (1942) and even earlier by Bourke (1890). These are names for what Goodwin terms *clans*, and Bourke terms *gentes*, referring to relationships of commonality between families who represent themselves as sharing maternal relatives (being of the same clan), or relationships of difference between families who represent themselves as not sharing maternal relatives (being of different clans). In Apache this kind of relationship between families is usually expressed with a verbal construction that includes: *hat'i'í*, literally *ha-* ('upward') + *-t'i-* ('moving as a long extension from a source') + *-í* (nominalizing enclitic, 'that which'). Bourke and Goodwin have pointed out that individual clan names are predominantly toponyms, often suffixed with an enclitic -*ń* to designate that a person or people are being referenced, or -*é* which indicates a name of longstanding use. Examples are *Nádots'osń*,[1] which can be translated as 'Slender Peak Standing Up People,' *Deestciidń*, 'Horizontally Red Rock People,' and *K'isdjint'i'é*, 'Alders Jutting Out People' (Goodwin 1942:604). It is apparent that these names are similar in form to the place names described by Basso; except that in this case the names, while creating a picture of a place, are used primarily to refer to an aggregate of people. A given group of maternal relatives are rarely living in the place described by their clan name. The fact that they share a particular clan designation implies that all are *extending up from a common source* in the form of a common place described by the toponym. It also implies that there is something that they all share by virtue of association with the same place.[2]

Importantly, clan names, like place names, are also storied. That is, they are associated with narratives that recount how a particular clan originated, or became associated with its particular place name, and its history of relationships with other clans.[3] Examples of the latter include *Dóótsdǫ'é*, 'Fly Infested Soup People,' and *T'anásgizn*, 'Washed People' (Goodwin 1942:604–605). An example of what Goodwin terms a "clan legend" involving many of the examples listed above is as follows:

> About seven hundred yards north of my camp, up the creek [Cibecue Creek], on a little bluff called *Dleecehilk'id* ("white paint hill"), a great many people were camped long ago. Bit by bit they moved away to other places, until only one lot was left. The old camp was infested with flies, so the remaining people became the *Dóócdǫ'é*. Many alders grew at the place where the upper settlement is now, so that place was called *K'isdjint'i'é* . . . Thus these people are related to the *Dóócdǫ'é*. Then some of the *Dóócdǫ'é* were witches. They washed these bad people and purified them, so they became *T'anásgizn*. They are still related to us *Dóócdǫ'é*. (Goodwin 1942:606)

Thus, clan names share many of the qualities that Basso describes for place names. They often describe the outward appearance of a place. They are associated with human events in the recent or distant past. And they are used to evoke interpretive frames for understanding ongoing relationships among people. A consideration of clan names places Basso's discussion of place names within a broader semiotic practice in which ongoing and emergent relations between people are constituted through stories linked to places.

In summary, the Apache language place names described by Basso and others pair reference to physical space with a narrative context that is mobilized through speaking to create interpretive frameworks for people's actions and for events as they unfold. Below I will argue that the exclusively

English language place names I describe below, while apparently at odds with their more traditional counterparts, in fact share with the latter common criteria for what makes a good place name, and represent the appropriation of media discourse within a local naming practice. However, while their means for constituting community are similar, the orientation is different. Apache language place names constitute a community grounded in the surrounding landscape, in ancestors, and in those who best know the how to apply the stories: those elder members of the community who are credited with possessing traditional knowledge. With these names, community is realized through imaginative application of an ancestral past on the landscape to everyday people and events. Samuels points out that this is also an assertion of indigenous autonomy in relation to the dominant society. It does this while playing to the expectations of the dominant society because Native American self- representations cast in terms of the traditional coincide with dominant ideological models of what it means to be Native American. In this way traditional place names comprise a "borderland genre" (a notion explicated through application to Coyote stories in Chapter 5) and operate as such by working with contrasting uses and terms of recognition across differently constituted regimes of meaning.

Apache English Bilingual Place-Naming

Samuels describes a different kind of place-naming strategy in his treatment of San Carlos Apache place names (Samuels 2001). It should be noted that San Carlos is immediately adjacent to the White Mountain Apache reservation and its residents share many of the same place names and naming practices. Samuels describes a number of strategies his consultants employed for subverting imposed English language place names. Perhaps the most common is to alternately use Apache language place names alongside imposed English forms. He terms these *translation pairs*. The Apache name within each pair is a well-formed place name along the model described by Basso. Its English counterpart is the official English language name that appears on maps and street signs, and that most non-Apaches are likely to use. He argues that the effect of alternatively using the two members of such a translation pair is to destabilize the air of naturalized reference accorded to the official name, and to flash between meanings and associations accorded to such places from alternate positions in the region's history of colonial imposition.

There are also many examples of such translation pairs on the White Mountain Apache reservation. In fact, most of the longstanding residential areas (discussed below) have corresponding English and Apache names that are alternated in everyday conversation. While most maps of the reservation display the English language names, people in casual conversation readily used Apache language names interchangeably with their English counterparts for the same places.

Samuels discusses a related place-naming strategy involving punning reinterpretations of official place names so that these are pronounced and interpreted with an Apache language meaning. For example, *Tucson* is interpreted as an Apache phrase: *tóó nzaad*, or 'water is far away.' I encountered the same strategy in my own field data. For instance, an abandoned settlement called *Seneca* on maps and street signs was interpreted as the Apache phrase *saan nakih*, or 'two old women.'

What is important about the place-naming strategies described by Samuels, and what distinguishes them from the names considered by Basso, and the media-derived names considered here, it that they predominantly target officially imposed names and destabilize their meaning. In so doing they create an imagination of community that grows in the cracks opened up through everyday unravelings of imposed meanings. The media-derived English language place names I am examining here contribute to the destabilization of officialized place names by posing an alternative cut from an entirely different cloth. They name a new kind of space: new housing developments. Most are obviously and deliberately jokes about these places "made-up" by local community members. They utilize English phrases and idioms like Jurassic Park, Bengay, or Lonesome Dove to name local spaces in a way that is markedly different from surrounding non-Apache communities. And while most of these newly coined names are circulated by word of mouth some are also institutionalized in maps, local news reports, and street signs. These quasi-institutionalizations are playful acts, but acts that also underscore reservation residents' abilities to author their own social landscape within new contexts and for their own purposes.

Contrasting Neighborhoods on the Reservation

Media-derived names are not used for established residential communities on the reservation but are applied only to newly constructed housing developments. In this section I sketch the differences between established and newly constructed neighborhoods and suggest that part of the motivation for the new place names is a comment upon these differences.

Longstanding Settlements

Within the more longstanding settlements on the reservation, such as East Fork, Diamond Creek, Cedar Creek, and others, residence patterns are organized into units, which are called *gową* and *gotaah*, 'households' and 'extended family compounds,' respectively. These are defined in terms of Apache principles of sociality, described as *k'íí*, and loosely translated as 'family.' These neighborhoods often have overlapping Apache and English language names,[4] and most of the former predate the establishment of the reservation. Examples include *Hawóó bi'ishęę'e*,[5] which can be translated as 'dove's call,' for an area in upper East Fork characterized by many doves; *Ch'ílwozh* is the Apache designation for the central town of Whiteriver, and describes the area accurately as one in which two ridges dip and come together in a valley; and *Bide'yóó* for Cedar Creek, translated as *on the other side* because Cedar Creek is on the other side of a mountain ridge from the central town of *Ch'ílwozh/Whiteriver*. The English language names are what appear on road signs and highway maps, and are used in the everyday speech of even older Apaches. But the Apache language names are well known, especially among older people, and circulated on the tribal radio station through a short, repeating segment in which a woman lists twenty-four Apache language names for more established neighborhood communities. I argue that these longstanding settlements, with their traditional Apache language names and officialized English language counterparts, serve as an important backdrop against which the marked and obviously humorous English language mass media inspired names acquire meaning and value in the local community.

New Housing Developments

In contrast with the more longstanding residential areas with their multi-generational extended family compounds, new tribally managed housing developments are age-segregated communities, comprised of small lots with single-family dwellings. They are often less sought after than spots in more established neighborhoods because different families are forced into close proximity without regard for kinship or other established forms of social relationship. For example, during my research period there was a recently built housing development that was persistently sparsely occupied despite being apparently ready for tenants. The absence of children running around and other bustle lent the development an air of bareness. In part this was because it was built in the middle of a flat juniper brush plain not far from the timber mill but very far away from any other housing. Because of these characteristics the development was called Lonesome Dove, after the famous

Western series. This name also contrastively indexes *Hawóó be'ishęę'e*, mentioned above. In fact, it was only a mile or so away from that more traditional neighborhood.

Another example is a housing complex within the town of Whiteriver reserved for senior citizens (the contrast with extended family residence patterns here is striking). At some point people began calling this neighborhood Bengay, for the ointment that many older people use to ease arthritic joints, and the name stuck. Another neighborhood in Whiteriver was notable for the fact that each house was painted a different color to differentiate a row of otherwise identical houses. This became Rainbow City. When a new row of houses was constructed just above this one on the lower sloping end of a butte, this neighborhood became Over the Rainbow. Another, built right against the butte so that it stands in shadow most of the day, is named Dark Shadows after the campy soap opera of the same name. A housing development built in the early 1980s and occupied primarily by young couples was called Knott's Landing. People explained to me that this is because the complex is poised on a hillside with sloping driveways similar to those of the television show, and because it was occupied primarily by young couples whose lives suggested comparison to that of characters in the prime-time soap opera.

Similarly, Chinatown is so named because, for some reason that no one has been able to assess, when the tribe built the houses they neglected to cover their lower levels. So, the houses all look like they are raised up from the ground as if expecting a flood; this despite the fact that the river close by flows through a deep canyon and the houses are situated on a slope many hundreds of feet above possible water contact. The name Chinatown indexes both the fact that the houses look like they could be found by the waterfront – similar to images of waterfront Chinatown in San Francisco or to houses in Southeast Asia encountered through television, and the fact that urban Chinatown in movies and television shows is associated with gangs and gang violence, a problem also associated with this housing development. Many of the Chinatown residents whom we knew described living there as a temporary measure, financially necessary until they can find a house in one of the more longstanding, safer neighborhoods, where they had family connections.

New Places, New Names

These English language names are coined anonymously and circulated by word of mouth. There are similar names for housing developments all over the reservation (for an example from Cibecue, see Basso 1996:151–152) and on the neighboring San Carlos Apache reservation (Samuels 2004), but the names for new developments within the main town of Whiteriver achieve the widest circulation. And some, as in the case of Knott's Landing and Bengay, can last for decades. These humorous names have become an expected accompaniment to new housing developments. Whenever a new development is built, people wait to hear "what they are calling it"; and knowing and getting the joke behind these names is part of contemporary communicative competence (Hymes 1972, 1973) in the reservation speech community. In fact, these place names are more than just jokes, and have become texts that are referenced in everyday conversation, on the tribe's radio station and in the tribal newspaper. Some appear on street signs, as well as BIA maps. Let me summarize what I take to be some of the salient qualities of these names, particularly in relationship to other, more long-standing place names, such as those described by Basso (1996) and Samuels (2001):

(1) All represent English language idioms – but *not* English language place name idioms.
(2) All refer to government housing projects built by the tribe in which a concentrated cluster of homes are constructed together and then allocated to individual occupants based on criteria other than kinship, and so contrast with more longstanding or traditional residential areas of the reservation.
(3) Unlike names discussed by Samuels (2001), for each there is no parallel Apache language alternative in circulation.
(4) Like the place names described by Basso, many are associated with narrative contexts, but these narratives are encountered not on the land, but in movies, television, or commercials.
(5) Like the place names described by Basso, and like clan names, each has multiple points of comparison with the neighborhood with which it is associated. Most index some aspect of the physical shape of the neighborhood, or its contiguity to other named spaces, as well as a quality of the people living there.

A summary of the names that I am aware of is presented in Table 4.1.[6] Here I have matched names of new neighborhoods with aspects of the spatial qualities of the neighborhood that they describe, narrative contexts elicited by the name, and the nontraditional residence pattern that they comment upon.

While the majority of these names do index aspects of the physical appearance of the neighborhood, or its spatial contiguity to other neighborhoods

Table 4.1 English language neighborhood names and their attributes

Name	Spatial description	Narrative context	Residence pattern
Lonesome Dove	isolated on a plain Near "Dove's call"	movie/Western	U, isolation from family and neighbors
Bengay		commercials product use	U, all older people age-segregation
Rainbow City	houses painted different colors		U
Over the Rainbow	built just above "Rainbow City"	*Wizard of Oz* movie song of same name	U
Dark Shadows	built in the shadow of a cliff	television show soap opera	U, atypical choice of location
Life Savers	houses painted different colors	commercials product packaging	U
Knott's Landing	sloping driveways	television show soap opera	U, all young adults age-segregation
Chinatown	Houses appear to be raised for water gaps in foundation	stilt houses SE Asia encountered through media, movie	U, atypical housing construction, low income, gangs
One Step Beyond	Houses next to graveyard	television show	U, older people age-segregation close to graves
Two Steps Beyond	built on the other side of graveyard from "One Step Beyond"		U, older people age-segregation close to graves
Satellite	can't get TV from the tribal transmitters so have satellite dishes	commercials reference to media itself	U, young families with jobs, copious television viewing
Ghost town	houses built over an old grave site	possible ref. to Westerns, tourism	U, houses built over a gravesite

Table 4.1 (*Continued*)

Name	Spatial description	Narrative context	Residence pattern
Jurassic Park	unknown	movie	unknown
Beverly Hills	on a hill	associated with movie stars rich people	U, tribal leaders, regarded as powerful, wealthy
Smurfville	unknown	television cartoon	unknown
Rainbow	built below where a fire had burned in multicolors	rainbow coalition political movement	U, non-Apaches live there – mixed "colors" or races
Corn on the Cob	Houses built in rows on either side of a road up a hill occupied by a family named "Cobb"		

Note: "U" indicates contiguity of families who do not regard one another as kin.
Source: Originally published as Nevins, Eleanor M. 2008. *Language in Society* 37(2):191–215. Cambridge University Press.

or places; a few, such as Bengay and Jurassic Park either do not, or the connection is unknown to me. Similarly, while a majority of the names reference a narrative context associated with mass media such as television, commercials, or movies, some, like Corn on the Cob, Rainbow Ghost Town, do not. The latter two still fit the general model put forward in this article in the sense that an English name or idiom is used contrastively with Apache to index an anomalous residence pattern. In the case of Ghost Town, like One Step Beyond, or Two Steps Beyond, residents tend to be older people, and the close proximity of their neighborhood to a graveyard and to remains of the dead is contrary to traditional residence patterns. Both names were described to me as humorous put-downs, indicating that the residents are so old or so otherwise decrepit as to be not just associated with the graveyard, but a step or two beyond it. Corn on the Cob is a little different. It is a new development built within the traditional community of East Fork/*Hawóó be'ishęę'e*. Many of the residents there are the sons and daughters of families of longstanding residence in surrounding neighborhoods. In this case the idiomatic English phrase Corn on the Cob is chosen less for its contrast with Apache than for the aptness of fit between the phrase and the fact that the hill was already called Cobb Hill, along with the fact that the houses were built closely lined up alongside the road resembling rows of corn kernels. I hope to show below that even these names that diverge in one way or another from the details of my argument with regards to mass media, still conform to my more general argument that these English language names, although superficially different from traditional Apache language place names, are formulated to fulfill many of the same expectations established in the genre of Apache language place names.

Commonalties between Apache Language and English Language Place Names

Place Names Are Associated with Narrative Contexts

As is the case with Apache language place names and clan names, each of the English language place names is associated with a narrative context, usually drawn from mass media. Many, like Lonesome Dove, Jurassic Park, Knott's Landing, and Dark Shadows are names of television shows, movies, or, like Over the Rainbow, the name of a song associated with a movie. Others, like Smurfville and Chinatown, are names for places within television shows or movies. Others are products like Bengay or Life Savers that are associated with narratives from commercials, or from common scenarios surrounding their use. Like the ancestors living in the past on the surrounding landscape, these narrative contexts are generally known, but fall outside the realm of gossip, because they concern people, scenes, and events that exist at a remove from the people and contexts of everyday life.

Most of the Place Names Describe Physical Attributes of a Neighborhood

It is striking that most of the place names evoke some aspect of the physical profile of the place that they name, or spatial relationships between housing developments. In some cases the particular media source discourse is chosen because there is a resemblance between places depicted in that narrative context and the neighborhood in question. These include Knott's Landing and Chinatown. In the majority of cases, however, indexing of place is accomplished through wordplay. Examples include Rainbow City and Life Savers for neighborhoods where each house is painted a different color,

Over the Rainbow for a neighborhood located above Rainbow City, Corn on the Cob for rows of houses built on a hill that used to be occupied by a family named Cobb.

Names Are Applied to People and Used as Interpretive Frames

In Apache language place names and those English language names considered here, naming is a symbolic act that often links aspects of the outward physical form of a place with persons and a markedly narrative context. In both "traditional" and media engaged cases this narrative context is imminently recontextualizable: in the case of narratives associated with Apache language place names, the narrative is associated with a past event on the land and is used in conversation to create new interpretations of persons in ongoing situations. In the case of clan names the narrative context and place are also devices by which to comment upon ongoing interpersonal and interfamilial relationships. In the English language names coined to describe newly constructed neighborhoods, naming similarly links aspects of the outward physical form of a place with persons and with a narrative context. The difference is that in the English language place names the narrative is usually decontextualized from mass media discourse rather than from stories imagined to have originally taken place on the surrounding landscape.

There are also key similarities in patterns of use. In Basso's account a place name can be deployed to suggest an apt fit between the story with which it is associated and an unfolding situation, particularly the behavior of someone under question. When the fit is perceived, a metaphoric relationship is established between the situation at hand and the events in the story. The story then proceeds to become the means by which current situations are interpreted. Again, in this respect the difference between "traditional" Apache place names and the English language names discussed here is primarily one of language and narrative source, not of motivating ideas and overriding patterns of use.

The new names for housing developments are similarly used to elicit moral interpretations of situations as they are unfolding, except that in this case the situation interpreted through the narrative is one of the contrasting lifestyles brought about by the housing development itself. While the English place names are more self-consciously humorous and the Apache names seem to carry more somber pedagogical purposes, both concern the creation of evaluative frames, particularly with respect to unfolding situations that are anomalous, or contrary to commonly held values.

In sum, both "traditional" Apache language place names and English language media-derived place names involve active metaphoric associations of narratives from a removed context, either the mythic or recent past on the land or from mass media, with situations, places, and people closer at hand. The productive creation of these associations to suggest interpretations of situations as they unfold is the driving force behind both naming practices. Both are informed by a common set of ideas about place names and their use: that these evoke both the physical features of a place and a narrative context. Both are also informed by an aesthetic preference for creative acts of naming, or speaking to a situation in which one compact act of speaking creates a striking fit between a given situation and a narrative context.

By tracing the similarities between Apache language and English language place names I am not suggesting that they are identical, only that precedents established by the former play an important role in shaping the latter, and they in fact represent the appropriation of media discourse to some of the same purposes and practices that are implicated in the use of Apache language place names. Each name bundles several qualities that are overlaid together, not because of intrinsic similarities, but by chance. Just as an act of interpretation is assumed to be one of contingency rendered meaningful in new moments of "getting it," the spatial and narrative facets bundled into a given name are also traces of past perceptions and insight, apprehensions, something some else made of prior contingencies, now coined in a name and carried forth into new utterances and moments.

Why English?

The significant difference between the Apache language place names described by Basso and the English language place names considered here is primarily a difference in language choice and orientation to place. In Basso's account, the landscape is mapped with place names and with myriad stories that people utilize to frame interpretations of ongoing events and situations. Government-constructed housing developments are similarly storied by means of their names, but the reservoir of common texts that people draw upon are associated not with an ancestral past on the land, but with stories circulated well beyond the local landscape through television, movies, and other English language commercial media. This raises the question of what the exclusive reliance upon English for these names reflects about the dynamics between Apache and English languages in the constitution of community on the reservation.

Initially, this difference in choice of language appears to reflect a broader pattern of language shift from Apache to English, one that is widely commented upon by all residents on the reservation. While most adults, mid-twenties and older, are bilingual in Apache and English,[7] there is great concern than younger people are not speaking Apache with the same degree of fluency. However, I argue that the situation is more complex than this would suggest (also see Nevins 2004). Because most people on the reservation are bilingual, and because most people have access to stories from both local and media contexts, we cannot ignore the fact that both languages and both sets of narrative contexts form part of the community's communicative and symbolic repertoire. The use of English in this case is a symbolic choice, not a capitulation to a sense of inevitable language shift.

I have argued that the English language idioms used for these names are symbolically deployed to highlight the contrast between these settlements and more longstanding neighborhood areas. English language and media contexts are also stylistic devices for suggesting not only a very funny apt identification between a housing development and a narrative context from commercial media, but in many cases lend a sardonic quality to the comparison. The contrastive tension between English and Apache has been commented upon by others, including Basso (1979), Farrer (1979), and Samuels (2001). Farrer describes a Mescalero Apache girl's puberty ceremony in which the only English that appears is written upon the body of one of the "sacred clowns" in the ceremony: Łibayé, 'The Grey One,' who is also a sort of trickster figure. On his body the words "Way to go Lynn!" are painted, in reference to the fact that the girl undergoing the ceremony had just won a beauty competition. According to Farrer, the English words made an evaluative comment upon Lynn's participation in a beauty pageant in a way that highlighted the conflicting values of womanhood between that context and the Apache puberty ceremony (Farrer 1979:4).

Using English media discourse for the new housing developments highlights their difference from more "traditional" residence patterns. It serves as a vehicle for comment upon the relative anomaly of the new residential patterns and the attendant lifestyles of the inhabitants. Just like the performative use of English by Apaches to create joking portraits of "the Whiteman" that foreground ways that Anglos were perceived to flout ethnical norms in their spoken behavior (Basso 1979) the use of English media discourse contributes to a playful, sometimes sardonic comment upon perceived changes and contrasts in contemporary Apache social life. In each case, the contrast with established residential norms contributes to the humor.

In sum, I argue that while English language names for new housing developments among the Western Apache reflect and celebrate familiarity with broadcast media discourse, these place names are nonetheless shaped by the same language ideology concerning contrasting indexical associations between Apache and English languages that inform joking portraits of "the

Whiteman" and the same precedents in narrative practice that inform "traditional" Apache language place names. So, rather than representing assimilation, this represents appropriation of media discourse for local purposes and meanings. The use of English rather than Apache in these names is informed, not by passive acquiescence to the glamour of English and the media or general patterns of language shift, but by the symbolic contrast with Apache values and practices that is mapped onto the contrast between English and Apache languages.

Why Mass Media Discourse?

Media, Joking, and Wordplay

Televisions, radios, and video players are ubiquitous in reservation households, far more common than telephones. Television shows are watched by groups of family members and friends, often with copious running commentary in Apache. Place names are not the only instances in which mass media is called into the service of verbal play. Familiar names from soap operas, sitcoms, daytime television, sports teams, and movies were frequently used to jokingly characterize people close at hand. For example, we worked most closely with the family of Rebekah Moody, who was sixty-five years old at the time of our fieldwork. Mrs. Moody spent many days with Bessie Oliver and Fiona Griggs, two women who lived nearby and who had been friends since childhood. All three women wore their hair in long braids and dressed exclusively in colorful and voluminous home-sewn dresses called *camp-dresses*. These and many other aspects of their comportment marked them off as traditional Apache women. All were widowed and would spend days together cooking outside for their grandchildren, gossiping and joking with one another. On more than one occasion, particularly at family gatherings, Rebekah Moody's eldest daughter could reliably start a group laughing by making the following comment: "Rebekah, Bessie, and Fiona 'Golden Girls' at'ee!" (where *at'ee* is a form of Apache copula). What made the comment funny was that it simultaneously foregrounds similarities between the two groups of women (older single women friends) and differences (traditional Apache women versus mainstream Anglo women). Here the difference between media worlds and everyday life is a productive one. The former are not emulated so much as utilized in the ongoing project of making playful metaphors between narrative contexts that exist at a remove and the people and scenes of everyday life.

In the course of three years of fieldwork, Rebekah Moody enjoyed using media discourse in a joking way, often to confound expectations (my own and her grandchildren's) for how a traditional Apache woman speaks. One day, after chiding me for saying "goodbye" and coaching me on how to properly take my leave in Apache, she brought me up short as I left her busy house by yelling a phrase we had encountered watching a body lotion advertisement on television. "See you later alligator," she yelled, and laughed at the surprise of all those around her. What made this funny was not the phrase itself, but that it was Rebekah Moody, breaking with her ostensible role as Apache elder and language teacher, saying it. The point here is that the difference posed by media discourse, both as a representation of and by non-Apaches, and as a world narrated at a remove from everyday life, is vital to its use by reservation residents in wordplay.

Media discourse also serves to index markedly non-Apache, or *ndah*, ways of doing things. In contemporary reservation discourse the prototypical *ndah* are White people. When I made the more than occasional etiquette gaffe, my *ndah* status was highlighted and I was often teased with comparisons to characters on television shows who behaved in ways my consultants judged to be nonsensical. This association between media discourse and *ndah*, or White people, is an important factor in the new place names. The use of media discourse, like the use of English, is a symbolic choice that casts these names as comments upon contrasts between ways of doing things embodied in the new housing developments as opposed to more longstanding traditional settlements.

Media Discourse Provides Shared Points of Reference

Because of the widespread presence of television, radio, and other media in Apache households, media discourse provides reservation residents who may not interact with one another directly with shared points of reference. The place names and other Apache uses of media discourse are relevant to a model, developed by Spitulnik, concerning the role played by media discourse in the construction and integration of large-scale communities (Spitulnik 1997:161). In her study of nationally broadcast radio shows in the new state of Zambia, she argues that mass media can serve as "both reservoirs and reference points for the circulation of words, phrases, and discourse styles" that act to integrate large-scale societies not only vertically through acts of direct media consumption, but laterally through the social circulation of media discourse outside contexts of direct consumption. The questions she poses are: (1) what is the process by which speech forms are transported from one context (mass media) to another (local use between persons), and (2) what conditions enable their decontextualization from the source context and recontextualization in everyday speech? The latter she characterizes as intrinsically heteroglossic (Bakhtin 1986), because recontextualization in everyday speech will vary according to the relevant repertoires and position of speakers and contexts in which it occurs. While lateral social circulation of media discourse leads to heteroglossic uses and interpretations of that discourse, she stresses the fact that these diverse uses are bound to one another through common reference to mass media discourse. This integration through common points of reference, she argues, is one of the enabling conditions for the imagination of a shared Zambian community.

This framework is in many respects particularly appropriate to Spitulnik's research site. The problem confronting this relatively new and ethnically diverse state of Zambia is how, given obvious diversity, do people share a sense of a common Zambian nation. The problem of relationship between one's own locality and surrounding social groups is posed differently to Native American reservation communities in the United States. Faced with the political and economic necessity of participating and exerting agency within encompassing political and economic regimes, the question confronting contemporary Apaches is how to become full participants in state, national, and international arenas while also remaining Apache, or "Indian." Attention to local discursive processes on the White Mountain Apache reservation prompts a different research question: how do local language ideologies, discursive practices, and genres inform the ways that media discourse is taken up (decontextualized) and reworked (recontextualized) and what sort of community is constituted through these recontextualizations?

Once these questions are given serious attention, they suggest further theoretical and methodological issues be brought to bear on research into the circulation of media discourse. Spitulnik focuses her analysis upon the media form itself, specifically how message forms in mass media facilitate social circulation. She suggests that certain kinds of message forms have "inherent reproducibility and transportability" and are more likely to be detached from their original context in media discourse and recentered in everyday speech. For Radio Zambia she identifies metapragmatic discourse as the most readily recirculated kind of media discourse. In her sample these include routines such as channel monitoring, dyadic turn-taking routines, and contextualization cues such as title announcements. Of these, title announcements are the most relevant to the Apache English language place names treated here.

Following Silverstein (1976, 1981), Spitulnik suggests three reasons metapragmatic discourse is particularly amenable to recirculation. One is that metapragmatic discourse has greater "transparency of form and function" than other forms of discourse, and tends to be more subject to awareness and manipulation. A second reason is the general applicability of metapragmatic discourse. Because it is discourse about discourse, it is more readily applicable to analogous functions in contexts of everyday speaking. And finally, the prominence of the medium itself, and a phrase's frequent repetition and association with celebrated characters and moments of drama, can enhance its detachability and repeatability outside media contexts. In the latter cases, she argues, a phrase is driven by the specific connotations that it bears in the original context.

In the Western Apache examples considered here the media discourse that is taken up and recentered in local speech is titles. These include titles of movies (*Jurassic Park*) and television shows (*Knott's Landing, Dark Shadows, Lonesome Dove*), names of places in movies or associated with movies or television (Smurfville, Beverly Hills), parts of the title of a song from a movie ("Over the Rainbow"), and names of commercial products (Bengay, Life Savers). As Spitulnik suggests, names for places, products, and movies do have a certain transparency of form and function that suggests their separability from surrounding discourse and facilitates repetition and recontextualization. This principle drives advertising and brand names generally. And certainly, their prominence and recognizability make them more viable candidates for recontextualization as new neighborhood place names than if the reference were obscure.

However, I argue that Spitulnik's analysis gives disproportionate explanatory weight to the message form as it appears in the source (mass media) discourse over and above selection criteria attributable to local genres and speech practices. If we consider the media-saturated environment of the contemporary United States, of which Apaches are fully a part, then it becomes clear that there are countless thousands of other such titles, names, or other metapragmatic discourse from which to choose. The criteria for selection is at best minimally set by its message form in the media. If we are to identify the key criteria for selection it is necessary to attend carefully to local cultural criteria including language ideology, circulation of prominent genres and discourse forms (whether or not these include media discourse) within the local community, the play of metaphor and other poetic principles already established in the community, and other local precedents. Media discourse provides common points of reference, but the uses to which these are put are defined locally.

Media Discourse Fulfills Place Name Genre Expectations

Media discourse is utilized for these place names because it fulfills existing criteria for naming already evident in traditional place names and clan names. Television, movie, and product titles come already attached to elaborate narrative and (depicted) spatial contexts that are generally familiar to most reservation residents. It is also important that the imagined media world exists at a remove from the people and events of everyday life, which makes it viable material for the creation of instances of metaphoric "apt fit" between a human context closer to hand and a more distant context in such a way as to create lasting evaluative (and often humorous) frames upon the former. The key factors in selection and use of media discourse in this case are located squarely in the local speech community's discursive practices.

The shaping influence of local genre orientations on the appropriation of media discourse in this case has implications for understanding how media discourse functions in the mediation of communities. In the case considered here, while the use of media discourse does index a kind of participation in a larger-scale imagined community, the use to which media discourse is put in this case also functions to differentiate a local reservation speech community from the surrounding society. Apache people who talked to me about the names were all conscious of the fact that the surrounding, predominantly Anglo, towns and communities do not name their neighborhoods in this fashion. And it is impossible for outsiders, otherwise familiar with the same media contexts, to "get" what the names mean without being initiated by someone familiar with local practices and precedents. Markedly contemporary rather than traditional, these names become part of the local imagining of the reservation as participating in national and international arenas but in a way that is clearly distinct from surrounding, non-Apache communities.

The names are a vehicle of differentiation packaged to be recognizable as different to outsiders as well. In most of the names, their context in mass media discourse is widely known as such even to people who are not insiders to the reservation, for whom their placement on street signs and mention in the newspaper is marked as odd or unusual.

A border zone encounter I witnessed is helpful here. During our fieldwork period our car, which was over ten years old, was consistently in and out of the shop. The best local mechanic was located on the outskirts of the town of Pinetop-Lakeside, within a mile of the reservation boundary. Most residents of Pinetop-Lakeside are non-Apache, but there is dense commerce between Pinetop-Lakeside and the reservation. Apaches are frequently in Pinetop-Lakeside to shop at Wal-Mart, go to the movies, and for other services. Pinetop-Lakeside residents make frequent trips to the reservation for fishing, hiking, camping, and to enjoy the tribe's restaurant, entertainment, and casino complex. So this auto-mechanics shop, staffed entirely by Anglos, was located on a constantly trafficked border. While I was sitting in the waiting room for the mechanic to finish replacing a CV joint, an Apache man unknown to me walked in and said his car had broken down and he would like to see about having it towed to this garage from his home in Whiteriver.[8] The man at the desk asked where his house was located. The Apache man said: "It's in Over the Rainbow, the house at the end of the row on the right." The man at the desk seemed mildly exasperated, and said something like "'Over the Rainbow', what's that?" To which the Apache man replied "That's where my house is in Whiteriver." The man at the desk: "I don't know what you are talking about. Where is it?" The Apache man tried to explain: "Just above the Health authority office there is a row of houses that are all different colors – this is 'Rainbow City,' get it? And just above them are the houses where I live – 'Over the Rainbow,' do you get it?" The man at the desk just shook his head and said: "How about you just ride down with the tow truck?"

In this example, despite that fact that both the men most likely knew the common reference to "Over the Rainbow" as a song associated with a famous movie, its use in this context was to differentiate the communities affiliated with each. That is, although they shared a common media reference point, the application of this in local usage was not immediately accessible (or not acknowledged as understandable) to the Pinetop resident. Nor would it be accessible to anyone who was not privy to, or did not care to identify themselves as, participants in reservation semiotics. In this case circulation of media discourse worked to differentiate the reservation community from surrounding towns and from the larger-scale society and polity surrounding them, even as it indexes familiarity with common media reference points. Media discourse is used as new material in the service of local poetics and it is this engagement of mass media and other introduced discourse forms with local language ideologies, genres, and discursive practices that must be attended to in order to render an accurate picture of the processes by which media discourse is circulated and how this bears upon the constitution of communities.

Appropriations of Media Discourse Are Political Acts

Bauman and Briggs explicate the relationship between recontextualization and power:

> To decontextualize and recontextualize a text is . . . an act of control, and in regard to the differential exercise of such control the issue of social power arises . . . we may recognize differential access to texts, differential legitimacy in claims to and use of texts, differential competence in the use of texts, and differential values attaching to various types of texts. (Bauman and Briggs 1990:76)

With English language media discourse-derived place names, residents of the reservation community exert control over English language idioms and media discourse by recontextualizing these in terms of a local place-naming genre. In so doing they create differentials of competence between themselves and surrounding communities while also defining themselves as comparable players on the modern or postmodern landscape. The playful nature of these place names, combined with sporadically applied officializing strategies (Hanks 1986) such as placement on street signs and maps, is a powerful assertion of self-definition, confounding mainstream presuppositions concerning what makes legitimate place names as well as what qualities should be attached to authentic Native American identities.

However, the political nature of the act of naming in this case is more than just substituting one authority for another. It also entails a different mode of political participation from that associated with place names in the surrounding society. Discourse genres are political because they implicitly define terms of participation. Place names, as circulated public words for the spaces people occupy, define participation in communities. The place names considered here focus community participation in the space that they mutually occupy in what Vizenor might term "trickster moves," with political entailments. As I tried to show in the previous chapter, there is a politics to translation. The translational model of the surrounding polity is predicated on relations of identity. On the one hand, this provides terms of coordination: Tucson is the same city, with the same name, so that everyone can find it if they want. On the other hand, the relation of identity also articulates a particular mode of power, in which those who are in a position to set those shared reference points exert differential control, defining a reality that must be navigated by everyone else. Documentation operates on the same principle, through it researchers define standards, abstracted out from contexts, through which language or culture is imagined to be identified, and according to which language or culture can be recognized as being reproduced, or not. It functions to provide a means of coordination and recognition vis-à-vis the nation-state, but also articulates its power. The place names considered here operate on a different principle, with different political entailments. Rather than assuming a relation of identical, shared meaning with regards to common references, these names foreground chance convergence, or contingent juxtaposition (Rumsey 2006), in which the meaning of a name emerges from acts of placement with regards to spaces, people, and events, all of which are set up to be inflected differently from any person's own placement relative to others. In this sense, the names discussed here can be considered an assertion of an alternative public (Gal and Woolard 1995) in that through them people engage with discourse circulated in commercial discourse nationally and internationally, but obviate these to establish alternative positions for participants in the reservation community.

Conclusion

In conclusion, English language place names taken from media discourse and applied to recently constructed housing developments represent one of at least three place-naming strategies deployed by residents of the White Mountain Apache reservation. These new place names represent an emergent genre that relies on precedents and expectations established by Apache language place names and clan names. It also makes use of a local language ideology in which the distinction between Apache and English languages can be used to index Apache versus White ways of enacting social relationships. Also informing this genre are existing genres of wordplay that utilize distinctions between Apache and English, including distinctions between local scenes and those portrayed in English language media discourse. As such, despite the fact that these names are often recirculations of English language media discourse, they do not represent simple assimilation to mainstream discursive norms. Instead, they represent the reconfiguration of media discourse to locally defined standards and purposes. As a strategy for engaging with the dominant society in the definition of place and community, these names celebrate participation in media discourse but in terms that privilege reservation insiders. Knowledge of the names defines an interpretive community in which participation and belonging relies on "getting" the same joke; where "getting the joke" implies engagement with ongoing commentaries, critiques, and interpretations of changes in contemporary social life as these unfold.

Discourse genre is a useful notion to bring into discussions of language shift and maintenance because it defines an analytic focus where language and culture are directly mutually implicated. Much of the endangerment literature relies on a deductive formula: if a language dies, a culture dies (e.g. Woodbury 1993) because language is taken to be the vehicle for cultural transmission. Some programs are justified as a sort of backward engineering, the logic being that if we could just reproduce the language in classrooms, the cultural institutions that depend on the language for transmission would also be shored up. This chapter demonstrates that the relation between language and culture is more complex and dynamic. Most obviously, this chapter demonstrates that people can appropriate, or indigenize, English, or another language imposed by settler colonialism, to their own, culturally defined purposes (see e.g. Field 2001) by incorporating it within local discourse genres. And whereas language documentation and maintenance programs tend to proceed on the assumption that languages and cultures are entities clearly bounded off from one another, and that keeping languages separate is key to maintaining quasi-national differences, these place names reveal another possibility. These place names also show that appropriation of languages associated with Others can be an integral part of the ongoing articulation of indigenous communities in their own terms and for their own purposes, including assertions of the mutual relevance of indigenous voices with respect to surrounding communities (see also Merlan 2005; Rumsey 2006; Stasch 2007; Weiner 2007).

And finally, these place names provide another vantage point from which to reflect upon language programs as forms of community mediation. If English language media discourse can be appropriated to an Apache place-naming genre in the service of an alternate way of enacting community, then the reverse is also possible. Apache language discourse can be appropriated to genres of the governing polity, in the service of enacting communities recognized through the technocratic apparatus of nation-states. Pointing this out does not delegitimize language documentation and maintenance, but locates them more accurately within the innovative dynamics of indigenous communities. Language documentation and maintenance play a part in the ongoing definition of indigenous communities, alongside other creative acts of language and community definition cast in other terms and according to different principles of translational and political articulation. This chapter has been an attempt to make the latter, which often goes unnoticed by researchers and policymakers, audible. The following chapter brings these considerations to bear directly upon language documentation and researcher–community relationships.

Notes

1   These names as given are taken from Goodwin (1942). Because he was not always consistent in his transcriptions I have opted to preserve his forms (and let others interpret them as they may) rather than replace them with my own best guess transcriptions.

2   For an example of the continuing currency of these ideas, when visiting a family on the San Carlos reservation for a gift exchange prior to a Sunrise Ceremony, one of the family members introduced himself to me as *Deschiidń*, and explained that while he lives in Phoenix and his other family lives on a flat plain in San Carlos, their clan name meant that their family once lived in a valley with lots of red rock.

3   Thanks to Charles Kaut for suggesting the applicability of this argument to clan names.

4   Almost none of these corresponding English and Apache names are direct translations, or calques, of one another (see Webster 2000).

5 A pamphlet published through the White Mountain Apache Culture Center gives the name *Hawóó bi'ishįį'e*, 'Dove's salt,' and this is repeated in a regular radio segment in which traditional neighborhood place names are listed. Residents of East Fork when questioned about the name as written were perplexed about the meaning of "salt." Some have suggested that whoever wrote the name down mistook *ishęę*, 'cry,' for *ishįį*, 'salt.' I've opted for the 'Dove's cry' version. There are also several traditional stories that make reference to Doves' cries.

6 Thanks are due particularly to the extended family of Rebekah Moody, who have acquired knowledge of many of these places by living in or near to them, and also to Charles Kaut and Phillip Greenfeld for willingness to share comments and knowledge of these places.

7 In fact, most conversations among younger and older adults are conducted primarily in Apache, and references to these neighborhoods in the course of conversation stand out as isolated chunks of English within an otherwise Apache flow of speech.

8 This interchange is reconstructed from my memory. What I present here is not a verbatim transcript of the conversation but my best attempt to render that conversation faithfully.

References

Abu-Lughod, Lila. 1995. The Objects of Soap Opera: Egyptian Television and the Cultural Politics of Modernity. In *Worlds Apart: Modernity through the Prism of the Local.* Daniel Miller, ed., pp. 190–210. New York: Routledge.

Anderson, Benedict R. 1991. *Imagined Communities: Reflections on the Origin and Spread of Nationalism.* London: Verso.

Askew, Kelly and Richard R. Wilk, eds. 2002. *The Anthropology of Media: A Reader.* Oxford: Blackwell.

Bakhtin, Mikhail. 1981. *The Dialogic Imagination: Four Essays.* Caryl Emerson and Michael Holquist, trans., Michael Holquist, ed. Austin: University of Texas Press.

Bakhtin, Mikhail. 1986. *Speech Genres and Other Late Essays.* Vern W. McGee, trans. Caryl Emerson and Michael Holquist, eds. Austin: University of Texas Press.

Basso, Keith. 1979. *Portraits of "the Whiteman": Linguistic Play and Cultural Symbols among the Western Apache.* New York: Cambridge University Press.

Basso, Keith. 1990. *Western Apache Language and Culture: Essays in Linguistic Anthropology.* Tucson: University of Arizona Press.

Basso, Keith. 1996. *Wisdom Sits in Places: Language and Landscape among the Western Apache.* Albuquerque: University of New Mexico Press.

Basso, Keith and Stephen Feld. 1996. *Senses of Place.* Santa Fe: SAR Press.

Bauman, Richard. 2004. *A World of Others' Words: Cross-Cultural Perspectives on Intertextuality.* Hoboken: John Wiley and Sons, Inc.

Bauman, Richard and Charles Briggs. 1990. Poetics and Performance as Critical Perspectives on Language and Social Life. *Annual Review of Anthropology* 19:59–88.

Bourke, John G. 1890. Notes on the Gentile Organization of the Apaches of Arizona. *Journal of American Folklore* 3(4):111–126.

Crystal, David. 2002. *Language Death*. Cambridge: Cambridge University Press.

Crystal, David. 2003. *English as a Global Language*. Cambridge: Cambridge University Press.

Farrer, Claire. 1979. Łibayé, the Playful Paradox: Aspects of the Mescalero Apache Ritual Clown. Paper presented at the annual meeting of the American Anthropological Association, Cincinnati, Ohio, November 24.

Field, Margaret. 2001. Triadic directives in Navajo language socialization. *Language in Society* 30(2):249–263.

Fishman, Joshua. 2001. *Can Threatened Languages Be Saved?* Philadelphia: Multilingual Matters.

Gal, Susan and Kathryn Woolard. 1995. Constructing Languages and Publics: Authority and Representation. *Pragmatics* 5(2):129–138.

Goodwin, Grenville. 1942. *The Social Organization of the Western Apache*. Memoirs of the American Folklore Society 33.

Gupta, Akhil and James Ferguson. 1992. Beyond "Culture": Space, Identity, and the Politics of Difference. *Cultural Anthropology* 7(1):6–14, 16–18, 20–23.

Hahn, Elizabeth. 1994. The Tongan Tradition of Going to the Movies. *Visual Anthropology Review* 10(1):103–111.

Hanks, William. 1986. *Intertexts: Writings on Language, Utterance and Context*. Lanham: Rowman & Littlefield.

Hymes, Dell H. 1972. On Communicative Competence. In *Sociolinguistics*. J.B. Pride and Janet Holmes, eds., pp. 269–285. Harmondsworth: Penguin Books.

Hymes, Dell H. 1973. On the Origins and Foundations of Inequality among Speakers. Special Issue: Language as a Human Problem. *Daedalas* 10(3): 59–85.

Johnstone, Barbara. 1990. *Stories, Community and Place*. Bloomington: Indiana University Press.

Kroskrity, Paul V. 2000. Regimenting Languages: Language Ideological Perspectives. In *Regimes of Language: Ideologies, Polities, and Identities*. Paul V. Kroskrity, ed., pp. 1–34. Santa Fe: School of American Research.

Kulick, Donald and Margaret Wilson. 1994. Rambo's Wife Saves the Day: Subjugating the Gaze and Subverting the Narrative in a Papua New Guinea Swamp. *Visual Anthropology Review* 10(2):1–13.

Liebe-Harkort, Marie-Louise. 1979. Bilingualism and Language Mixing among the White Mountain Apaches. *Folia Linguistica* 13:345–356.

Mankekar, Purnina. 1999. *Screening Culture, Viewing Politics: An Ethnography of Television, Womanhood, and Nation in Postcolonial India*. Durham: Duke University Press.

Merlan, Francesca. 2005. Explorations towards Intercultural Accounts of Sociocultural Reproduction and Change. *Oceania* 75(3):167–182.

Modan, Gabriella. 2006. *Turf Wars: Discourse, Diversity and the Politics of Place*. Oxford: Blackwell.

Nevins, M. Eleanor. 2004. Learning to Listen: Confronting Two Meanings of Language Loss in the Contemporary White Mountain Apache Speech Community. *Journal of Linguistic Anthropology* 14:269–288.

Nevins, M. Eleanor. 2008. "They Live in Lonesome Dove": Media and Contemporary Western Apache Place-naming Practices. *Language in Society* 37: 191–215.

Nevins, Thomas J. 2005. A World Made of Prayer: Alterity and the Dialectics of Encounter in the Invention of Contemporary Western Apache Culture. Dissertation, University of Virginia.

Phillipson, Robert. 1992. *Linguistic Imperialism*. Oxford: Oxford University Press.

Powdermaker, Hortense. 1950. *Hollywood: The Dream Factory. An Anthropologist Looks at the Movie Makers*. Boston: Little Brown.

Roth-Gordon, Jennifer. 2002. Slang and the Struggle over Meaning: Race, Language, and Power in Brazil. Doctoral dissertation, Department of Anthropology, Stanford University.

Rumsey, Alan. 2006. The Articulation of Indigenous and Exogenous Orders in Papua New Guinea and beyond. *Australian Journal of Anthropology* 17(1): 47–69.

Samuels, David. 2001. Indeterminacy and History in Britton Goode's Western Apache Placenames. *American Ethnologist* 28(2):277–302.

Samuels, David. 2004. *Putting a Song on Top of It: Expression and Identity on the San Carlos Apache Reservation*. Tucson: University of Arizona Press.

Silverstein, Michael. 1976. Shifters, Linguistic Categories, and Cultural Description. In *Meaning in Anthropology*. Keith H. Basso and Hugh A. Selby, eds., pp. 11–55. Albuquerque: University of New Mexico Press.

Silverstein, Michael. 1981. *The Limits of Awareness*. Texas Working Papers in Sociolinguistics 84. Austin: Southwest Educational Development Laboratory.

Silverstein, Michael and Greg Urban. 1996. The Natural History of Discourse. In *Natural Histories of Discourse*. Michael Silverstein and Greg Urban, eds., pp. 1–17. Chicago: University of Chicago Press.

Spitulnik, Debra. 1993. Anthropology and Mass Media. *Annual Review of Anthropology* 22:293–315.

Spitulnik, Debra. 1997. The Social Circulation of Media Discourse and the Mediation of Communities. *Journal of Linguistic Anthropology* 6:161–187.

Stasch, Rupert. 2007. Demon Language: The Otherness of Indonesian in a Papuan Community. In *Consequences of Contact: Language Ideologies and Sociocultural Transformations in Pacific Societies*. Miki Makihara and Bambi B. Schieffelin, eds., pp. 96–124. New York: Oxford University Press.

Vizenor, Gerald, ed. 1998. *Fugitive Poses: Native American Scenes of Absence and Presence*. Lincoln: University of Nebraska Press.

Webster, Anthony K. 2000. The Politics of Apache Place Names: Or Why "Dripping Springs" Does Not Equal "*Tónoogah*." In *Proceedings of the Seventh Annual Symposium about Language and Society – Austin (SALSA)*. Texas Linguistic Forum 43:223–232.

Weiner, James. 1991. *The Empty Place: Poetry, Space and Being among the Foi of Papua New Guinea*. Bloomington: Indiana University Press.

Weiner, James. 2007. The Foi Incorporated Land Group: Group Definition and Collective Action in the Kutubu Oil Project Area, Png. In *Customary Land Tenure and Registration in Australia and Papua New Guinea: Anthropological Perspectives. Asia Pacific Environment Monograph 3*. James F. Weiner and Kate Glaskin, eds., pp. 117–134. Canberra: Australian National University E Press.

Woodbury, Anthony. C. 1993. A Defense of the Proposition, When a Language Dies, a Culture Dies. In *Proceedings of the First Annual Symposium about Language and Society – Austin (SALSA)*. Robin Queen and Rusty Barrett, eds. *Texas Linguistic Forum* 33:101–129.

Woolard, Kathryn. 1998. Introduction: Language Ideology as a Field of Inquiry. In *Language Ideologies: Practice and Theory*. Bambi B. Schieffelin, Kathryn A. Woolard, and Paul V. Kroskrity, eds., pp. 3–49. Oxford: Oxford University Press.

5

Stories in the Moment of Encounter
Documentation Boundary Work

God made it [the writing] but it came down to our earth. I liken this to what has happened in the religions we have now. In the center of the earth, when it first began, when the earth was first made there was absolutely nothing in the world. There was no written language. So it was in 1904 that I became aware of the writing, it was then that I heard about it from God. (Silas John Edwards, translated and quoted in Basso and Anderson 1973:1014)

Philological need gave birth to linguistics, rocked its cradle, and left its philological flute wrapped in its swaddling clothes. That flute was supposed to be able to awaken the dead. (V.N. Voloshinov 1973:71)

Living Histories

The two men featured in the epigraphs to this chapter, Silas John Edwards and V.N. Voloshinov, were contemporaries in the 1920s:[1] one on the Fort Apache reservation and the other in Leningrad, in what was then the Soviet Union. Both were engaged, from their respective positions within the late colonial order, with problems of language, writing, and moral agency. Silas John Edwards was a religious leader trained as a Traditionalist *diyiń* and also worked for several years as a translator for the minister of the East Fork Lutheran mission. Mr. Edwards posed an alternative to Lutheran claims

---

Lessons from Fort Apache: Beyond Language Endangerment and Maintenance, First Edition. M. Eleanor Nevins.
© 2013 John Wiley & Sons, Inc. Published 2013 by John Wiley & Sons, Inc.

about the superiority of the Bible and Christianity. He told people about a vision in which a new set of ceremonies was revealed to him, along with a writing system for teaching the songs to initiates, and he began to hold weekly meetings at consecrated sites, or Holy Grounds. In so doing he founded a new Traditionalist movement, the "Holy Ground Movement," that spread across several Apache reservations in the southwestern United States.

Voloshinov, on the other hand, was a scholar and participant in what is sometimes described as the Bakhtin circle. The quote in our epigraph is taken from a work in which he attempts to lay foundations for a study of language grounded in utterance, dialogue, and in the situation of language in social relations among speakers. It is part of a critique of what had just been established, via Saussure's students, as modern structural linguistics. Voloshinov situates structural linguistics, which he terms "abstract objectivism," within the broader political history of philology and points to ways that key social premises of philology had been carried over into it.[2] Philology, he wrote, arose as a means of decoding alien or dead languages in order to establish access to texts that from the perspective of the analyst were permanently bounded off from the personal contexts from which they emerged. From its beginnings in classical philology, and extended to Oriental and colonial linguistics, philology selects out utterances from their contextual places in ongoing dialogues and recasts them as monologues and as monuments to the past.[3] Put alongside the language endangerment and maintenance literature (for example, recall the book titles listed in Chapter 2), Voloshinov's description of the "philological flute" wrapped in the swaddling clothes of linguistics that was "supposed to be able to awaken the dead" rings presciently.

I open the chapter with these two quotes because both require us to think about indigenous language documentation through a history of encounter (T. Nevins 2004; Silverstein 1996b). That history proceeds from the colonial philology associated with Orientalist and missionary translation efforts, to the salvage documentary philology of the Americanist tradition, to contemporary concerns with documenting languages in response to concerns about language endangerment. Both statements stand in relation to colonial philology, but askance from it: prompting us to consider the symbolic use made of documentation to project historical and expected future relations between peoples. Silas John Edwards was speaking for himself and his movement in response to challenges posed to the authority of Apache religious leadership by the Lutheran mission. Voloshinov, on the other hand, was painting a critical portrait of the project pursued by his continental linguistic colleagues. Taken together, the two vantage points allow us to draw illuminating parallels and contrasts between what were contemporaneous projects: colonial philology and Silas John's Holy Ground Movement.

The colonial philologist, whether missionary, army officer or scholar, documents languages through encounters with the colonized. The social process of circulating and refining objects of documentation among scholars, archivists, translators, and publishers, establishes the products of documentation as stable objects. Colonial philology defined languages through products of documentation and drew relations between languages within an extended, temporally deep framework.[4] This temporalizing maneuver has a parallel and an alternate in the action of a person like Silas John Edwards. His announcement of a new religion emerged out of his own encounters with philological documentation. In proclaiming receipt of new songs and a writing system he defines terms of a new ceremony. By circulating these among networks of practitioners and other *diyiń*, and by suggesting parallels to the Christian Bible and to other ceremonies, our epigraph shows that he established for himself and for those who followed him, temporally deep relations between languages and religions.[5]

I draw the parallel in a spirit of symmetry, but also because drawing broad similarities allows us to perceive more clearly a difference between the terms of mediation posed by Silas John Edwards' action in contrast to that of linguistic or philological documentation, not in order to criticize either, but to specify both in their respective positions in a wider context of community mediation. While many contemporary linguists might not recognize their own motivations in Voloshinov's portrait: "That flute was supposed to able to awaken the dead," the portrait is consistent with the broader rhetoric of language endangerment. Voloshinov's argument challenges us to reflect upon questions of voice and agency in the knowledge produced through documentary encounters with others and to consider the question of whose voices are cast as dead or dying and whose agency is expressed in the "saving" act of documentation, or in the "revitalizing" purposes of language programs.

In contrast, Silas John Edwards asserts continuity with a more extended past, not by reviving something dead or dying, but by posing himself in a listening orientation to an active but temporally deep voice. For Silas John Edwards the agency that animated the past is still relevant, and in this sense not dead, because states of affairs established by ancestral actions continue to make present lives possible. His songs share with Traditionalist ceremony more generally a concern with enabling precedents, in which sustaining relations among family figure prominently, as do moral involvements with other living beings upon whom people depend. Traditionalist ceremonies trace these back to precedents in the actions of ancestors and to necessary relations between soil, sun, and water on the earth's surface. As in other Traditionalist ceremonies, the deep temporal agency of ancestors and the life-sustaining conditions they established through their thoughts, plans, and prayers on the surface of the earth are continuous with elders and the recently dead, and prominent in the songs of the Holy Ground Movement. For Silas John and other *diyiń,* and for the people who listened to them, the lingering effects of ancestral actions were in this sense alive, their voices still speaking. The challenge and opportunity posed to people was to perceive them.

Temporalities and Political Relations

Silas John Edwards' response to the mission encounter demonstrates that temporality is not an impersonal fact, but a means of political and intersubjective coordination in encounters with others. Through temporal orientation expectations as to whose voices are relevant to ongoing matters of concern are established. As such, temporality in colonial and postcolonial encounters is subject to negotiation and struggle. In many Apache families the voices of elders as well as the voices of ancestors are described as shaping the present in ways that range from everyday speech to prayers, songs, stories, but also more diffusely as footprints, breath, and all the traces their actions left on the world (Basso 1996). The rupture with the past asserted through the rhetoric of Lutheran conversion provoked counterarguments and responses, not from an impulse to resist change and hold to tradition, but because it provoked an argument about where and with whom to attribute the agency to shape the present and future.

In this chapter our focus is upon language documentation as acts in the mediation of indigenous communities. In Chapter 2 I argued that a temporal argument framing indigenous languages as belonging to a past that has been disrupted and superseded by a modern present is implicit to the language endangerment literature. Community members looking to support an indigenous language through funded programs often confront paradoxes of expertise, temporality, and objectives in their attempts to either assume the position of, or work with, university accredited language experts. Documentation requires encounter between university-credentialed language experts and those speakers of indigenous languages who derive their authority from other sources. This chapter traces a history of Apache language documentation, from missionary efforts to assimilation era salvage philology to contemporary endangered language documentation. I attend to three Apache voices: Silas John Edwards, Lawrence Mithlo, and Rebekah Moody, whose engagements with documentation span more than a century of encounters. I do this in the hopes of prompting a shift in perspective upon language documentation away from the "discovery" of a language by linguists and towards the invention of what counts as knowledge of language through encounters between persons engaged in different regimes of meaning (following Wagner 1981). My purpose is to draw attention to relativities in perspective that are both preconditions and entailments of documentary encounters, but not programmatically addressed in the language endangerment literature.

In efforts to document endangered languages, awareness of differences in interpretive stance between linguists and many speakers of indigenous languages is an inevitable part of the actual practice of linguistic fieldwork. It is often expressed in informal ways, as in the cartoon in Figure 5.1, put

Figure 5.1 "The Phantom Linguist." With kind permission from Nick Thieberger, 2002.

together by Nicholas Thieberger in 2002 and circulated in his workshops on linguistic fieldwork.

In this example of linguistic self-parody, the fieldworker is presented in the guise of a comic book superhero: The Phantom. There is quite a lot being commented upon in this improvised comic, but I want to draw attention to the fact that it elicits awareness of interpretive disjuncture. The cartoon's rendering of the linguist as superhero and as the person of whom it is said: "finally someone who will save our language!" is funny because it puts the claims of endangered language documentation as these are presented in some popular books (e.g. Abley 2003; Harrison 2010) and in films (e.g. *The Linguists*) in a face-to-face village setting, and confronts the reader with the implausibility that members of such a community will see the problem in the same terms and accord to the linguist the same heroic role. It elaborates the disjuncture between the linguist's concerns, motivated by his placement within a network of other linguists, and the concerns of many other persons who speak the language. Our phantom linguist says to the assembled community members: "I'm from the university and I'm here to help you." He deliberates aloud about specialized technocratic standards: "should we be OLAC compliant? And what about the GOLD ontology?"[6] In so doing, the author of the cartoon foregrounds the extent to which the linguist, as technocrat, is engaged in concerns that exclude most community members.

Polysemic Mediation – Language Documentation as Boundary Works

The cartoon elicits awareness in its audience that nonlinguist indigenous community members very likely approach documentary encounters with different meanings and purposes than those of the linguist. However, the question of what these alternate purposes might consist in remains a cipher. This chapter is aimed at that gap. Acts of language documentation are acts of mediating a community as an indigenous one within encompassing sociopolitical orders, and occurs in a complex, diverse social setting. Documentation emerges from encounters between linguists and other participants in indigenous communities, who bring different concerns and purposes.

Alongside forms of political integration accomplished by documentation throughout the assimilation era and subsequently through provisions for recognizing difference on the quasi-national model of ethnicity and language standardization, parallel histories of differentiation can be found in religious movements like the Holy Ground movement, through extended family pedagogies and politics as discussed in Chapter 3, through novel place-naming practices like those discussed in Chapter 4 (also Basso 1996; Samuels 2001), and in place names embedded in moral involvements with land described by Basso (1996). As the previous chapters, together with our epigraph in this chapter from Silas John Edwards, demonstrate, those alternate means of enacting community are not in outlook smaller in scale nor more private than their nationalist counterparts. Founded in alternative participatory pragmatics, they mutually implicate local scenes and more extended cosmopolitan realities (see also De la Cadena 2010; Poirier 2008; Rumsey 2006).

Writing at the Boundary of Dueling Temporalities

Our opening epigraph shows Silas John Edwards' voice asserted in the context of an adversarial colonial dialogue in which temporal framing and the moral authority of his voice, and of elders and ancestors, were at stake. Silas John Edwards's innovations demonstrate (following Hanks 2010 and Morgan 2009) that the colonial encounter was also a documentary encounter. He demonstrates that this was true not only for the colonial agents recognized as authors of those documents but also for indigenous colonial subjects. Prior to establishing the Holy Ground Movement, Silas John Edwards had worked across different religious traditions: first as apprentice to his father, a *diyiń*, and, following that, in the first decade of the twentieth century as translator working with Rev. Edgar Guenther at the East Fork Lutheran mission. As a *diyiń* he had memorized the songs, stories, and visual symbols for several ceremonies. As a mission translator he helped the Lutheran minister in his efforts to write Apache language and to establish terms of translation for rendering the Lutheran message in Apache moral idioms.

Rev. Edgar Guenther, like Lutheran ministers elsewhere, employed philological methods within a modernist temporal framework through which he assigned different temporal statuses to the various languages he regularly dealt with. On the one hand, his seminary training in Hebrew and Greek provided access to the ancient written languages of the Bible, which he treated as the transcendent word of God definitive not only of the true meaning of past events, but also of the present and future. On the other hand, to make his mission work useful to other missions on other Apache reservations (see Samuels 2006) he applied his philological training to improvise written accounts of the language of his Apache congregation. He did not, of course, accord the language of Apache Traditionalist ceremony the same status he accorded biblical Hebrew and Greek. Rather, the mission, in its capacity as an evangelizing institution and as a day school, cast Apache language and ceremonialism as aspects of a primitive past that would be superseded by conversion to Christianity.

The Fort Apache reservation was established late in 1891, at a time when English-Only assimilationism dominated national policy, affecting settlers who spoke language varieties other than standardized American English[7] as well as Native Americans (Morgan 2009). In this period army officers, missionaries, and linguists wrote down Apache in a manner that was not intended for use by the vast majority of persons who spoke it. The East Fork Lutheran day school was like many other reservation schools in the time period in that indigenous children were taught that reading and writing English was necessary to their future (Meek 2010). English literacy was put to use in Sunday church services through reciting creeds, written minister calls and congregation responses, and for singing hymns from hymnals. Between obligatory schooling and the conversion rhetoric of Lutheran church services, writing was a powerful symbol of temporal rupture. Students were taught to expect the succession of primitive, illiterate ways by a life that was modern, literate, and Christian.

Silas John Edwards' work with Rev. Guenther at the mission was a kind of boundary work (Hanks 1986; Star and Griesemer 1989) to which each brought different purposes. Subsequently, each conveyed different recontextualizations of what each received from that encounter to others. For Silas John Edwards, as for other *diyiń* of his time (Samuels 2006), biblical figures suggested similarities to key figures of Apache cosmological narratives and ceremonies. He formalized a translational pairing between *Bik'ehgohidaań* 'because of whom there is life' and God; between *Nayenezghaní*, or 'he overcomes evils/obstacles' and Jesus. The ancient but continually relevant temporal status that the Lutheran minister accorded to the Christian Bible harmonized with the status that Silas John Edwards, his father and other *diyiń* attributed to the songs and stories of Traditionalist ceremonies. Following upon the mission encounter, divinely inspired script took on new life in the series of visions with which Mr. Edwards established the Holy Ground Movement and added to Traditionalism a way of writing down songs and ceremonies. Mr. Edwards' writing integrated elements of the Roman script he encountered at the mission with visual elements from Traditionalist ceremony.

For example, in Figure 5.2 Roman cursive script for the first person pronoun *shi* is combined with an image for prayer, which often appears in sand paintings, on the crowns of crown-dancers, and painted on the bodies of dancers in Traditionalist ceremonies.[8] His use of writing, together with

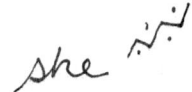

Figure 5.2 Credited to Silas John Edwards, "My Prayer," as reported in Basso, Keith and Ned Anderson. 1973. A Western Apache Writing System. *Science* 180(4090): 1013–1022.

the translational pairs noted above, posed terms of commensurability between the songs and narratives of Traditionalist ceremony and the Bible (Basso and Anderson 1973; Nevins 2010b).

In addition to appropriating the Bible as symbol, and claiming their own access to divine script, participants in the Holy Ground Movement also made use of another kind of document: letter writing. In the example below, a group of men on the San Carlos reservation use English language literacy to petition the reservation superintendent to allow their ceremonies to take place. The excerpts are taken from a letter signed by twenty-five San Carlos Apaches to the superintendent of that reservation in 1921:

> We the undersigned hereby request that we be permitted to hold Indian Prayer Service every Sunday on our Prayer Grounds . . . The purpose of this meeting is to teach everyone of our Creator and the life of Jesus Christ, and that each one must worship only two highest beings. As heretofore we have been worshipping things such as the sun, different movements of clouds, winds, stars and many other things which God created, the same as we are; at the same time, we are rapidly doing away with the medicine men, who in years past have been among us, and from practicing medicine have taken from us the best we had in horses, cattle, saddles and money. . . The missionaries have been among us, a failure it seems. They tend more to learn our language and tend more to introduce our singing. . . . So in the year 1920 we . . . called together a group of our leading Indians and decided to take this step: to call together a Prayer Meeting every Sunday which is open to all our Indians who desire to come here . . . The service is conducted in the Indian tongue as the leaders are all non-English speaking. (Spicer 1962:533)

Indigenous documentary acts figure importantly in assertions of the moral authority of their voices across boundaries between *ndee*/Apache and *ndah*/White, or across Traditionalist and Christian (Nevins 2010b; Nevins and Nevins 2009). Taking the view of Apache religion projected by the officers at Fort Apache, by the reservation agent, and by missionaries, Silas John Edwards and other leading participants in the Holy Ground Movement recast it, answering with alternative claims to biblical authority, the means to which were controlled by Apache religious leadership.

As is evident in the legacy of Silas John Edwards, the subjects of colonization respond to literacy and to acts of language documentation in complex and strategic ways, appropriating tropes and elements from that encounter to their own purposes. Mr. Edwards' appropriation of writing was part of a broader strategy to counter-temporalize the relation between Apache religion and Christianity and to assert the continuing relevance of Apache leadership to Apache futures. That Silas John Edwards and participants in the Holy Ground Movement were successful in doing this is borne out in the fact that the movement quickly spread across the Fort Apache, San Carlos Apache and Mescalero Apache reservations (Spicer 1962: 532–535), where its members continue to hold leadership positions across tribal offices at the time of my writing this book, nearly ninety years later.

The Lutheran minister responded to the early success of Silas John Edwards by lodging complaints with the reservation agent (Spicer 1962:532). Not long after, Mr. Edwards was jailed for nearly twenty years on what were later determined to be trumped up murder charges. The movement flourished despite his imprisonment, during which time he kept up correspondence with movement practitioners through letters and visits. The coercive nature of the actions taken against Silas John Edwards deserves criticism but should not obscure from view the fact that they were in response to the agency exercised by Apache speakers in their own continuing control of what Hymes (1972a) terms their "means of speech." That is, these acts and other repressive policies were in response to Apache abilities to shape their ongoing relations with one another and with more extended communities using instrumentalities that fell outside the purview of the forts, the missions, and the administrators of the reservation. Uses of writing by participants in the Holy Ground Movement shows that documentary encounters, even under the more politically disadvantageous conditions set by official assimilation policies, may present opportunities for indigenous political assertions not anticipated by colonial agents.

Encountering Others across Contrasting Regimes of Meaning

The historical relationship between the Holy Ground Movement and the Lutheran mission at East Fork speaks to the motivating relation to otherness in the formation of social selves across both missionary (Keane 2007) and indigenous regimes of meaning (see T. Nevins 2010; Nevins and Nevins forthcoming, cf. Stasch 2009; Weiner and Glaskin 2007). Traditionalist *diyiń* define their agency through relation to others according to a strategy that differs from that of the missionaries. Their claims rest upon their ability to speak across and reposition boundaries with respect to variously figured others. For example, in the *Na'i'ees*, a girl's coming of age ritual involving the extended families, or clans, of the girl undergoing the ceremony and woman chosen to be her godmother, *diyiń*, and other leaders, elicits boundaries between the two clans in order to speak across them, posing not mutual identity, but commensurate moral relations between them going forward (Nevins and Nevins forthcoming). In cases of bodily and psychological healing, *diyiń* move across and reassert perceptual and tactile boundaries between human beings and differently embodied beings like deer, snake, and lightning (Goddard 1920:394–400; Goodwin 1942) where knowledge of the other side of such boundaries is woven into life stories and possibilities moving forward. What is now labeled "Traditionalist" religion[9] is full of elements emerging out of historical and ongoing engagements with the otherness posed by neighboring Apachean as well as Puebloan ceremonial practices (see Goodwin 1938). In the same way, contemporary *diyiń*, as was the case with Silas John Edwards, define themselves and their agency through invoking and repositioning boundaries between Traditionalist and Christian religions (Nevins 2010b; Nevins and Nevins 2009) in a way that answers charges of primitivism or idolatry with arguments that demonstrate mutual commensurability in the past extending to the present and relevant to future orientation. In all of these cases agency, or power, emanating from ancestors, is assumed to be carried in words: in the songs of ceremony, in the prayers of elders and ancestors, in the quoted past words of others. Speaking places the present moment in a flow of social agency enabled by ancestral actions and works, shaping the present and with implications for the future.

Lutheran missionaries define themselves through their actions in the mission field, in which they identify what is pagan amongst the people who make up their prospective congregation and put forth terms for conversion. As in other Protestant missionary efforts (following Keane 2007) the central critique leveled upon indigenous religious practice was the charge of "fetishism." Keane shows how what is at stake is the question of where, how, and across what kinds of boundaries legitimate attributions of agency can be made.

> the concept of fetish arises in a comparative context, as an observer's response to seeing *other* people attribute false values to objects. Such discourses of

fetishism and idolatry are marked by their doubleness: they require both a fetishist and an outside observer in whose eyes the fetishist is trapped in misrecognition. (Keane 2007:225)

Within the ideology of Protestantism and the modern state, charges of idolatry or fetishism carry the assumption of a given, prior separation of human agency from objects or things and its attributed containment within the boundaries of individual minds. Charges of fetishism proceed from this assumption and are taken by those who wield them as instruments through which to root out false belief. In relation to indigenous families and ceremonial practices, charges of idolatry are used to redirect the flow of recognized agency away from the contingent involvements of persons in family and ancestors, towards containment within the boundaries of individual persons, or citizens.

In this way ministers attempted to establish the conditions of what their seminary deemed acceptable conversion, in which their mission subjects might, free of the shackles of tradition and from ancestors and family, each individually voice a sincere belief in the truth of the Bible and through this act become incorporated as believers within the body of the church to assume the benefits and obligations that church membership entails. Conversion to Lutheranism participates in a poetics of political integration in that converts are incorporated as individual souls into the body of the church. Ministers and the converted are continually invented through acts of purification in which encroachments of the traditional, the ancestral, or the pagan are rooted out and individuals are brought within the body of the church. They make use of orientation to others to assert an exclusive space on one side of a temporal boundary between the modern/Christian and the Traditional/pagan.

In the mission field and in the field of social action defined by Traditionalist ceremony, each provides an occasion for their opposite number to act, and each provides an occasion for the self-definition of the other. And while their actions are mutually articulated, they not identical – each is playing a different game, carrying different assumptions, and pursuing different kinds of actions across a jointly occupied social field. I suggest that it is helpful to view language documentation in parallel terms: as a form of encounter in which the researcher and the speaker each figure as necessary others, and in which each addresses their respective other with different purposes, in different terms, and with respect to different regimes of meaning in which the location of agency figures as a difference with political ramifications. Language as constituted in linguistics is a material thing. It is through encounter with indigenous others and through materializing their speech in disciplinary terms as "elements of language" that fieldworkers and the knowledge claims of documentation are granted legitimacy.

Once language has been cast as an object, and once the researcher establishes her stake in that object, interpretive disjuncture emerges with those consultants who see things differently. As Keane notes: "it is precisely because material things seem to be endowed with objective, culture-free values . . . that the encounter with others who evaluate things differently can be so troubling" (2007:226). Linguistic researchers engaged in indigenous language documentation are forced into adopting some stance with respect to the alternative posed by the people they work with. Proceeding without making a provision for difference effects an erasure of the point of view of one's consultants in the process of documenting their speech. However, confronting differences in the imputed status of one's research object from those who have a strong moral claim to it can transform the interpersonal boundaries of a research encounter into one of diplomatic exchange, in which the documentary object's status as a representation of "language" is subsumed to the agentive role played by words, or speech, in an exchange of perspectives with those deemed "other," and in which the overriding concerns are ethical and political.

For the remainder of this chapter I look to a process and product of linguistic documentation: text collections, to illustrate ways that speakers of indigenous languages who work with linguists have engaged with documentation in complex ways. I will examine two collected Apache language texts. One was spoken by Lawrence Mithlo and transcribed by Harry Hoijer in the 1930s during the era of salvage documentation, and another was spoken by Rebekah Moody and transcribed by me in the 1990s amidst an environment informed by a concern with the threatened status of Apache language. By looking to the rhetorical strategies employed by the speakers as evident in the two texts, I show that both speakers bring purposes and temporal arguments that contrast with those they anticipate to be held by the researcher as they attempt to engage the researcher in an exchange of perspectives.

The Temporal Argument of Salvage Documentation

An assertion of rupture with an indigenous past parallel to that of the Lutheran mission and day school was forwarded in the simultaneous project of salvage ethnology. It was not inconsistent to support, as did John Wesley Powell as director of the Bureau of American Ethnology (from 1879 to

1902), salvage ethnology as a research project while also advocating termination via allotment with regards to Indian lands (Morgan 2009). Franz Boas, when he took on the role of honorary philologist for the Bureau of American Ethnology in 1901, broke with Powell in this respect, effecting a greater separation of linguistic and ethnological research interests from land policy (Darnell 1990). In his published correspondence, Boas expressed opposition to the allotment system and blamed what he saw as the destructive repression of American Indian languages in residential schools on the influence of missionaries (Lewis 2001). But he evidently did not see an opportunity to exert influence on policies towards American Indians, at least not only until very late in his career in the New Deal era when John Collier held the position of Commissioner of Indian Affairs (1933–1945).

Boas gave the collection of texts in American Indian languages primacy in the research program he established when he founded the Columbia University anthropology department in 1889 (Bauman and Briggs 2003; Darnell 1990). Through text collections in American Indian languages he attempted to establish the study of Native American languages, oral folk literature, and culture on comparable footing with that of the classical tradition (Bauman and Briggs 2003). Texts would provide a basis for grammatical descriptions, oral literatures, and cultural analysis. Transcribing Native language texts forced the fieldworker to attend to details of the terms of expression employed by the Native American people who worked with them. According to Lowie, Boas displayed concern throughout his career for interrogating the epistemological basis of claims about American Indian cultures (Lowie 1947). Text collection was intended to provide a check upon some of the distortions of translation arising from what he saw as the inevitable relativity of enculturated perspectives between the researcher and members of the target community (Darnell 1990; Lewis 2001). This chapter represents an extension of that concern, but directed to the pragmatics of encounter and dialogue between researcher and consultant, and making a space for reconfiguring our ability to hear research subjects not only for the information they provide, but as participatory public voices.

Even given Boas' positions on Indian policy and skepticism as to conditions of ethnological knowledge, the historical ends Boas assumed for Native American languages and cultures continued to indirectly reflect the same assumptions about their eminent demise that were embedded in missions and other ongoing projects of federal governance. In fact he designed some of his projects to directly articulate with them. For example, Boas designed the first *Handbook of North American Indian Languages* (Boas 1911) to be of general use not only to scholars but also to others positioned between Native American communities and the surrounding economy, society, and government, including missionaries, traders, and reservation administrators

(Darnell 1990:132).[10] From his position in a network of scholars, opinion makers, and government agencies, Boas retained and made effective use of the assumption that Native American languages and cultures were disappearing and in urgent need of documentation. In common with the contemporary rhetoric of language endangerment, the felt urgency of ethnological salvage inspired a generation of anthropology and linguistic doctorates to energetic efforts, and justified funding for research, archive space, and publication. The salvage project motivated the collection of ethnological accounts, grammars, and texts in American Indian languages through the Bureau of American Ethnology and the Museum of Natural History from the late nineteenth into the twentieth century.

Language Documentation in an Apache History of Plural Mediation

In the first decade of the twentieth century, when Silas John Edwards was working as a mission translator, Pliny Earle Goddard (1919, 1920) collected White Mountain Apache (the ethnolinguistic group with which Silas John Edwards identified) texts from people living on the neighboring San Carlos Apache reservation in the neighborhood of Turkey Creek. After Silas John Edwards' imprisonment, and while the Holy Ground Movement was spreading to other Apache reservations, more specialized and elaborate Apachean language documentation was carried out by Harry Hoijer, who integrated Edward Sapir's Navajo field materials with his own work across Apache reservations in Arizona, Oklahoma, and New Mexico (Hoijer n.d., 1938a, 1938b, 1945a, 1945b, 1946a, 1946b, 1946c, 1947, 1948, 1949). While the image conjured of salvage work is that of a field researcher working with one of a handful of remaining speakers of an indigenous language, for most of the Apache reservations of the southwest in the first half of the twentieth century, indigenous language fluency was dramatically more prevalent than English language fluency among adults. The salvage goals of Americanist linguistics in the Apache case, and for other reservations in the West, projected a future of language shift that was not yet manifest.

Silas John Edwards' rhetoric is relevant to contemporary concerns with language endangerment because the alternative that he poses throws presuppositions implicit to both the mission context and salvage linguistics into relief. The past of the Holy Ground Movement is different from the past of Lutheranism or of scientific humanism. The letter presented above to the reservation superintendent show that while the Holy Ground Movement was presented by participants as innovative, the rupture they effected was not with the past, but with respect to their contemporaries: the missionaries and with other practicing *diyiń*. The difference that Silas John Edwards asserted between his vision and Lutheranism, or between his movement and the ceremonies of other *diyiń*, was via his claim to having uncovered a new way to manifest the agency of a temporally deep cosmological source. In politic relation to the mission, his act of temporal positioning is an equalizing one, and implies that the practitioners of all "the religions we have now" might, if they were to attempt it, recognize one another in mutual orientation to that source (Nevins and Nevins 2009, forthcoming).

In this respect, as an alternative act in the mediation of an indigenous community, the Holy Ground Movement reflects the orientation of Apache persons situated within a colonized community responding to the claims of Christian missionaries and reservation administrators, and recasting that relation by means of extending and innovating upon a repertoire of existing discursive genres and practices. The administrators and missionaries, of course, were themselves orienting to Silas John Edwards and other Apaches via the expectations placed upon them and with instruments put at their disposal by the assimilationist regime of the early twentieth-century United States.

I present this history in order to propose that salvage documentary research elicits not only linguistic data, but also consultants' prior experience with colonial agents and discourses and with discourse genres, styles, and practices. The account of Apache lives spoken by Lawrence Mithlo to Harry Hoijer in the 1930s and published as "Old Apache Customs" in *Chiricahua and Mescalero Apache Texts* (1938a), and another spoken by Rebekah Moody to me in 1996, illustrate this. Although separated by sixty years and differences in historical paths, there are striking parallels between the two speeches. I propose that these are the result of loosely shared commonalities in what Hymes (1972a) termed the "means of speech" by which both engaged with the otherness of the researcher and the temporal politics of the ethnographic encounter. I will present excerpts of both texts, pointing to commonalities in the way that each speaker attempted to intercept what they took to be the assumptions of the researcher and assert an alternative temporal orientation for their relation going forward, in which the agency of their own families through time proves relevant. However (following Silverstein 1996a), I will also show that the speaker's own rhetorical efforts compete with the contextual frame imposed by the researcher and by the publication format of a text collection, and for this reason can be difficult to recognize, effectively hidden in plain sight.[11]

Attention to these texts as records of acts of speaking situated in the documentary encounter reveals that both speakers address themselves to the researcher and attempt to alter the terms of their relationship and the purpose of their encounter. In particular, both speakers attempt to anticipate and intercept the view of themselves and their own group in which their own past is figured in terms of ignorance and lack and replace that view with an alternative drawn in terms of morally valorized sustaining acts among family. Each employs a rhetorical strategy reflected upon among my consultants as *bá'hadziih* or 'speak for them' to temporally refigure the research relationship by posing past commensurabilities between themselves and the researcher, and between Apaches/*ndee* and White people/*ndah* as a basis for mutual moral recognition and oriented to possible relations moving forward.

Rethinking Text Collections in the Mediation of Communities

Two of my dissertation advisors, Dell and Virginia Hymes, had been students of Hoijer at UCLA (University of California, Los Angeles) where Dell held a postdoctoral position in the late 1950s. Hoijer's articles on Apachean grammar and his collected texts were part of my graduate preparation prior to fieldwork. I paid close attention to his 1938 *Chiricahua and Mescalero Apache Texts*. The Chiricahua texts in the collection carried unique moral weight because the contributors had all endured more than twenty years of imprisonment in the wake of the so-called "Apache wars." In the collection, only the text contributed by Lawrence Mithlo and considered here, as well as several of Sam Kenoi's contributions, translated as "stories of the Foolish People" make reference to violent encounters with White people/*ndah* and imprisonment. Chiricahua families had been relocated to the San Carlos Apache reservation, which shares a border with the Fort Apache reservation, with many ties of family and marriage across Apache persons situated in both.

My "fieldwork project" was addressed to innovations in Apache language use, especially in the use of oral narratives in the contemporary reservation community. I saw myself as attending to what Ron Scollon, discussing his and Suzanne Scollon's Alaskan documentary work, termed "the language people speak today." For the Fort Apache reservation this included an interplay of languages people identified as Apache and English, and, more sporadically, Navajo and Spanish and a range of discourse genres spanning familial, bureaucratic, religious, and mass media settings. Quite a bit of what I did was text collection. Together with those Apache persons who were interested or willing, we recorded Christian testimonies,

Traditionalist narratives, oratory and songs, mock telephone conversations, family stories (Watt 2004), and accounts of extraordinary encounters with things like burning bushes or UFOs.[12] These were usually followed up with time-intensive translation sessions. All my consultants voiced particular interest in translation and comparison between Apache and English. They also expressed concerns about language endangerment and entertained the idea that creating more written materials in Apache language with accompanied English translation would in a general way be beneficial to the cause of supporting continued Apache language use. Tape-recordings of these performances were circulated informally among family and church networks. For my purposes, I thought I would be able to use these materials to say something about discursive innovation, poetics, and the creativity of locally established discourse genres (following Bauman 1984, 1986; Hanks 1986). I noticed but did not fully appreciate the significance of the fact that my consultants prefaced every spoken performance that they recorded with me with a prayer. I also noticed that many of their performances ended in entreaties directed to me and to the larger prospective audience. What I did not appreciate was the extent to which this sort of address to those figured as *ndah* was not an exceptional adjustment to my presence, but integral to the ongoing "language that people speak today," extended to the research encounter.

When I returned to the University of Virginia after my field term, I spent a year working at the Electronic Text Center[13] to create an electronic version of Harry Hoijer's *Chiricahua and Mescalero Apache Texts*.[14] Retaining Hoijer's numbered units, we represented them on the screen in line and verse format (following Hymes 1981), and provided options for coordinating the Apache and English side by side with one another and with corresponding linguistic notes. However, as it turns out, the most important innovation we introduced was to place the name of the Apache contributor at the beginning of each text with which he was associated, so that anyone viewing the text would also view the contributor's name. This contrasted with Hoijer's print version, in which he had restricted acknowledgement of the individual contributors to a paragraph in his introduction. The texts in the print version had been presented on the page as numbered ethnological items: Chiricahua texts 1–39, Mescalero texts 1–8, with individual titles, but without attributed authorship (cf. Sarris 1993). I intended the electronic version of *Chiricahua and Mescalero Apache Texts* to be multifunctional: useful to linguists for analysis, and to community members as meaningful stories, songs, and speeches. It would take an unexpected phone call to alert me to the significance of the collection as a document of encounter between its Apache contributors and the researcher, who the former treated as an intermediary for *Indah*,[15] or 'White people.'

How I Got a Clue

I worked at the Electronic Text Center Tuesdays and Thursdays, part-time. A couple of weeks after we had posted the Hoijer texts online, I arrived to work my Tuesday shift and my co-workers told me that a woman from the Mescalero reservation had called many times, first on the previous Friday and then on Monday (the day prior) asking to talk to me. She would probably call again today. Given the complex politics surrounding Native American research and representation and my own experiences with the tribal attorney's office with respect to the Ndee Biyati' project, I did not know what to expect. She did call that day and identified herself to me as a relative of many of the men who contributed texts to the collection. She said she wanted me to know how important it was to have their names appearing on the screen with their contributions. That, she said, made it "more than just words on a page." She said she wanted me to know that these were all important men whose names: Lawrence Mithlo, Duncan Belacho, David Fatty, Sam Kenoi, Charles Smith, and Horace Torres, are still remembered and respected on the Mescalero reservation. She said that these men talked to Morris Opler and to Harry Hoijer because many of them had been prisoners of war for much of their lives and knew that the way Apaches were depicted in newspapers had worked against them. She wanted me to know that the men treated their work with researchers as a kind of diplomacy in which they attempted to have a hand in how they were understood.[16] She said that even though some people do not like to publish traditional stories and songs today, she had respect for these men and what they were trying to do. She said she used the online texts in Apache language and culture lessons with her own children, and that her children brought these projects into their classrooms.

This prompted me to think about a conversation with Rebekah Moody as we both stood on her front porch just days before Tom and I were to return to Virginia after nearly three years there, spent largely with her family. Much had happened in that time, conflicts and tragedies as well as celebrations. She said to me: "When you write about us, don't just talk about our trash. Be proud of us." As will become clear below, "be proud of us" is not only addressed to the objects of representation that I would produce, though it has implications for them. Instead, her statement more directly reflects her concern that I speak about them from a position of moral involvement. I note this here because the researcher's position of moral involvement is what Rebekah Moody and Lawrence Mithlo address in the two "texts" considered below.

Misrecognized Dialogues in Elicitation Sessions

In keeping with our opening epigraph from Voloshinov, I note that text collections take an utterance that was elicited as part of a dialogue between researcher and speaking contributor and recontextualize it as monologue and as monument to the past. Here, following the speakers' contextualizing cues in the progression of their performances (Duranti and Goodwin 1992; Silverstein 1996a), I attempt to re-place texts collected from Rebekah Moody and Lawrence Mithlo within the ongoing dialogue of their research encounters. I am aided in doing so by bringing these speeches into relation with what I learned about Apache speech genres through a broader engagement with residents of the Fort Apache reservation through research concerns defined by the ethnography of speaking (following Basso 1979, 1996; Hymes 1972b).

There are significant differences and parallels between the two speakers and speeches considered here. As a child Mithlo was among the Chiricahua who suffered removal from Arizona and twenty years of detention in the wake of the "Apache wars." As an adult he moved from Fort Sill, Oklahoma to the Mescalero reservation in New Mexico and became part of the leadership there. He was exposed throughout his life to the politics of modernizing temporalities, including not only the rhetoric of his captors concerning his people's imprisonment, but his participation in Western-style schooling, in Catholic missions, and through engagement with anthropologists. He addressed himself to Harry Hoijer after having also worked with Morris Opler, who provided ethnological notes to his speech.

Rebekah Moody, on the other hand, did not suffer removal and imprisonment but, like Mithlo, she describes deprivations as a child and as a young woman. Like Mithlo, she was exposed to modernizing temporalities through many contexts, including the East Fork Lutheran Mission, of which she was a longtime member and where she attended school in the 1940s, twenty years after Silas John's period of employment there, and where she worked as an aide in the orphanage and nursery. Like Mithlo, as an adult Rebekah Moody became part of the leadership of her community. Her late husband had been tribal chairman for many years and her home served as a diplomatic venue where she hosted visiting leaders, missionaries, and more than a few ethnographers: Charles Kaut, Ray Birdwhistell, Keith Basso, Tom Nevins, and me.

While the two speeches and speakers are separated in time, location, gender, and in dimensions of personal history, what is held constant is that both accounts are provided to an anthropological researcher by a person with long experience in the discursive strategies of community leadership, including oratory. Both speakers apply an oratorical strategy used to negotiate relations between a group with which the speaker identifies, and those figured as other. This way of speaking was reflected upon among my consultants as *bá'hadziih*, or 'speak for them.' People are expected to *bá'hadziih* at ceremonial exchanges between clans (Nevins and Nevins forthcoming), when giving testimonies in Apache Independent Christian churches (Nevins 2010b), and in political speeches.

To identify commonalities between Mithlo's and Moody's speeches that they share with *bá'hadziih* across other contexts, I adapt Harding's (1987) tactic for the analysis of conversion rhetoric. That is, I identify a progression of rhetorical moves that shape one side of an implied dialogue between speaker and responsive listener. Like conversion rhetoric, *bá'hadziih* is persuasive speech, a bundle of rhetorical strategies for shifting the interpretive position of the addressee. Leaving the differences between the two speeches aside, I identify four rhetorical moves they have in common in order to reveal an intersubjective strategy that both speakers employed in the research encounter. I also suggest contrasts between the rhetorical purpose of *bá'hadziih* and the default interpretive frame implicit to ethnolinguistic text collections as a publication genre in documentary linguistics.

First Rhetorical Move – Difference of Perspective Established and Marked

At the very beginning of their speeches both speakers identify a portion of their audience as *ndah/indaa*, or strangers. *Ndah* is translationally paired (Samuels 2001) in both reservation communities with 'White person.' For example, here is how Lawrence Mithlo begins his speech:[17]

'Iłk'idą́, in"daaí Vit'ago hąhé łą́ daolaahát'édadą́
Long ago, at a time long before there were many white men,

"Déí 'ił'ango 'ádaahooghéí díík'eh joogobago daahi"dáná'a.
all of the different ones who are called Indians lived poorly, they say.

'Íyąąda k'adi, Chidikáágo hooghéí 'ásht'į́.
But anyhow, I am one of those called Chiricahua.

Shin"déí, biłn"dénshłį́í,
My people, those people with whom I live,

dásídá'át'égo 'iłk'idą́ daahiⁿdáná'aí baanałdaagoshⁿdi.
I shall tell you exactly how they are said to have lived long ago.[18]

And here is how Rebekah Moody begins her speech:

Díí ndaahíí hágot'éégo doníína
This white person, how it was long time ago

"Nágowągohíí baago shiłnágo" shiłndi, 'ákoo
"Tell me all about all it" she said to me, and so

Setting aside differences in tone and authority claims, what I want to draw attention to is the fact that both begin by marking a difference in position and perspective between themselves and a portion of their audience who are figured as other, or *ndah*. In so doing they frame the speech situation as a particular kind of dialogue.

Second Rhetorical Move – Self from the Other's Point of View

Near the beginning of each speech the speaker depicts his/her own group's past as it might likely appear in the unsympathetic gaze of White people. Both speakers elaborate themes of material poverty and ignorance.
For example, Lawrence Mithlo:

Daanahitsóyéí dáłeezhíighe'yá daahindáná'a.
Our grandfathers lived in the dirt, they say.

Dátł'ohná beekooghąshį́ dá'ádaa'ílaa.
Their houses were made only of grass.

Tł'oh bégoos'eelyá naasjé.
They lay on grass that had been spread out.

Ch'ide yá'édį.
There were no blankets.

Beekooghaní yá'édį.
There were no tents.

Dooha'shį ła'jóláhát'éda.
None could be secured anywhere.

'Iban 'ádaat'éí gotł'aazhį k'édaadeesdizná'a.
Things like deerskin were wrapped about them, they say.

Naagołtį́go, tóí gok'izhį nkeedanlį́.
When it rained, the water flowed down upon them.

Zas naałtį́go, zasí gokázhį naadaałtį.
When it snowed, the snow fell on them.

Hago, dákǫǫná daagoch'ide.
In the winter, only the fire was their blanket.

And Rebekah Moody:

Dá''ostagyóó 'onékał łehni', ádách'itishé.
We used to go to school when we were little.

Bus dohwaada.
There was no bus.

Daní' 'onékaa łehni'.
We used to walk.

Zhot'éé nagołt'įįh.
It would be really raining.

Ch'íh binádasiłdíígo onékaa łehni'.
We used to walk with a blanket draped over us.

Ná'íícho hat'í' 'ágodzééhí dohwaa bé dá'ǫǫzida.
We don't even know what 'jacket' was. (starting to cry)

Áná zh-t'éé dáńdí łehni', iłdó' . . .
And we used to be just poor . . .

In each case, the speaker marks the account of deprivation with his or her affective orientation to the other's gaze. For example, consider the following passages from Lawrence Mithlo:

'I"daanałį́í goostáńdiłtałí hah'áálgo, díík'ehnyá
White men, carrying six-shooters, from this

> *"dédáłeendasijaaí beenaał'a'áłádą́.*
> by means of them you (dual) could make slaves of a whole camp of Indians.

'Ágołdish"dí:
I say thus to them:

> *"Naał'a'ánahałaaí nahí Chidikááǥo hongéí doobaayándzįda.*
> "We who are called Chiricahua are not ashamed that you (sg) made us slaves.
>
> *Han k'aa nahá'ágólaan 1'ań 'áńá yaayáńzįhálí."*
> Perhaps whoever is said to have made arrows for us is ashamed."

Mithlo's alternating use of dual and singular verb stems plays a contextualizing role in this direct address to his audience. He clearly includes Hoijer and the prospective audience for the speech within *Iⁿdaa*, or 'White men' but provides a means to differentiate that field with his use of the dual verb form when he presents the act of making slaves of camps of Indians.[19] By using the dual stem he allows for there to be White men who made slaves of Indians and other White men who did not. When he poses an address to the former, those who did enslave Indians, saying: "I say thus to them: 'we are not ashamed,'" he does not use second person address. That is, he does not say in the context of his speech to Hoijer "I say thus to you." Rather, he uses the prefix *go-*, often described as an "environmental prefix" because it indexes a perceptual surround. In this case it figures his speech as broadcast with regard to a perceptual surround. Within that projected speech, he uses the singular stem in the verb "you made us slaves," delimiting the direct addressees to those White men who enslaved them and addressing them within the listening presence of an audience that includes those who did not, inviting moral alignments.

A little farther along in the speech, after listing traditional foodstuffs, including wood rats and burros, he makes a similar declaration, saying:

> *'Ádíídíí díík'eh nahidáń.*
> All of these [were] our food.
>
> *'Áí nahí doobaayándzįda.*
> We are not ashamed of that.
>
> *Dá'ághát'éǥo, nahidáń nahá'ájílaaná'a.*
> In that way, they made our food for us, they say.
>
> *Jooba'éⁿdéłąí í yee'isdahóóka.*
> Many poor people lived by means of it.

In this passage the implicit contrast was between Mithlo's self-positioning with poverty associated with an Indian past and the imagined unsympathetic gaze of White men. While the record does not preserve Mithlo's vocal quality, through word choice he establishes an affective orientation to that view of himself and an Indian past from the imagined perspective of *Iⁿdaa*: a sympathetically defiant stance against the looming prospect of shame.

Like Mithlo, Rebekah Moody conveys an emotional stance towards what she is saying in her choice of words, but also by her vocal delivery, in which words were accompanied by restrained crying. She continues:

Kodííbi 'áshich'íshí íbiye'hóó,
When I was small

> *zhǫ t'édat'iyéhyóó łehni', nokée baa dowhaada łaí*
> we used to be very poor, when we were little and we didn't have any shoes, and

> *diyáágo zhó'dágową t'ééda'ch*ǫǫ*' éízh*ǫ*.*
> all our clothes were just ruined and wearing out.

Łeh náshijeí łehni' íí schoolyóó daa.
That's what we used to wear to school.

Diyáágé naketano ndah da'idééhgo. éí beena ółtag.
Those white people used to give just some clothes, and then, that's what we'd wear to school.

Dółghaiyé nóhwił nakih 'i shódohwaa hayóó háń init'įįh binída émá.
We used to ride, two at a time, on a donkey, nobody used to tease us for that.

. . .

Áíyóówóyóóhíí bikeé dikáhá nádaidéé łehni'
We used to get shoes too from those same people

> *d*ǫǫ*zht'éé ádikeé.*
> they weren't good but I had to wear them

*Nch*ǫǫ *'égat'éé.*
They weren't good.

Dohaa deez ndíhí dikée dadohwaada.
The shoes were not the right size.

Dohaa k'ehgot'éégo bikee dayóó ts'onts'a degá hágo bee ánóch'itaá be nách'oghah bee.
You don't have to be shy about it, you have to leave it on and then walk around with it.

Zhǫ tédant'íhyóó nagh'áh azhǫ́.
We were raised just poor.

What is accomplished, or attempted, here by each speaker is the alteration of an outside view, or objectification, of an Apache past in the prospective gaze of the researcher, or white people. They alter this by animating for that outside audience the emotional orientation that goes along with being the recipient of that gaze.

Third Rhetorical Move

In what I have identified as a third rhetorical move that the two speeches share in common, the speaker attempts to transform the terms in which their own and other Apache lives are perceived by moving the gaze of the addressed others, in this case the anthropologist, from what had been apparent, but which the speaker had just rendered morally or emotionally problematic, to what had not been apparent, but which the speaker reveals to have been true and important all along. This elicits a different moral alignment with an Apache past.

Lawrence Mithlo does this by juxtaposing the image of Apache poverty against a morally valorized portrait of Apache families:

'Ádą́ 'iłk'idą́, joogobago daajíⁿdáná'a.
At that time long ago, they lived poorly.

Ndah "déí 'isdzą́ą́yóí biche'shkéne gózhǫ́go yaahihⁿdíná'a.
But Apache women taught their children well, they say.

. . .

"*Shishke'é, doo'jódzįda.*
"My child, one does not curse.

Doháń k'eshíⁿdiida.
One hates no one.

Doháń bich'įįlójigoda.
One behaves foolishly to no one.

Doháń baajadloda.
One laughs at no one.

Dohyáabaajó'įįlee'át'édań goshinsį́.
One treats with respect those to whom one can do nothing.

Yóósń Tóbájiishchinéń bichįį'itédahdlii.
Pray to God [and] Child of the Water.

Áń dá'gobiłk'eh gok'ehgodaanⁿdá.
We live because of those two.

Niigosjáńí yáí 'ágoił'į."
They made the earth [and] the sky."

daayiił'díná'a.
they said to them, they say.

. . .

'ⁿdaanałįí, dákogo,
You who are white people, then,

  díídíí 'iłk'idą́ "dé doo'ikóńzįdaí gółį ndah,
  even though these ancient people knew nothing,

  dá'át'égo koogha̱ gótǫ́ǫ́yéí goos'ą́í bighe'yá
  still, inside their poor camps,

  dá'át'égo gózhǫ́go biche'shkéne yaahihⁿdíí,
  still, they taught their children in a good way,

nahí doobégonasįda.
you do not realize this.

Here teaching and good words, as acts of sustenance, are presented as a realization about Apache families (see Witherspoon 1975) that "White people" have so far not been able or willing to make. In saying "you who are white people . . . do not realize this" he is of course inviting them to realize it now, or to at least be aware that there is something they do not understand.

Rebekah Moody also remembers and calls attention to new thoughts about a prior state, also thematically figured in terms of familial acts of sustenance:

Dat'įshdí tł'égó shichóstííńí dohwaada dobí ná'daghá.
I used to be kind to my grandfather because he doesn't see.

Shimaa bikįh nadááhyóó,
When he used to come to my mom's house,

> *bits'il got'áá nasgis łéne*
> I used to wash his hair
>
> *Hankerchief dách'ęę łehda nits'óo sé bátánizgis.*
> When he used to carry around the dirty handkerchief, I used to wash it for him too.
>
> *Soap bee bátánísgis baa clean ánáslé godaá iłts'os.*
> I used to wash it with soap and then give it back to him.
>
> *Dííjįįyóó yich'odahńdii' ashłįį́ nágonsee*
> Today I was thinking about how it was good that I did that for him.

In a more intimate idiom of personal experience, Rebekah Moody also draws attention to acts of familial sustenance that she figures with "today I was thinking about . . ." as a new realization about past actions. In revealing what had previously been submerged or hidden as something newly reflected upon and salient to the ongoing dialogue, the speakers also present their lives with respect to the researcher via an alternate temporal frame. They describe Apache prior acts that are not yet over because their own selves, and their present encounter with the researcher, are not alienated from them. They replace apparent ignorance with knowing family, and apparent helplessness and poverty with an image of themselves or their own group as having done certain important things very well. They invite the researcher to make a shift in moral alignment to orient themselves differently to the Apache past just revealed by allowing it to speak to them.

Fourth Rhetorical Move

Finally, at the end of both speeches, the speakers elaborate a direct address to their interlocutor. In doing so each attempts to involve that interlocutor in a mutual anticipatory stance, and attempts to establish terms of plausible moral commensurability between their group and that of the researcher, or more broadly "White people," moving forward.

On this count Lawrence Mithlo seems less optimistic than Rebekah Moody. Just after the passage quoted above depicting good thoughts and teaching in Chiricahua families, he lays out for his audience an assertion and a choice. He says:

> *Danghéí, chi"dáí, gok'azí, goosdoí, joobaí, díík'eh goniińłt'é ndah,*
> Though hardship, hunger, cold, heat, poverty all overmastered them,
>
> *Yóósń Tóbájiishchinéń goche'shkéneí beebich'įįyájiłti.*
> they talked to their children about God [and] Child of the Water.

Bikooghąí baajoogobááyéégo naagoos'ą ndah,
Though their camps were everywhere poor,

> *bighe'shį saanzhóní hí"dínzhóní yeeyádaałti.*
> they inside of them spoke by means of good words [and] good thoughts.

Yeenaatsékees.
They thought by means of them.

Yee'aahih"díná'a.
They taught by means of them.

'Ádíídíí díík'eh dáá"dí.
All of this is true.

Dálóó'stso téjółgayé daahiiłghał naldish"díí dásí'ághát'égo dáá"dí.
It is true just as that which I told you [about] our eating wood rats [and] burros is true.

Mithlo here counterposes what he has tried to reveal about the moral foundedness of Apache familial life against the account of an implicitly deficient material culture, which he accurately takes to be of interest to his anthropological interlocutors. The strength of his assertions "you do not understand" and his rhetorical emphasis through successions of parallel contrastive statements, suggests that he is aware that the ethnological frame of his interview with Hoijer, and perhaps the text collection that will result from it, works against his purposes in this regard. Hoijer's title for this text, "Old Apache Customs," bears this out, in its suggestion of neutral, objective reportage. Mithlo's authorship does not appear as a byline with the text but is buried within a paragraph in the introduction to the collection. And in their annotations Hoijer and Opler confine themselves to clarifying matters of reference. Neither acknowledge that a direct address to them or to the audience has been made, nor do they take up and elaborate the alternate themes Mithlo introduces. And it would have worked against the genre conventions of text collections at the time to have done otherwise. What Hoijer does remain faithful to, though, is the sequential flow of Mithlo's speech. He does not edit out Mithlo's direct address from the text.

Rebekah Moody also ends with an anticipatory stance. She makes use of a prayer formula described in the Apachean literature as *sa'ąh naghaaí bik'eh gózhǫǫ́* (Hoijer 1938a; Farella 1990; Farrer 1991; Witherspoon 1977), which loosely translates as "maturation and growth, walking with it so that goodness/health is forthcoming." She makes use of a contextualized version of this to sacralize the intimate familial action between herself and her grandfather, and to exhort her audience (the verb stems that connote the prayer formula appear in bold):

*Dándii, kíł **gózhǫ́ǫ́**, baa dózhǫ́, 'abegoz'**ąh** ch'agé; ch'o**ghaał** gołda*
Truly, you should do good for people, grow with that, walk with that

"niłgózhǫ́" baa ch'adii 'ídágo . . .
so that "it's good with you" is what people say about you . . .

Doníína, dołjíín
Long time ago, those days

łáni' bich'osdii na
I used to help a lot of people back then

dágową
all of them.

Mrs. Moody sets her own past action, guided as it was by the example of her elders, as a teaching precedent for all people – including the audience of *ndah*. In doing so she also shifts perspective from the portrait of herself and her family as poor and needing help to figuring herself as a provider of help, and as a person who teaches others. This figures her in a leadership role in the encounter with the researcher, who is figured as a person parallel to herself (but younger) oriented to pragmatic questions concerning how to live morally with others. She allows her own past to speak in the present, to impinge upon the present and future of her audience in how they grow and as something carried when they walk forward. The exhortation to "grow" and "walk with it" harmonized with other rhetorical figures that people in Rebekah Moody's family used to frame the research encounter. Throughout our time in her extended household we were often described as "the kids" and quite a bit of joking as well as serious attention was paid to how we might mature. Another ethnographer of longstanding association was described to us in parallel terms: "He's been coming here since he was a kid. We had a hand in raising him."

Archives as Boundary Works

What an examination of these spoken encounters reveals is that while both speakers invoke something we might label as "the past," they do so in the service of posing an alternate temporal semiotics (Bloch 1977; Fabian 1983;

Gell 1992) in the research encounter. In moves parallel to those of Silas John Edwards, Rebekah Moody and Lawrence Mithlo render an Apache past, not as something already completed and discrete, and not as something that only implicates one side of a boundary between Apache and White. Prior acts and states are invoked in ways that reveal moral commensurabilities in the past in order to speak to the ongoing present of Lawrence Mithlo's encounter with Hoijer, or Rebekah Moody's encounter with me, in order to establish the moral context for the relationship moving forward. While noting the ruptures that they (accurately) take to be of interest to their interlocutors, they work to dissolve the "objectivity" of that rupture by filling it in with their own emotional stances.[20]

Their concern with speaking truly, "$dá^ndí$," is never divorced from awareness of the difference in perspective between themselves and those others in the audience (cf. Rosaldo 1973). There is a looming perspectival boundary between the parties that both speakers attend to and attempt to modify with their words. Moody and Mithlo are concerned with tracing and making visible for their audience a previously un-presented or unrealized aspect of their own group that they are now presenting as true and inalienable from themselves and also very much at stake in the ongoing interaction. This is a strategy for establishing what Strathern (1988) terms "an exchange of perspectives." They pose morally plausible relations going forward that are imaginable, but not determined or yet fulfilled. They offer the researcher a new morally symmetrical basis for their mutual gaze.[21]

Many of our examples of Apache *bá'hadziih* across other contexts temporalize social relations in similar ways (Nevins and Nevins forthcoming). It is ironic that, like *bá'hadziih*, so many discourse genres classed under the modernist label "traditional" like myths, tales, and songs, are used in ways that are similarly anticipatory, subjunctive, and oriented to possible futures (e.g. Basso 1996). Many are similarly "means of speech" for fashioning selves through ongoing relations with others (Merlan 2005; T. Nevins 2010; Rumsey 2006; Stasch 2007; Vivieros de Castro 1996) and have been employed as such in dealings with researchers.

Encounter in Documentation: Text Collections in the Americanist Tradition

Such considerations bring to the fore the ironies and political effects of the notion of tradition in the articulation of indigenous communities within colonial and postcolonial orders. On the one hand, being "traditional" makes statements like Mithlo's appear recognizable, admissible, and fit for the public record. On the other, understanding his statements as a straightforward account of "Old Apache Customs" guarantees misrecognition of some of his purposes and instrumentalities in speaking. In a manner relevant to how we think about saving endangered languages, salvage documentation has historically contextualized native speech, not as contemporary voices engaged in ongoing dialogue, but as a referential record of a traditional past, which is assumed to have been disrupted and superseded by the modern (Gruber 1970). According to Bauman and Briggs:

> Americanist texts thus helped define modernity in a purely negative fashion. Boas's textual practices constructed anthropology as a science of culture rather than of colonial encounter, an historical mode of inquiry that rested on a principled effort to construct modernity in opposition to a pre-contact, romanticized past, thereby excluding the anthropologist and the constructed nature of anthropology's social and textual objects from its purview. (Bauman and Briggs 2003:282)

As Hymes noted (1981), the presentational format of text is shaped to that purpose and not to the question of what their contributors might have been trying to pose to the researcher, or to more extended audiences. As actions in the mediation of communities, salvage text collections can circulate traces of indigenous speech to new contexts, but often framed in a way that, in Blommaert's terms (2010), limits the mobility of indigenous voices, by working at cross-purposes with their rhetoric strategies. However, I have tried to show in this chapter that this did not preclude the people working with researchers from making attempts to speak to them. It also does not prevent texts from taking on new lives through new contextualizations.

A unique strength of the Boasian textual tradition is the record it produced of extended speech from members of indigenous communities. Granted, any given speech performance is radically recontextualized by the researcher and by other parties to the production and circulation of a text collection (Haviland 1996; Urban 1996). Still, a disciplinary commitment to fidelity in transcription to the syntagmatic flow of an utterance retains a portion of the speaker's contextualizing information that can now be looked for (Duranti and Goodwin 1992; Hymes 1975b; Silverstein 1996a). Embedded within the distorting ideological "salvage" frame of the text collection are alternative voices that can be attended to by modifying the framework in which we interpret them.

Attention to Mithlo's and Moody's rhetoric allows us to recognize how they addressed the researcher for the purpose of altering the latter's perspective. This suggests that the records of extended speech in the Americanist tradition are full of potential alternative voices if approached with similar concerns in mind. If we interpret the items in text collections as rhetorical acts towards an exchange of perspectives, perhaps realizations about what has been true all along but previously unreflected upon might contribute to an ethical basis for yet other relations moving forward.

In actual practice, linguistic elicitation is a sort of interview, the terms of which are to a significant extent improvisationally negotiated between consultant and linguist. What emerges through documenting language is not something that existed prior to that encounter, but an equivocal entity Hanks (2010:10–12) terms a "translanguage" in which elements of the consultant's speech are matched to the researcher's own terms and framing concepts. Considered as encounters, each text stands as a kind of record of an occasion in when an indigenous speaker was asked to perform an extended stretch of speech for a researcher. In addressing the researcher, the indigenous speaker draws upon precedents and tools, including discourse genres, associated with their own network, which stand in the position of what Vizenor seizes upon as a sort of obviative fourth person pronoun (Vizenor 1998) writ large, something felt via its absence, with respect to the research encounter. The trace is felt as conflations of the researcher's own genre expectations tugging against interpretive closure.

The products of language documentation are boundary works that emerge through encounters between actors embedded within alternate networks – something I attempt to capture with the notion of plural, or complex, mediation. Both are engaged in the production of texts, or in making speech that is marked off in some way from other aspects of context, but the means and use, the genre frame on these texts, differs for researcher and indigenous speaker; and the text becomes a common object through which they misunderstand one another (Nevins 2010a). Therefore the "facts" that emerge from documentation can be heard speaking in more than one way, and via by more than one personal network.

Notes

1. Silas John specifies 1904 as the date of his visions, but it was in the 1920s that his religious movement rose to public prominence.
2. Parallel treatments of linguistics with respect to philology can be found in disciplinary histories written by Hymes (1963, 1975a), elaborated with respect to colonialism by Errington (2008), and with respect to the politics of modernity by Bauman and Briggs (2003).
3. For a parallel argument applied to saving endangered languages, see Moore (2006).
4. In the case of the colonial philology, even though linguists in the Americanist tradition tended to be critical of cultural evolutionism, the prevalence of the latter in popular

understandings of difference, along with missionary interests in religious succession, inflected the meaning of indigenous languages.

5 A relevant discussion of the political nature of Silas John Edwards' writing in relation to temporality and colonialism can be found in Collins and Blot (2003).

6 OLAC is an acronym for "Open Language Archives Community" and GOLD ontology refers to "General Ontology for Linguistic Description."

7 Including the German-heritage Lutheran ministers who ran the East Fork mission.

8 Even outside Silas John's movement other *diyiń* and Traditionalists pointed to painted symbols on bodies and ritual paraphenalia, or symbols carved into trees, as "writing."

9 The label "Traditionalist" emerges out of dialogue with modernizing agents like missionaries and schools. It was more common to hear people use the names of particular *diyiń* and ceremonies than to use the term "Traditionalist." When it was used it was to express affiliation with *diyiń* and their ceremonies. Contemporary Traditionalists assert continuities with Apache ceremonies through time, while also using them in self-consciously innovative ways, for example for court cases and in preparing members of the armed forces for overseas deployment.

10 Boas excluded Edward Sapir's contribution from the first volume on the grounds that it departed from the standard presentation format he had designed and would be thereby less accessible to the nonspecialist (Darnell 1990).

11 Briggs (1986) has addressed misunderstandings in research interviews arising from disjunctures between the assumptions and pragmatic expectations that researcher-interviewers and community member-interviewees bring to the encounter concerning how learning is achieved and how questions are asked and answered. He points to the use his Mexicano consultants made of local speech genres like proverbs and stories to recontextualize his research concerns within what were to them more acceptable knowledge practices and forms of authority. I extend that concern by looking at the use Apache interviewees make of their own communicative repertoires, in this case a speech genre, for addressing the otherness of the researcher and potential extended audiences.

12 Certain kinds of talk were excluded, including gossip and stories described as *godiyįhgo* 'holy,' or 'medicine world,' which are the province of *diyiń*.

13 Under the direction of then director, David Seaman, and with the design help of Tom Nevins.

14 These can be viewed at: http://etext.virginia.edu/apache/index.html (accessed November 6, 2012).

15 The *ndah* form reflects common pronunciation and spelling conventions on the Fort Apache reservation and the *indaa* form reflects Hoijer's representation of the speech of the Chiricahua and Mescalero Apache people who worked with him. The same pronunciation could be heard on the Fort Apache reservation in the 1990s and when written was usually represented as *ndah*. For simplicity of presentation, I default to *ndah* in my own descriptions but retain Hoijer's orthographic rendering in the quoted text.

16 For example, Opler (1938).

17 Following Hymes (1981), the relevant presentational unit for these speeches is taken to be the spoken line, which often corresponds to full sentences. Lines are marked here by a hard return, and with their beginnings in alignment with the print on the far left of the page. Within lines, the beginning of rhythmic units within a line or subordinate clauses within a sentence are marked with indentation. For Rebekah Moody's passages, nonverbal aspects of her presentation taken to be especially relevant are noted within parentheses.

18 In Hoijer, Harry. 1938a. *Chiricahua and Mescalero Apache Texts with Ethnological Notes by Morris Opler*. Chicago: University of Chicago Press. With kind permission from University of Chicago Press.
19 This use of alternations between singular, dual, plural, and environmental person in oratory follows Merlan and Rumsey's discussion on "the grammar of segmentary person" (1991: 95–98).
20 The extended discussion this requires will rely upon Hymes (1966) and Keane (1995) for entextualizations and relativities of language function, Hanks (1986) for boundary works.
21 This also suggests that field research and text collection can be reinterpreted along similar lines as techniques for manipulating the perspectival boundary between differently arrived at subjects (T. Nevins 2010; Wagner 1981).

References

Abley, Mark. 2003. *Spoken Here: Travels among Threatened Languages*. Boston: Houghton Mifflin Harcourt.
Basso, Keith. 1979. *Portraits of "the Whiteman": Linguistic Play and Cultural Symbols among the Western Apache*. New York: Cambridge University Press.
Basso, Keith. 1996. *Wisdom Sits in Places: Language and Landscape among the Western Apache*. Albuquerque: University of New Mexico Press.
Basso, Keith and Ned Anderson. 1973. A Western Apache Writing System. *Science* 180(4090):1013–1022.
Basso, Keith and Nashley Tessay, Sr. 1994. Joseph Hoffman's "The Birth of He Triumphs over Evils": A Western Apache Origin Story. In *Coming to Light: Contemporary Translations of the Native Literatures of North America*. Brian Swann, ed., pp. 636–656. New York: Random House.
Bauman, Richard. 1984. *Verbal Art as Performance*. Salem: Waveland Press.
Bauman, Richard. 1986. *Story, Performance and Event: Contextual Studies of Oral Narrative*. Cambridge: Cambridge University Press.
Bauman, Richard and Charles Briggs. 2003. *Voices of Modernity: Language Ideologies and the Politics of Inequality*. Cambridge: Cambridge University Press.
Bloch, Maurice. 1977. The Past and the Present in the Present. *Man* 12:278–92.
Blommaert, Jan. 2010. *The Sociolinguistics of Globalization*. Cambridge: Cambridge University Press.
Boas, Franz, ed. 1911. *Handbook of North American Indian Languages*. Bureau of American Ethnology Bulletin 40, Part 1. Washington DC: GPO.
Briggs, Charles L. 1986. *Learning How to Ask: A Sociolinguistic Appraisal of the Role of the Interview in Social Science Research*. Cambridge: Cambridge University Press.
Collins, James and Richard Blot. 2003. *Literacy and Literacies: Texts, Power and Identity*. Cambridge: Cambridge University Press.
Darnell, Regna. 1990. Franz Boas, Edward Sapir, and the Americanist Text Tradition. *Historiographia Linguistica* 17(1/2):129–144.

De la Cadena, Marisol. 2010. Indigenous Cosmopolitics in the Andes: Conceptual Reflections beyond "Politics." *Cultural Anthropology* 25(2):334–370.

Duranti, Alessandro and Charles Goodwin. 1992. Rethinking Context: An Introduction. In *Rethinking Context: Language as an Interactive Phenomenon*. Alessandro Duranti and Charles Goodwin, eds., pp. 1–42. Cambridge: Cambridge University Press.

Errington, Joseph. 2008. *Linguistics in a Colonial World: A Story of Language, Meaning and Power*. Oxford: Wiley-Blackwell.

Fabian, Johannes. 1983. *Time and The Other: How Anthropology Makes Its Object*. New York: Columbia University Press.

Farella, John. 1990. *The Main Stalk: A Synthesis of Navajo Philosophy*. Tucson: University of Arizona Press.

Farrer, Claire. 1991. *Living Life's Circle: Mescalero Apache Cosmovision*. Albuquerque: University of New Mexico Press.

Gell, Alfred. 1992. *The Anthropology of Time: Cultural Constructions of Temporal Maps and Images*. Oxford: Berg.

Goddard, Pliny. 1919. San Carlos Apache Texts. *Anthropological Papers of the American Museum of Natural History* 24(3):141–367.

Goddard, Pliny. 1920. White Mountain Apache Texts. *Anthropological Papers of the American Museum of Natural History* (24)4:369–527.

Goodwin, Grenville. 1938. White Mountain Apache Religion. *American Anthropologist* 40(1):24–37.

Goodwin, Grenville. 1942. The Social Organization of the Western Apache. *Memoirs of the American Folklore Society* 33.

Gruber, Jacob. 1970. Ethnographic Salvage and the Shaping of Anthropology. *American Anthropologist*, New Series 72(6):1289–1299.

Hanks, William. 1986. *Intertexts: Writings on Language, Utterance and Context*. Lanham: Rowman & Littlefield.

Hanks, William. 2010. *Converting Words: Maya in the Age of the Cross*. Berkeley: University of California Press.

Harding, Susan. 1987. Convicted by the Holy Spirit: The Rhetoric of Fundamental Baptist Conversion. *American Ethnologist* 14(1):167–181.

Harrison, K. David. 2010. *The Last Speakers: The Quest to Save the World's Most Endangered Languages*. Washington DC: National Geographic.

Haviland, John. 1996. Text from Talk in Tzotzil. In *Natural Histories of Discourse*. Michael Silverstein and Greg Urban, eds., pp. 45–78. Chicago: University of Chicago Press.

Hoijer, Harry. n.d. San Carlos Texts. Unpublished manuscript [except for one narrative which is published in Basso and Tessay 1994] in the Hoijer Papers at the Library of the American Philosophical Society.

Hoijer, Harry. 1938a. *Chiricahua and Mescalero Apache Texts with Ethnological Notes by Morris Opler*. Chicago: University of Chicago Publications in Anthropology, Linguistic Series.

Hoijer, Harry. 1938b. The Southern Athapaskan Languages. *American Anthropologist* 40:75–87.

Hoijer, Harry. 1945a. The Apachean Verb, Part I: Verb Structure and Pronominal Prefixes. *International Journal of American Linguistics* 11:193–203.

Hoijer, Harry. 1945b. Classificatory Verb Stems in Apachean. *International Journal of American Linguistics* 11:12–23.

Hoijer, Harry. 1946a. The Apachean Verb, Part II: The Prefixes for Mode and Tense. *International Journal of American Linguistics* 12:1–13.

Hoijer, Harry. 1946b. Chiricahua Apache. In *Linguistic Structures of Native America*. Harry Hoijer, ed., pp. 55–84. New York: Viking Publications in Anthropology 6.

Hoijer, Harry. 1946c. The Apachean Verb, Part III: The Classifiers. *International Journal of American Linguistics* 12:51–59.

Hoijer, Harry. 1947. The Structure of the Noun in the Apachean Languages. In *Actes du XXVIII Congres International des Americanistes*. Paris.

Hoijer, Harry. 1948. The Apachean Verb, Part IV: Major Form Classes. *International Journal of American Linguistics* 14:247–259.

Hoijer, Harry. 1949. The Apachean Verb, Part V: The Theme and Prefix Complex. *International Journal of American Linguistics* 15:12–22.

Hymes, Dell H. 1963. Notes toward a History of Linguistic Anthropology. *Anthropological Linguistics* 5:59–103.

Hymes, Dell H. 1966. Two Types of Linguistic Relativity. In *Sociolinguistics*. W. Bright, ed., pp. 114–157. The Hague: Mouton de Gruyter.

Hymes, Dell H. 1972a. Editorial Introduction. *Language in Society* 1(1):1–14.

Hymes, Dell H. 1972b. Models of the Interaction of Language and Social Life. In *Directions in Sociolinguistics: The Ethnography of Communication*. John. J. Gumperz and Dell Hymes, eds., pp. 35–71. New York: Holt, Rinehart & Winston.

Hymes, Dell H. 1975a. Pre-war Prague School and Post-war American Anthropological Linguistics. In *The Transformational-Generative Paradigm and Modern Linguistic Theory*. E. Koerner, ed., pp. 359–380. Amsterdam: John Benjamins.

Hymes, Dell H. 1975b. "Breakthrough into Performance." In Dan Ben-Amos and Kenneth Goldstein (eds) *Folklore: Performance and Communication*. The Hague: Mouton. Pp. 11–74.

Hymes, Dell H. 1981. *In Vain I Tried to Tell You: Essays in Native American Ethnopoetics*. Philadelphia: University of Pennsylvania Press.

Keane, Webb. 1995. The Spoken House: Text, Act and Object in Eastern Indonesia. *American Ethnologist* 22(1):102–124.

Keane, Webb. 2007. *Christian Moderns: Freedom and Fetish in the Mission Encounter*. Berkeley: University of California Press.

Lewis, Herbert S. 2001. The Passion of Franz Boas. *American Anthropologist* 103(2):447–467.

Lowie, Robert. 1947. Biographical Memoir of Franz Boas. *National Academy of Sciences of the United States of America Biographical Memoir*, vol. XXIV, 9th memoir.

Meek, Barbara. 2010 *We Are Our Language: An Ethnography of Language Revitalization in a Northern Athabascan Community*. Tucson: University of Arizona Press.

Merlan, Francesca. 2005. Explorations towards Intercultural Accounts of Sociocultural Reproduction and Change. *Oceania* 75(3):167–182.

Merlan, Francesca and Alan Rumsey. 1991. *Ku Waru: Language and Segmentary Politics in the Western Nebilyer Valley, Papua New Guinea*. Cambridge: Cambridge University Press.

Moore, Robert E. 2006. Disappearing, Inc.: Glimpsing the Sublime in the Politics of Access to Endangered Languages. *Language and Communication* 26: 296–315.

Morgan, Mindy J. 2009. *The Bearer of this Letter: Language Ideologies, Literacy Practices, and the Fort Belknap Indian Community*. Lincoln: University of Nebraska Press.

Nevins, M. Eleanor. 2010a. Editorial: Intertextuality and Misunderstanding. *Language and Communication* 30(1):1–6.

Nevins, M. Eleanor. 2010b. The Bible in Two Keys: Traditionalism and Apache Evangelical Christianity on the Fort Apache Reservation. *Language and Communication* 30(1):19–32.

Nevins, Thomas J. 2004. World Made of Prayer: Alterity and the Dialectics of Encounter in the Invention of Contemporary Western Apache Culture. Dissertation, Anthropology Department, University of Virginia.

Nevins, Thomas J. 2010. Between Love and Culture: Misunderstanding, Textuality and the Dialectics of Ethnographic Knowledge. *Language and Communication* 30(1):58–68.

Nevins, Thomas and M. Eleanor Nevins. 2009. "We Have Always Had the Bible": Christianity and the Composition of White Mountain Apache Heritage. *Heritage Management* 2(1):11–33.

Nevins, Thomas and M. Eleanor Nevins. forthcoming. Speaking in the Mirror of the Other: Dialectics of Intersubjectivity and Temporality in Western Apache Metapragmatics. Special issue of *Language and Communication*, "Intersubjectivity: Cultural Extensions and Construals." Alan Rumsey and Eve Danziger, eds.

Opler, Morris. 1938. A Chiricahua Apache's Account of the Geronimo Campaign of 1886. Narrated by Samuel E. Kenoi. *New Mexico Historical Review* 13(4):360–386. http://etext.virginia.edu/toc/modeng/public/OplKeno.html (accessed November 6, 2012).

Poirier, Sylvie. 2008. Reflections on Indigenous Cosmopolitics: Poetics. *Anthropologica* 50(1):75–85.

Rosaldo, Michelle. 1973. "I Have Nothing to Hide": The Language of Illongot Oratory. *Language in Society* 2(2):193–223.

Rumsey, Alan. 2006. The Articulation of Indigenous and Exogenous Orders in Papua New Guinea and beyond. *Australian Journal of Anthropology* 17(1): 47–69.

Samuels, David. 2001. Indeterminacy and History in Britton Goode's Western Apache Placenames. *American Ethnologist* 28(2):277–302.

Samuels, David. 2006. Bible Translation and Medicine Man Talk: Missionaries, Indexicality, and the "Language Expert" on the San Carlos Apache Reservation. *Language in Society* 35(4):529–557.

Sarris, Greg. 1993. *Keeping Slug Woman Alive: A Holistic Approach to American Indian Texts*. Berkeley: University of California Press.

Silverstein, Michael. 1996a. The Secret Life of Texts. In *Natural Histories of Discourse*. Michael Silverstein and Greg Urban, eds., pp. 81–105. Chicago: University of Chicago Press.

Silverstein, Michael. 1996b. Encountering Languages and Languages of Encounter in North American Ethnohistory. *Journal of Linguistic Anthropology* 6(2): 126–144.

Spicer, Edward H. 1962. *Cycles of Conquest: The Impact of Spain, Mexico and the United States on Indians of the Southwest 1533–1960*. Tucson: University of Arizona Press.

Star, Susan Leigh and James R. Griesemer. 1989. Institutional Ecology, "Translations" and Boundary Objects: Amateurs and Professionals in Berkeley's Museum of Vertebrate Zoology, 1907–39. *Social Studies of Science* 19(3): 387–420.

Stasch, Rupert. 2007. Demon Language: The Otherness of Indonesian in a Papuan Community. In *Consequences of Contact: Language Ideologies and Sociocultural Transformations in Pacific Societies*. Miki Makihara and Bambi B. Schieffelin, eds., pp. 96–124. New York: Oxford University Press.

Stasch, Rupert. 2009. *Society of Others: Kinship and Mourning in a West Papuan Place*. Berkeley: University of California Press.

Strathern, Marilyn. 1988. *The Gender of the Gift: Problems with Women and Problems with Society in Melanesia*. Berkeley: University of California Press.

Urban, Greg. 1996. Entextualization, Replication and Power. In *Natural Histories of Discourse*. Michael Silverstein and Greg Urban, eds., pp. 21–43. Chicago: University of Chicago Press.

Viveiros de Castro, Eduardo. 1996. Cosmological Deixis and Amerindian Perspectivism. *Journal of the Royal Anthropological Institute* 4:469–488.

Vizenor, Gerald. 1998. *Fugitive Poses: Native American Scenes of Absence and Presence*. Lincoln: University of Nebraska Press.

Voloshinov, V.N. 1973. *Marxism and the Philosophy of Language*. L. Matejka and I. R. Titunik, trans. New York: Seminar Press. (Original work published 1929.)

Wagner, Roy. 1981. *The Invention of Culture*, revised and expanded edition. Chicago: University of Chicago Press.

Watt, E.T., with assistance from K.H. Basso. 2004. *Don't Let the Sun Step over You: A White Mountain Apache Family Life, 1860–1975*. Tucson: University of Arizona Press.

Weiner, James F. and Kate Glaskin. 2007. Customary Land Tenure and Registration in Australia and Papua New Guinea: Anthropological Perspectives. In *Customary Land Tenure and Registration in Australia and Papua New Guinea: Anthropological Perspectives. Asia Pacific Environment Monograph 3*. James F. Weiner and Kate Glaskin, eds., pp. 1–14. Canberra: Australian National University E Press.

Witherspoon, Gary. 1975. *Navajo Kinship and Marriage*. Chicago: University of Chicago Press.

Witherspoon, Gary. 1977. *Language and Art in the Navajo Universe*. Ann Arbor: University of Michigan Press.

6

What No Coyote Story Means
The Borderland Genre of Traditional Storytelling

All the *diyiń* were holding a council at the Sun's house.
They were all there.

When they were through holding the council, they got a paper from above.
On it were written words, just like a letter.
The *diyiń* wanted to read the letter and know what it said.
One of them said: "I will try."

They had a chair there and they told him to sit in it and take the paper.
The *diyiń* sat down and took the paper.
He looked it all over, but could not read it.
Then another *diyiń* sat down and tried to read the paper, but could not.

Finally Coyote, who was a *diyiń*, was the only one left.
They said: "You ought to be able to read this paper, Coyote."

Coyote sat down in the chair and took the paper.
He looked at it a while and then started to read it.
He rested his head in one hand and held the paper before him with the other hand. Coyote read the paper right off without trouble.

He knew how.

(adapted from Goodwin 1994:173[1])

Lessons from Fort Apache: Beyond Language Endangerment and Maintenance,
First Edition. M. Eleanor Nevins.
© 2013 John Wiley & Sons, Inc. Published 2013 by John Wiley & Sons, Inc.

The title of this chapter alludes to a widely circulated article by linguistic anthropologist Shirley Brice Heath entitled "What No Bedtime Story Means: Narrative Skills at Home and School" (1982). In it she investigates communicative relativity at the interface between schools and neighborhood communities in Piedmont, North Carolina in the decade following desegregation of public schools. I draw upon her work to frame this chapter because the constellation of issues: narrative, literacy, disjuncture between homes/neighborhoods and schools, are salient concerns across her study and this one. Following Heath, this chapter addresses differences in contextualizing practices that embed stories within a network of relations extending well beyond the immediate context of telling and shape orientations in consequential ways. The power of Heath's study lay in the linkages she drew between everyday acts and articulations of persons within broader-scale socioeconomic orders. Intimate everyday narrative acts do not determine socioeconomic placement, but contribute in nontrivial ways by layering up precedents that establish expectations, habits, and terms of recognition between members of minority or working class communities and teaching professionals in schools.

This study follows upon hers in drawing linkages between the ways in which stories are taken up in communicative context and the nontrivial role this plays in the articulation of indigenous communities within broader sociopolitical orders. The participants in her study: teachers, families across neighborhood communities, students, and workplace managers shared a concern with gaps in student achievement. By contrast the shared concerns surrounding stories reflected upon as "traditional" and the role accorded indigenous languages in their performance are made more complex because of the place that such stories hold in representing the difference that an indigenous community poses with respect to a history of colonization. Remembering, avoiding, or even disavowing Traditional stories and songs is often intertwined with concerns for keeping up an indigenous language (Kroskrity 2012) and can become involved with religious and political positions in complicated ways.

Coyote Literacy

In the previous chapter documentation and literacy were established as key symbols utilized by differently positioned persons to different ends in the history of colonial encounter across Apache reservations in the southwest extending to the present day. Here I consider narratives assigned the status of "Traditional," and demonstrate their dynamic and ambivalent role in the mediation of Apache reservations as indigenous communities with respect to surrounding sociocultural orders. Consider the Coyote story that appears as an extended epigraph to this chapter. It is taken from Grenville Goodwin's *Myths and Tales of the White Mountain Apache* (1994), first published in 1939, where it appeared under the title "Coyote Reads the Letter as He Sits," told by Francis Drake in 1929. Goodwin, like Goddard ten years prior, studied with people who identified as White Mountain Apache on the San Carlos Apache reservation near its border with the Fort Apache reservation. Goodwin's work was anchored in a trading post in the neighborhood of Bylas, where he stayed for nearly three years from 1929 to 1932. Goodwin was the first anthropologist to conduct intimate, long-term research among White Mountain Apache persons. The consultants who worked with him: Anna Price, Francis Drake, Palmer Valor, Bane Tithla, Richard Bylas, Neil Buck, Clyne Jose, and Thomas Riley, like those who worked with Opler and Hoijer on the Mescalero reservation, were respected community leaders. Two of them: Anna Price and Palmer Valor, were centenarians.

Trading posts, like the Lutheran mission described in Chapter 4, were sites in which the colonial encounter was also a documentary encounter (Morgan 2009). Record keeping accompanied all transactions and so was an important condition upon the means by which Apache persons obtained provisions necessary for their livelihood after access to land necessary for longstanding practices of horticulture, hunting, and seasonal gathering was compromised by the imposition of the reservation. Trading posts also served as post offices and as meeting places where documents such as letters or petitions might be drawn up. Francis Drake's Coyote story, like Silas John Edwards' script, and like the letter signed by those Apache men petitioning the superintendent for permission to assemble for Holy Ground ceremonies, brings Apache colonial engagements with reading and writing into view.

"Coyote Reads the Letter as He Sits" was performed in 1929, at a time when government policy was assimilationist. However, the conditions of telling and the events within the story reflect engagements with literacy that do not fit "assimilation" in any straightforward way. Instead, this story reflects an environment in which alternative acts of mediation authored through indigenous leadership were as salient to everyday life as were the fort, the mission, and the trading post. Goodwin reports that an alternate title for this story was: "The Paper from Above Arrives at the Sun's House." Messages from afar that initially present themselves in inscrutable form, but which are subsequently understood by a person who discovers that he "knows" how to listen to them, occur across other Apache stories and in everyday talk (Nevins et al. in press). Other stories in Goodwin's collection involve messages that require acts of translation and boundary crossing in order for their message to be understood. The *diyiń* in the story do not base their authority as such upon an identity with an Apache past purified of contact with *ndah*/White settlers, nor do they keep to one side of a boundary between Apache and White. Instead, they work at that boundary, move across and reposition it. Along the way they reveal something that Coyote had known all along.

New revelations about commensurabilities with those encountered as *ndah*, like "Coyote knew how to read" are acts of mediation in an alternate, differentiating mode. The boundary he crosses and speaks across is exactly the boundary that Apache persons at San Carlos encountered regularly in literacy events (Heath 1983) at the fort and at the trading post. In both contexts, a White person/*ndah* sat behind a desk or counter with an Apache person on the other side. The *ndah*/White person read or wrote something along with their transaction. And the transaction between them often had tangible consequences for that particular Apache person's future and livelihood. In "Coyote Reads the Letter as He Sits" Coyote assumes the postures of *ndaa*, or 'White men' in similar acts of reading: "Coyote sat down in the chair and took the paper . . . He rested his head on one hand and held the paper before him with the other hand." With the bodily postures attributed to him in the story, Coyote is portrayed as having crossed to the other side of that desk. Acts such as these are both metaphorical and political. They bring together what had been given as separate (*ndee* and *ndah* in Bylas in the 1920s), revealing past commensurabilities (Coyote knew how) and posing possible futures (see Merlan and Rumsey 1991:238–244; Nevins and Nevins forthcoming). This story, and that of Silas John Edwards, can be taken as moments in what Morgan (2009), Bender (2002), and others describe as indigenous engagements with literacy; with the proviso that what we identify as "literacy" remains open to be defined in alternate, unexpected terms.

Coyote's Boundary Voice

Coyote's role in the story is consistent with the position he occupies as a narrative figure more generally, where he can be found at the boundary of familiar persons and others. For example, a series of stories in the 1938 Hoijer text collection figure Coyote as a "bungling host" (Hymes and Simpson 1984; Thompson 1966; Webster 1999) who repeatedly visits persons like Owl, Frog, and Beaver, all of whom live at a far remove from his family (so different from his own family that they have different kinds of bodies). When he visits, he is hosted by them in a manner that he finds appealing. When they later come to visit him, he attempts to reciprocate, hosting them in what he takes to be the same manner in which they hosted him, but without first considering differences of knowledge (in these cases he does not know how to do what they did for him), affective disposition, and perspective between them and himself (having different bodily habits, they like different foods, for example). The results are comical and often involve him unintentionally injuring himself and members of his own family or offering his guests something they find useless or disgusting. His repeated bungling is reflected upon in the following passage, which is taken from a story performed by Charles Smith and appears in the Hoijer (1938) collection as Mescalero text 5: "Coyote and the Creation." To conserve space I present only the English translation. Turns at talk are separated by empty lines, and my omissions of portions of the sequence of talk are represented by ellipses. Here is the conversational exchange between Coyote and his wife:

"I am going away again," said Coyote, it's said.

"Why are you going to tire yourself out?
Just now you were very tired.
You no sooner come in and sit down on the ground at home
      than you dash out again.
Just now I've become tired of you.
You are continually leaving us in an empty camp.
We too would like to see other places.
Take us with you over there," said Coyote's wife to him, it's said.

Coyote said to her, it's said: "How are you to do that?
I want you to go over there with me.
[But] the children are small.
The place to which I am going is far away.
There are many broad rivers on [the road].
There are many big canyons.
And the mountains also are very high.
There are many steep cliffs.
And there are also dense forests.
You see, some of those children of mine are small.
Some of them cannot swim.
There is much that frightens them.
They soon become tired."
. . .
"Good things are said about the Frog people.
Because of that, I shall go to them.
I shall bring back something for you."

. . .

Coyote's wife spoke thus to him, it's said:
"All right, go ahead.
[But] do not imitate anyone again.
Though I do not do it, I am ashamed at your failures."

"Very well, I shall not do so again.
When I have been to these people, then I shall not go anywhere from you again.
We will return to our own people.
I do not know where the camp is but someone somewhere will tell us about it.
Later, when I return, I will tell you the story.
Therefore, all of you embrace me well.
Then I'll leave you." (Hoijer 1938:170–171)[2]

In this passage Coyote's wife alludes to previous disastrous attempts Coyote had made to host visitors from afar by "imitating" them, when this led to embarrassment because their knowledge, powers, and proclivities were different from his. Note the emphasis placed on the distances Coyote travels and his reliance on "what is said" about a people in his determination about who to visit next. Coyote is part of an imagining of an extended social world and of encounters at the far edge of imagined familiarity.

The otherness of less familiar people and their different embodied habits are cued in the performance styles of Goodwin's consultants as they tell Coyote stories. In portraying Coyote's voice it was common for storytellers to allude to what were for them speech patterns stereotypically associated with neighboring peoples. For the White Mountain Apache persons Goodwin worked with it was common to give Coyote an exaggeratedly nasal whining voice that they associated with Chiricahua Apache (Goodwin 1994). Chiricahua were described by his consultants as *ndee*, so clearly more recognizably familiar and "like us" to his consultants than White people, who were described as *ndah*, 'others/enemies/strangers.' Chiricahua Apache spoke a language that was easy for Goodwin's White Mountain consultants to understand, even with some differences in pronunciation. They had similar stories and ceremonies, even if they told them and performed them a little differently. Marriages between Chiricahua and White Mountain Apache were commonplace, and some of the same clan names were in use among them. But whereas White Mountain Apache had a longstanding relationship to the Bylas area, Chiricahua Apaches were relocated to the San Carlos reservation after having been removed from their territories to the south. After the final confrontation with Geronimo, many Chiricahua persons were forcibly removed from San Carlos and taken by train to prison camps in Florida and then Oklahoma. So not only were Chiricahua Apaches from a less familiar place, they also had a different relationship to *ndah*, the ever present unavoidable others in White Mountain Apache lives. Through these kinds of relational positions Chiricahua were cast as *ndee*, but different enough to merit comment and to serve as recognizable foils in some trickster stories. So the figure of Coyote brings orientations to more proximate others into the pragmatics of the storytelling event. In this way, Coyote stories are an idiom of extended sociality, orienting participants to one another via recourse to imaginations of others. Animation of Coyote through speech styles stereotypically associated with neighboring peoples is widely attested throughout the Native North American West (e.g. Hinton 1994:45–47; Hymes 1981:65–78; Ramsey 1977; Sapir 1909:293, n.41, 1915).

Coyote moves at the edges of presently knowable life, traversing and altering the outer limits of awareness between oneself, one's own and less familiar others – where things often go awry. Coyote brings encounters with less well-known others into view. Given that in the colonial encounter Anglo settlers, or "White people" became the unavoidable *ndah*/other, it is not surprising that Coyote stories would be used to figure relations with them. In addition to "Coyote Reads the Letter as He Sits," two of the other Coyote stories in the Goodwin collection: "Coyote Steals Wheat/ Coyote Feces under His Hat" and "Coyote Herds Sheep for a White Man" also place Coyote in the role of a relatively less familiar *ndee* (maybe Chiricahua) in relation to 'White men'/*ndah*.[3]

In other stories Coyote similarly plays out the consequences of experiential limits on knowing, where the self bumps up against the nonself. This can involve familiar small-scale details of human life, like the fact that our shoes wear out from our travels and must be remade, as in this performance by John Altaha, of "Coyote and the Shoes," recorded with Tom Nevins, Mary Altaha, and the author in 1999:

JOHN: That's a little short one too. It's about the shoes.

JOHN: Coyote, it's Coyote again.
When you're have a shoes, those days,[4]
Shoes don't wear out, you know.
One pair you buy, lasts forever.

So, this Coyote, what he did is ah,
He got him ah, a new pair of shoes,
And he just wear it, maybe two days.

Then one day he started where there are a lot of rocks, you know,
He took his shoes off.
Put on the very sharp, sharp edge of a stone, anahi
Beat on it and make a big hole on both sides.

That's when the shoes [laughs] starts wearin' out, you know.
He started that
Before, the shoes wouldn't wear out.
He did that too, so [laughs].

[everyone laughing]

MARY: From then on we start wearing out our shoes.

Other stories locate Coyote similarly, as the source of the "push-back" that one encounters from the world as one works from forming a goal to accomplishing it. This is the subject of the story "Coyote and Mescal" treated at length later in the chapter. As in the case of the bungling host stories, Coyote involves storytelling participants in an imagination of encountering partial limits as their experiences and actions are extended through space and time.

These confrontations of the self with the not-self scales out from immediate experience in intimate contextual surrounds to larger kinds of push-back, including limits upon a person's life span (e.g. Hymes 1994) or upon the comprehensibility of other beings. Further on in Smith's "Coyote and Creation" story, it is through Coyote's actions that people called "Frog" or "Bear," who had in previously appeared human to one another, and who had been able to understand one another's speech, were translated into their present animal forms in which they are no longer capable of understanding each other. The passage begins with Coyote speaking:

"Earth! Now, for some reason,
 that which lies upon your surface,
 those who live upon your surface,
 [and] those animate beings who exist upon your surface,
 none of them disappearing,
  will all be transformed in a place similar to this one
  which he[5] will make somewhere.

The people to whom I am going,
 on the very day that I come to them,
  will become like those in that place.

Then, when they have spoken to me and I have spoken to them,
 from that moment on,
  they, their words and their bodies by means of which they
  customarily move about on the surface of the earth,
   will change.

I will not have heard them.
. . .

He went to the fourth of the four streams that flowed into the lake.
At the edge of the stream, in a wide place, there were four clumps of tule.
The Frog chief was sitting on a black rock which lay on the east side of the clump
        [of tule] which lay on the edge of the [river] bank.
[Coyote] stopped before him.

Then the Frog chief was transformed exactly as [Coyote] had said he would
        be transformed.
Right at that moment he became an ordinary frog.

[Coyote] was unable to talk to him at all.
And therefore he did not talk to him.
[The frog] jumped away from him into the water.

So that one was the first of all living creatures to be transformed.
From this time on, everyone that [Coyote] looks at, whoever it is,
        will be changed in this way.

He walked about sadly.
He looked at the water.
He also tried in vain to speak.
  . . . (Hoijer 1938:173–174)

Coyote himself undergoes the same transformation as Frog and other creatures he encounters, away from what to storytelling participants comprises the familiar and the known. Like Frog, Coyote's body and voice are transformed and reduced, pulled away from full human recognizability:

"Now I have become very tired.
He has made me in the form of a man.
Therefore, I shall make my body small.
[So will change] my ears, my nose, my eyes, my body hair, [and] my teeth:
My legs will be four,
My tail will be bushy,
I shall howl and bark,
My feet will be bunched,
        and I shall close up my arms and my hands.
Coyote is no more.

Now I will return as coyote the animal [to] my wife [and] my children.
Wherever I go, wherever I live, I will sleep well everywhere.
Only all varieties of meat will be my food and I will drink only water.
I will howl." (Hoijer 1938:176–177)

As in many other stories about Coyote, the transformations his actions effect in the world happen without his intention. Towards the end of the same narrative passage, the agent acting through Coyote to bring about these changes speaks for the first time with a voice split off and separate from Coyote's at a point in the unfolding story when Coyote's own voice and body rescind beyond the far side of human recognizability:

"Now you have given yourself the name 'Coyote.'
You will like it that way.
Because I think [so], I shall give you those portions that you have not created."

"Who are you who move me about the places I have not created?
Yours is a voice that I constantly hear.
Who is this person who is speaking to me again?
Now, come before me!"

From inside a cloud there was a roar of thunder.
A rainbow had come down on both sides from inside the cloud.
He who was its power came down.
The whole earth began to shake.
The winds, breezes, and sands began to move.

"Perhaps you will also create still more that I shall give to you."

Then the cloud moved down to the surface of the earth before him.
The earth roared.
It shook.
The cloud moved upward.

The being who had just come,
    he of whom one could certainly not say that he was an evil man,
        had come down.
He stood facing [Coyote].

"Now, since you do not want to be human, now you may go away.
Humankind will do to you whatever they will.
They will give you troubles that do not exist for human beings."

> At this point, Coyote trotted away.
> There stood Child of the Water.
> Everything had stopped its motion.
> Nothing made a noise. (Hoijer 1938:177)

"Everything stopped its motion. Nothing made a noise" punctuates a default state of movement (Hoijer 1951; Weiner 1991) establishing temporal rupture as an erected barrier in the conditions of mutual knowing between those who would be henceforth stand to each other across a radical boundary as differently embodied and differently perceiving beings.

As blundering and painful as Coyote's predicaments can sometimes seem, these are not cautionary or forbidding tales. Encounters with others, and extension of selves across space and time, while full of potential trouble, are sought after and figured as desired, interesting, and necessary to life. Through encounters with others, persons differentiate from what is known, and elaborate the temporal unfolding, epitomized in idioms of walking and growth, of that place in the path of humanity from which a person stands. It is perhaps worth pointing out, and in keeping with an attempted "symmetrical anthropology" (Latour 1993:102) that Coyote here, and in the bungling host stories, has something in common with the Phantom Linguist cartoon of the previous chapter. In both cases disjunctures in perspective are brought to the fore, even as both parties to a disjuncture are brought into the same narrative field of view.

Coyote stories are part of histories of differentiation emerging from encounters with variously scaled others, from other persons, to families, to clans, to ndee/'people like us,' to *ndah*/'enemies/strangers,' to differently embodied and perceiving beings, to the not-self pushing back at our perceptual experience of the phenomenal world from landscape and from limitations on human bodies and lifespan. That Coyote stories have been used to reflect upon encounters with others prior to and throughout the colonial era can be found in the broad rhizomic (Deleuze and Guattari 1987) spread of the motifs, themes, and plots of stories anchored in the figure of Coyote throughout the Native North American West (Goodwin 1994; Hymes 1994; Lévi-Strauss 1990; Ramsey 1977; Thompson 1966; Underhill 1985; Webster 1999).

Histories of Differentiating Media

Contemplating the broad geographic distribution of Coyote stories throughout the Native American narrative traditions of the North American West, it is difficult to imagine how such a thing happens without print, radio, telephones, television, movies, and the Internet to spread the word. Labeling such stories as "oral literatures" is part of the way indigenous communities are imagined in relation to politically integrating institutions like tribal governments and schools. As political rhetoric, "oral literature" serves an equalizing function. It locates an orally transmitted kind of cultural literacy in indigenous histories. However, it is all too easy to project notions of mechanical reproduction, or of broadcast mass media, from a standardized, centralized source onto what Kroskrity (2012) calls our "story about the way stories are told."

Here I sketch a different meta-story and cast the wide range of Coyote stories within a consideration of indigenous histories of differentiation. The idea that there is a unified thing called "Coyote stories" is in a sense in the eye of the beholder, emergent through ethnological and folkloric research. Many different names have been attached to apparently similar characters and stories. ᵐBa, ᵐba ts'ǫǫsé, shǫǫde, ᵐba ts'ǫǫsé łighaí are all terms averaged out to the translational equivalent "Coyote" in the Apachean literature, with ramifying differences and variations beyond. Even more often the main character of a story is not named.

Ethnographers and linguists (including Opler, Hoijer, and Sapir) have commented upon the fact that Apache narrators accentuate the differences between stories. Opler, who worked across several Apache reservations in the 1930s, describes how each narrator linked his or her stories to the specific person who taught them the story, and remarked upon variations between their way of telling the story and others'. To tell a story is also to assemble previous tellers and distribute the voice of the story out to them (and to Coyote). According to Opler (in Hoijer 1938:214):

> It must not be supposed that all Mescalero Apache tell the coyote cycle in exactly the same way or even relate the episodes in the same order. There is considerable individual variation, and I have listened to animated arguments between various Apache concerning the proper manner in which the cycle should be told. . . . When I was recording the cycle, my informant might interrupt his discourse to say, "Now I learned my story from Old Man T. Others told it differently. One man put in a different story at this place." Then would follow a variant or an additional episode with the name of the old storyteller whose narrative included it.

He describes how story variation and personal attribution together form a track record of mutually contingent actions and imaginings. One person is aware of telling a story differently from another, one family is aware of telling it differently from another family, one camp is aware of telling it differently from a neighboring camp – so that each telling exists in dialogic relation to an extended world of other's words (Bakhtin 1981). A given story is told in an already populated field of other parallel stories and other parallel tellers.

Opler (in Hoijer 1938:214) elaborates upon another relationship expressed through storytelling: that any given Coyote story or episode was told in relation to precedents established by other episodes in what he described as a cycle:

> I have said something concerning the continuity of the cycle and the definite order of the episodes. This is an aspect of the coyote stories not fully appreciated, a circumstance which has resulted in violence to the rich esthetic and ethnological content of the cycle. . . . Since, in the full body of the myth, such plots often run through more than one episode and there is much interweaving of the whole cycle by reference to what has gone before, the procedure of isolating separate coyote stories ends in truncating and mutilating them. For instance, in one of the last episodes of the cycle, Coyote meets Beetle, and, after making some caustic references to a previous encounter of the two, eats him. The allusion is not clear unless one is familiar with the details of an earlier episode in which Beetle outwitted Coyote and escaped from him.

In other words, an aspect of the meaning taken from any given telling was intertextual. The layering on and remembering of tellers is asserted through the parallel, contextual, and intertextual layering of each story or episode in light of others.

Expectations surrounding Coyote as an actor, as a voice with power, and as a possible danger that must be treated carefully, rests on a number of mutually supportive and progressively scaled pragmatic inferences and relations among persons. There is a temporal, spatial, and personal scaling from the present teller to the previous named storytellers, to unnamed ancestors, to cosmological figures like Coyote. Many Coyote stories play out mishaps at the limits of selves and misrecognition at the edge of familiar experience, reflecting an intersubjective pragmatics in which the relative knowability of differently placed and embodied others continually presents itself. Coyote establishes boundary play alongside the notion that long ago all had been human to each other. In this way Coyote stands as a condition of qualified possible recognition across difference of varying scales. Each storyteller is poised at the emergent tip of a pathway of previous tellings, each of which can be projected back to its enabling precedents. And ultimately, a storyteller is talking at the tip of that path about Coyote. And in turn, Coyote, way back at the boundary between his and our humanity, may be listening. This is why Coyote stories are described as *godiyįhgo*, or 'holy' and why most people who are described as "really believing in them," as well as those who just play it safe, will only tell them in the winter, when the power that animates Coyote is less likely to overhear and respond in uncontainable ways.

Ethnopoetics and Research Diplomacy

Stories recognized as "traditional," like languages recognized as "indigenous," are symbols in the mediation of indigenous communities within encompassing polities. The traditional stories documented under the assimilationist regime of the early twentieth century were packaged and circulated in a form intended for use by scholars and by those involved in colonial administration. The political climate shifted following the civil rights movement and the American Indian movement. Native American literature emerged as a distinct print literary market (Vizenor 1997). In this climate some scholars and writers began to reinterpret earlier products of linguistic and cultural documentation, and re-present them for circulation to audiences for whom they had become newly relevant. Ethnopoetics, as developed by Dell Hymes (1981, 1996) and Dennis Tedlock (1983, 1999), emerged as a focus of study that bridged interests in literary art with commitments to accuracy in translation for anthropological and linguistic documentation. Interest in Native American oral literatures also coincided with concerns for language rights and for supporting and maintaining indigenous languages (Hinton 1994; Kroskrity 2012; Woodbury 1993).

Hymes (1981, 1996) argued that the presentational format of Americanist linguistic text collections, in which narratives and speeches were crammed into columns in block paragraph form, obscured their rhetorical composition. He reexamined documented narratives looking for relations of disjuncture, cohesion, and parallelism among clauses and sentences and among more extended, inclusive units. From this he identified a dimension of poetic patterning he termed "measured verse." To better reflect the poetics of narrative on the printed page he advocated representing texts as lines of poetry and in units of verse, stanza, and scene. For Hymes, because presenting a narrative in ethnopoetic format was more faithful to the rhetorical shape given the story by the teller, it was therefore a less distorting medium for the teller's voice.

If following Hanks (1986, 2010) we look at colonial genres like text collections as boundary works in the political mediation of indigenous communities, then another aspect of the difference introduced with ethnopoetics emerges into view. Recasting a transcribed text into verse format introduces a difference in its genre, and its implied relationship to broader audiences, reinterpretting collected texts as poetry. Some might feel cautious, as did I, about projecting onto indigenous narrators and stories given categories like "literary artist" and "literary art." However, the fact that these very categories are also in play for members of indigenous communities, some of whom make their living as literary artists or purchase and read literary art, means that reframing oral narratives in this way places them in a translational politics salient to community members as well as researchers. It was Hymes' intention to change not only the way such narratives might be appreciated by a general literary audience, but also to return them to their community of origin in a new form, which he hoped would be a more accessible and apt vehicle for the voices of storytellers. Ethnopoetic approaches to Native American oral narratives and song establish connections between the Americanist tradition of text collection and the emerging genre of literary publications recognized as Native American Literature[6] by locating "oral literature" in the former. More broadly, ethnopoetics provides a bridge between salvage documentation and contemporary concerns about voice and agency.

From his own experiences during annual summer visits to the Warm Springs reservation, Dell Hymes suggested that I bring with me to the Fort Apache reservation some of Hoijer's and Goddard's texts that I had re-presented in ethnopoetic format. He suggested that these might generate interest and provide a basis for mutual collaboration. I followed his advice and did see bilingual verse presentations of Goddard's (1920) White Mountain Apache narratives circulated informally with positive but qualified evaluative responses within several tribal education offices.[7] Interest in reading such texts, and in recording and transcribing new ones, was consistent with my consultants' oft-stated interest in Apache–English comparison and translation (cf. Samuels 2006). And in the Fort Apache community, where nearly everyone, including Traditionalists, identified as Christian (Nevins 2010), verse presentation not only evoked comparisons with literature, but also the Bible.

Ethnopoetics proved to be a basis for collaboration with one of our consultants, John Altaha, also a *diyiń*. We met him through work on an Apache language education project, through a teacher who had been taking language lessons with him. With him and Mary Altaha we recorded and translated oral narratives he judged to be appropriate for publication, and have published two of his longer narratives in collections of Native American oral literature (Nevins et al. 2004; Nevins et al. 2012).

Texts as Boundary Works

During my ethnographic term, I did not witness an extended family storytelling session involving Coyote. And of the families I knew, only two, both with *diyiń* in the family, reported performing and hearing Coyote and associated cosmological stories at home.[8] There are other contexts in which traditional cosmological narratives are told, one of which is associated with sweat lodges and initiation as *diyiń* or as singers/disciples who support *diyiń* in the performance of public ceremonies. Most young people were more likely to encounter Coyote stories in the culture center, through children's books, or (for the few school programs in which it was permissible) during storytelling sessions with an elder in their weekly Apache Culture class at school. When Coyote stories are met with in these contexts they are accompanied by translations in form and meaning, which includes framing as "traditional" and as items of Apache culture. Recentering storytelling from home to school and from personal to traditional is consistent with the rhetoric of language endangerment and maintenance in the sense that where a story or language is no longer spoken in the home, it is up to educational institutions to maintain them. Some of my consultants reflected upon the association of traditional stories with culture centers and schools in just that way. One of my consultants, who grew up speaking Apache and listening to stories spoken in Apache among his friends and family in East Fork, nonetheless described his time working as an intern at the culture center and museum as the time when "I was getting to know my culture."

In the contemporary reservation community, traditional stories are circulated across familial and ceremonial contexts, on the one hand, and in the culture center and more sporadically in school contexts, on the other. The fact that "the same" story may be performed in either set of contexts masks the extent to which the act of performing it serves different purposes within each. The movement of stories from extended family and ceremonial contexts to school and museum involves a sort of "radical translation," following Keane's (2007) discussion of radical conversion, in the sense that it involves recontextualization across different semiotic regimes in which the purpose of speaking, the status of words, and attributions of agency are configured differently. This process can involve changes in the form of a story, such as translation to printed English and inclusion in a literary anthology or children's book. Or it may involve fidelity to the form of performance, but where the same formal features are repurposed within a new controlling context.

An example of such a transformation across a text trajectory with implications for language material development is the change a traditional story, in this case a story about Coyote, undergoes as it moves from an extended family environment to a classroom or culture center. In this section I focus upon a particular Coyote story: "Coyote and Mescal," in order to explore the boundary role occupied by "traditional storytelling" in the complex mediation of the reservation community. The story was told at the kitchen table of the home of a prominent family, whose members included John Altaha, a well-respected *diyiń* called upon to perform ceremonies across the Apache reservations of the southwest, Mary Altaha, who had attained a nursing degree at Haskell Indian Academy, and their sons, who were principal members of an Apache Country Western band with national distribution (see Samuels 2004). The venue, then, was a familial environment in which John and Mary had the status of grandparents and elders, a sanctified space where local and sometimes international guests approached John in his capacity as a *diyiń*,[9] and an occasional recording studio. The stories told in this venue were therefore poised between a number of suggested contextualizing environments. John and Mary Altaha approached our work mindful of differences in perspective and with an expressed interest in translation, which is what we spent the majority of our time together doing. Mary Altaha cast her concern with translation in relation to matters of language shift in the following way:

> A lot of these words I guess were just everyday words at one time, I guess; but now we don't talk like that. That's why it's hard to translate it. We throw in a lot of English words to make it easy for us to talk. Then now we try to talk with our kids and we have to talk English and that's hard. And we can't tell stories like this to them because it loses the meaning or the fun part in it, the joke in it, you know, it loses that as you try to speak it in English because it's meant to be told in Apache, I guess. It had more meaning in Apache.

She also reflected upon the fact that young people do not read Apache either, so that writing down the story in Apache was not a straightforward solution to the problem. She noted that certain neighborhood communities on the reservation, particularly Cibecue, still spoke the language and young people there were speaking it and able to listen to stories in Apache.

At the time of our fieldwork, John Altaha was seventy-two years old, and a prominent *diyiń*. As a *diyiń*, or ceremonial specialist, he was known to be an excellent singer and storyteller, and he traveled through the Apache reservations of the southwest where he would officiate a number of ceremonies. Corresponding to his status as a *diyiń* and elder, was his recognition according to another status: that of "cultural expert," a status that also formed the basis for invitations extended to him to speak at neighboring universities or consult on Native American Graves Protection and Repatriation Act implementation. This put him in the role of cultural broker (Gershon 2006; Silverstein 1998), in that he was positioned to translate between different regimes of meaning.

Various offices of the tribe called upon him to serve as a cultural expert. In this capacity he visited some of the schools on the reservation to perform songs and short traditional stories that he deemed appropriate for that context. We recorded a number of interviews, stories, and songs under conditions he judged to be appropriate and safe, and created translated texts that he deemed appropriate for publication and for sharing with students in a classroom.[10] Although such narratives were certainly part of his repertoire as a *diyin*, he did not share with us or bring into his work for the schools the sort of extended cosmological narrative like "Coyote and the Creation" (excerpted above) that Hoijer transcribed from Charles Smith more than sixty years prior. Instead, he performed a handful of short, lighthearted coyote stories. Even for these, he would only meet with us to record them or work on translations of them in the winter months. April 15 was the cut-off date.

So in winter months over the course of two years we worked with John Altaha and his wife, Mary Altaha, three or four hours at a sitting once a week recording, transcribing, and translating selected songs and stories. These included a series of short stories that Mr. Altaha learned from his father, all of which elaborated the theme: "How Coyote Ruined It." These stories described the transition from a seemingly idyllic easier prior state, when shoes (and people) never wore out and food gathered itself, to a more familiar way of life in which the world presents itself with more resistance and opacity, and goals require more mediation and effort in order to be fulfilled. In these stories it was Coyote who ruined many previously easy jobs by acting differently than everyone else – often for no apparent reason; and in so doing so established precedents for the kinds of push-back encountered as one goes along in life today. First, drawing upon several sources, I present a sketch of familial contextualizing practices and show how these are mutually constitutive in performance with particular linguistic features in John Altaha's storytelling style. Following that I will characterize the functional transformation of the same performance features repurposed as items of cultural knowledge in schools and culture center museums.

In an extended family environment, Coyote and other such stories are told mostly at night and always in the winter, and these restrictions remind participants of the possibility of the listening presence of ancestral agencies (such that a person should take care in speaking of them). The stories themselves are told within an intimate interpersonal surround, with the looming prospect that the speaker may be "shooting" the story at one of the listeners (Basso 1996; Opler 1996:440–441), and suggesting to everyone assembled the aptness of the fit between the story and the person's behavior. Storytelling features and style are part of a rhetorical strategy to downplay the agency of the speaker and invite listeners to imaginatively trade places with ancestors, a process that affects changes in the way the listener thinks. Interpretive conventions militate against abstracting out a "moral" that should be the same for every listener (Basso 1996). Instead, the entire story is taken up as a whole (Toelken and Scott 1981). Used this way, even apparently incidental features of dress, manner, landscape, or predicament might variously speak to different people, prompting each to recognize an aspect of his or her life in the story and "replace themselves" through the story and thereby become affected in different ways by ancestors' voices in imaginations of themselves in their ongoing involvements with others.

Traditional stories told in familial and ceremonial contexts provide an opportunity for allowing ancestors to speak to people (if a person is "listening") and to play a shaping role in a person's awareness and interpretation of ongoing events (Basso 1996; Opler 1996; Toelken and Scott 1981). The delicate task of the storyteller is to avoid directly interposing herself or himself between the ancestors and listeners' imaginations of the unfolding story. Accordingly, storytelling style is spare, with maximal gaps between utterances that listeners are expected to fill in with their own imaginations. Common reference points in familiar places and scenes are utilized to orient listeners to the ancestors, the remnants of whose actions are located in those places, and to key listeners to fill in context imaginatively. Some storytellers make extensive use of quotative particles, like *ch'idii*, or 'people say,' that locate the source of the story outside the storyteller and that index prior acts of speaking extending from the present day to the imagined time of the ancestors.

Another task of the storyteller is to bring listeners into imaginative relation with ancestors so that they can see what the ancestors saw, hear their voices, stand where they stood (Basso 1996). This concern that listeners become anchored in the perceptual surround of the story is reflected in the Apache metadiscursive term for story: *nágoldi'e*, literally 'perceptual surround spoken by him/her again' (where the construction is built around the verb of speaking *-di'*, the *ná-* prefix establishes that this act of speaking repeats something done before and is therefore expectable, and where the *-go-* 'environmental' prefix is what figures the action as establishing an orientation to a perceptual surround). This is also reflected in the association of some stories with place names, which specify a particular position on the surrounding landscape and a particular orientation to its features (Basso 1988). Observing seasonal constraints orients listeners to ancestors as potential participants who must be approached correctly, and whose awareness waxes and wanes with the seasons. Care must be taken, and respect demonstrated, in careful timing and in careful wording, because one wants to exert control over the extent and manner in which the powers associated with ancestors enter into one's life.

Below is a short Coyote story performed by John Altaha in the winter at his kitchen table with members of his family present. It was also recorded for the purpose of transcription and materials development. To the latter end, he proposed a title for it: *ᵐBa' Ts'ǫǫsé, Donzhǫǫnyóó 'Anei'a'tsada Nyeigo, Naiziigo 'Agoola*, or 'Coyote, How He Ruined an Easy Job.' The storyteller makes special use of metapragmatic, reflexive language (Silverstein 1993). This includes hearsay constructions (*ch'idii*, 'they say'; *golsee*, 'it's called'; *nágoldįį*, 'they tell stories about it'), evidentials (*shą'*, *lę́*, *lééni'*), temporal framing words (*dóniiná*), repeated formulaic pronouncements of names or characterizations (*ᵐBa' Ts'ǫǫsé* 'Coyote,' *ní iłch'ǫǫ'* 'he ruined it'; *Dził nadaaháá*, place name), a construction linking the story to the context of telling (*yaalé*, 'extending rope-like from him'), and opening and closing formula (*'Ałkínáálą́ą́* and *shigoshgan dashjah*, respectively). Also important is the term *k'ad*, or 'now' because it marks a departure from repeated and expected acts, through which a difference is established (it intercepts conditions otherwise established through the *-ná-*, usative, iterative prefix). And finally, *Dzą́ą́yéko* "right here" is spoken with extra emphasis at the end of the story, locating the imaged story as well as the storyteller's labor (my yucca fruit lay piled up right there) on a particular place in the surrounding landscape. After presenting the story, I will first discuss how these metapragmatic features in family storytelling anchor the moment of speaking in a charged interpersonal and temporal surround that places listeners in an indexical flow of sociality continuous with the ancestral actions of Coyote.

Here is the story (metapragmatic discourse features discussed above are in bold):

'Ałkínáálą́ą́ ch'idiigo
It happened that way, people say

ᵐBa' Ts'ǫǫsé, shą'
Coyote [himself]

Díínóniiná ⁿ*deehíí: nadaah, hayídíłkááł*
Long Ago, these People: they chop out mescal

Nzaayóó, dził bę́ęzhyóó, hayídíłkááł
Far away, on the side of a hill, they chop it out

Ná' golííní gwa'á'shááyóó, barbecue pit o'áń yaagogeetá
And, near to the place where they live, a barbecue pit is dug

Éí hayóó nadaah hayiskaałí 'iyaayóó yééd1yíí **lę́**
From over there, that mescal that they have cut, they would just give it a push downhill

Nádík'e daí barbeque baa' 'ánólzaa, da'bínik'e
Just by itself, its would move towards the barbecue pit, just move by itself

'Ákoo nihik'ego 'at'éélį́, godiyááná **dóníiná** *daits'énáyóó*
So, that was their way then, when things first got started, in the beginning long ago.

'Ákoo 'ééníishą' **ᵐBa' Ts'ǫǫsé**
And so along came Coyote

Áń, dágową, háń **ni'iłchǫǫń**, *nágoghaálé áná'ałdo*
That one, everything, the one who ruined things, he goes about everywhere, even then

'Ákoo **ᵐBa' Ts'ǫǫsé, shą'**
So then, Coyote, [himself]

Táts'a níí' γii'γįį
Burden basket, had his very own

Dziłkáíyé ni'otakgo
He went to the top of the hill

Kóó ni'ogolged.
Here he had dug a hole

Náłdziłkáí ni'otakgo
He went back to the top of that hill

Éí éílá, nadaah, nááhayidzíłkááłé.
From there, mescal, he cut it out

Níγík'eeł 'γé táts'a bighée nį'oyíídíiłgo
He cleared it the area of mescal and stacked them inside his basket

Eé' níiyideesghę nábighee'í barbecue o'i'áńgo, pit nágólaa', 'ákoona nayidééhoo
Then he started carrying it, putting it inside the barbecue pit, going back and forth

'Ékó'á náyideestį́
That's where he went fetching and carrying several times

'Ákoo 'áíγéé, godiyáágo 'ik'ehgo, nadaah niká 'onak'áíγóó, níhayidziłkaałá:
From there onwards, it began to be that way, whenever they go after mescal, they would cut it out:

Ch'é yanáiyił, yinadaiyił, donadilyeeda
In vain, they try to push it, they push it, it will not roll

*Éíya dazh*ǫǫ *'anak'oh,* **ch'idii ne'**
Then it just falls over, people say

ᵐ***Ba' Ts'***ǫǫ***sé,*** *nío yihi gheehgo, ai'iyé* **ni' iłch'**ǫǫ **lééni'**
Coyote, him packing it in, that's how he ruined it

Éí eik'ehgo nikee oníí, nín daayiighéé, 'ik'ehgo **nyaalé**
Then afterwards, they started to haul it in from that time on

Dóniiná 'ak'ehgo, ᵐ***Ba' Ts'***ǫǫ***sé, ní iłch'***ǫǫ***' lę***
Long time ago, according to it, Coyote, he ruined it

ᵐ***Ba' Ts'***ǫǫ***sé,*** *ní atíné, daagowá* **hání'iłch**ǫǫ**'**
Coyote, he did it, everything, he ruined it

*Ní'iłch*ǫǫ ***ł'ęęłę́***
That's how it got ruined

Kóné **k'ad** *dza* **lę́**: *nadaahí, nádík'eh'an'í, dohah nádík'ehda, ní'á'íí* **yaalé**
So this is what he did: mescal, that used to go, won't go again, from there on

"*Éí* ᵐ***Ba' Ts'***ǫǫ***sé ní'atįį,*" **golseego,** ᵐ*Baa* **nágoldįįgo**
"That is the Coyote, he did it," they say, they tell the story,

Dzą́áyéko Dził nadáháá, bęęzhiyóó, **shigoshgan dashjah**
Right here, Silver Butte, at the middle of it, my yucca fruit, I put them there

Mr. Altaha's use of hearsay constructions not only disavows personal knowledge of the story, but also points to the fact that this story has a life that extends beyond the immediate context of telling it at night at the kitchen table, implying prior acts of speaking and the likelihood that others also tell this story.[11] *Shą'* is an evidential particle with a dual function. First, through it the speaker disavows personal knowledge of what is being said. Combined with temporal frames set by *dóniiná*, or 'long time ago,' it qualifies the speaker's lack of personal knowledge with the sense that the story events occurred prior to the lifetime of the people assembled. The repetition of "that's how he ruined it" and the verbal construction *yaalé*, 'a rope-like shape extends from it,' ties the conditions of life experienced by the listeners in the room as the continual outcome of Coyote's actions, bringing them to a limiting aspect of their own experience that Coyote brought to them. Together these features have the effect of distancing the listener's imagination from the person of the speaker and bringing it closer to the character of Coyote via ways his actions bear upon their experience.

That is, metadiscursive idioms are used to cast the animating agency of the story, not in the storyteller, but in what our storyteller described in his translation of *shą'* as "Coyote himself." The evidential particles *lę́* and *lę́ę́ni'* are variants of the same evidential particle (de Reuse 2003). It orients listeners to the events of the story as a "deferred realization," something that happened, but whose significance one comes to awareness of later – a new realization of what had been true all along that one comes to by the unfolding of experience. These features, together with the expectation that the speaker may be telling the story for a reason, prompt listeners into imaginative engagement with Coyote, and, through Coyote, to humorous and critical reflections upon one another. A storytelling performance is judged successful to the extent that participants are able to see, hear, and vividly imagine the actions of ancestors; and to the extent that the force of the story – bundled in with places and recognizable actions, exerts a lasting (salutary) effect on the listeners, including subsequent moments of remembering the story upon encountering the place associated with it and vice versa (Basso 1988). Here speaking is an invitation to each listener to imagine, to orient themselves through awareness of place and ancestral actions, and as the story unfolds to come to their own revelatory meaning, to get what Mary Altaha described as "the joke in it."

Extended Sociality, Equivocation, and the Poetics of Stories

All of the features discussed above help to orient participants beyond the proximate context of telling to more distant, extended relations. The poetics and style of the story are the means by which an immediate spoken interaction orients participants to more extended temporal, spatial, and ultimately social relations. Hearsay constructions evoke the speech of other people, evidentials evoke the experiences of more distant, less intimate persons, temporal depth evokes people and events that happened before anyone today was alive, the figure of Coyote evokes a temporally deep ancestor and the contemporary differently embodied being that trots along the edge of homes and settlements, and Silver Butte (literally 'mescal mountain') – placing one's yucca fruit right there – all of these orient participants to an extended spatial, temporal, and interpersonal surround.

Storytelling style, then, consists in a bundle of strategies for orientating participants to distant, extended persons and agents. The discursive means through which extended orientations are established – instances of the situationally extrinsic that is intrinsic to language – is reflected upon by linguistic anthropologists as "entextualization" (Bauman and Briggs 1990). Entextualization consists in means of speech (Hymes 1972) through which a difference is introduced into an ongoing interaction, bringing to bear upon that interaction other persons, events, scenes, and precedents that scale participant orientation from familiar to less known and knowable relations. As noted above, the most readily elicited Apache language translational equivalent to "story" is *nágoldi'é*, or 'telling a perceptual surround again.' A story, or "perceptual surround spoken again," is an interpretive frame upon ongoing speech, and invites a particular form of participation. Stylistic features of stories are tools of participatory orientation to more extended, less intimately known, social relations. In this way, entextualized discourse is a way that extended sociality is introduced into the ongoing flow of a communicative interaction.[12]

In addition to appearing to be bound off from surrounding context, there is another way that stories correspond to what Keane (2007) and Silverstein and Urban (1996) describe as the "thing-y" or object-like quality of entextualized discourse. Stories are object-like in that they present their own measure of causal force, their own push-back upon the perceptual world of contemporary listeners and tellers. They are taken to exert effects that are not entirely contained or anticipated in the intentions of storyteller or listeners.[13] As Basso shows (1996), stories are described among neighborhoods of the Fort Apache reservation as being shot like arrows and the places associated with them described as stalking people. In the spoken practice of many of our consultants, stories and land invited realizations in listeners of who they are in relation to those who made their lives possible. It was assumed that ancestors are "already there" unnoticed and unnamed, waiting to be revealed and remembered. And this is something each person, at various scales and via different idioms, is involved in doing with their own minds as they mature.

What No Coyote Story Means: Speech Repurposed

Storytelling is a kind of extended sociality that involves distant interlocutors, including those who are no longer living, but whose agency may still be manifest via other media, including the land, some interactions with animals, and in other ways. In this way, stories about ancestors are an example of what Keane (1995) describes as ritual speech. Stories share with ceremony and prayer the fact that they introduce into spoken interaction terms of participation between proximate human actors and distant, deceased, or invisible agents. I have tried to show with the discussion of Coyote and Mescal that the stylistic features of stories about ancestors orient participants to places and persons at a temporal remove from proximate contemporary interpersonal interaction. The discursive means, in this case the bundling of stylistic features in a conventionalized genre like traditional storytelling, allows recursive applications across different spoken contexts and so are also the means of recontextualization across diverse and successive interactions.

What Keane notes for recontextualization of ritual speech applies to Traditionalist narrative:

> Their textual character is in part a function of the perceived challenges of communicating with distant interlocutors, such as the dead, and of obtaining from them recognition and responses. The character of ritual words in turn facilitates their use in new contexts, supplying an emergent folkloric discourse with materials that are interesting primarily for what they denote or as a code awaiting exegesis. It should be no surprise that the speech performances that most lend themselves to entextualization are favored as lasting cultural objects. (Keane 2007:262)

Keane points out that the same means by which stories, songs, and other forms of ritual speech bring persons into indexical flows with ontologically different beings (the dead, ancestors) also confer an object-like, or bundle-like, quality to that language, and a consciousness of such stories and songs as distinct and broadly recursive kinds of speaking. Their entextualization features make stories of ancestors suggestive candidates for inclusion in the folkloric project of culture centers, archives, and school curricula (see also Silverstein 1996).

However, when a story is recontextualized as an object of cultural knowledge within an institution of state, it is poised to undergo a conversion in participatory pragmatics. In this sense, traditional storytelling is an example of what Hanks (1987) terms a "threshold genre" in that storytelling circulates between different discursive regimes, with different interpretative consequences within each. Traditional stories told within a school classroom, to a researcher, or in a culture center museum are necessarily recontextualized through orientation to a language ideological regime (Kroskrity 2000) that differs from that of the familial storytelling context described above. Here the speaker's role is transformed from that of elder family member to "cultural expert." The primary function of language, which authorizes the speaker and justifies his or her expert status with respect to "Apache culture," is referential with respect to an imagined stable object that is Apache culture and language (Keane 1995). The story is transformed into an item within an inventory of cultural knowledge that might be documented by researchers, and transmitted to students in the schools and to laypeople in the culture center.

In some cases storytellers alter the style and form of their stories to fulfill what they anticipate as the genre expectations associated with the new context, such as translating Coyote stories into the form of moral fables, fairytales, folklore, or Bible stories. In other cases care may be taken to replicate the formal features of traditional storytelling (as in Hymes 1981), but in this context their function within the controlling context of school or culture center as a state institution are as markers of traditional authenticity. So telling the same story using the same words in a classroom – or as we did, recording a story and translating it for use as classroom materials – reconfigures its purpose and meaning (Keane 1995). That is, the occasion of storytelling is defined as a lesson in Apache culture; here understood, not as a relationship between ancestral agencies and listeners, but as a culturally distinct and authentic Apache story, a part of a larger body of traditional knowledge.

Recontextualized as items of cultural expertise in culture center or school performance, genre-specific contextualizing features like hearsay constructions and evidential particles like *shą'* are less about anchoring the listeners in a charged contextual surround involving the possible involvement of ancestors, and more about telling the story "correctly" in terms of standards of accuracy and representation. Here also, the possibility of the storyteller shooting the story at a target is precluded by the fact that there is very little interpersonal familiarity between the students and the storyteller. Items of cultural knowledge in archives and school curricula are often taken to stand in for the "language and culture" of the broader community, obscuring the full range of practices in the community and obscuring the transformations such discourse undergoes when it is recontextualized in Western educational institutions. This process has been described as "erasure" in the language ideology literature (Irvine and Gal 2000; Kuipers 1998).

However, while "erasure" of contextual variation and difference may be an apt description of the interpretive position of researchers and administrators viewing the community from a distance, it is less adequate to the manifest differences in point of view among community members on site, who confront community critique and intervention that bring those "erased" contextual differences to the fore. Objects of documentation, from stories to orthographies, present points of reflection within a dynamic, contested terrain. Among the language programs on the Fort Apache reservation that I was familiar with in the late 1990s, traditional stories were only sporadically brought in. When included in classes, stories were not part of the repeated, objective curriculum, but introduced with guest speakers. In such cases storytelling carried a dangerous edge, because telling traditional stories in the classroom was not without controversy. The moral responsibility for telling stories in a classroom was placed in the teller, so that the decision to bring someone in to talk to a class was less about the "what" of their talk but the quality of that person as a "who" and that person's reputation for good judgment. As I will show in Chapter 7, the voice of Coyote in the wider reservation community carries risks to people who would like to include Coyote stories in museum or school curricula.

Indigenous Language Programs as Equivocal Translational Spaces

Heath's (1983) monograph: *Ways with Words: Language, Life and Work in Classrooms and Communities*, is salient to language maintenance for the account it contains of how teachers, students, and community members brought ethnographic methods into school practice to ameliorate school–community disjuncture. Heath's ten-year involvement with her field site allowed her to collaborate with teachers and parents to establish classrooms as explicitly translational spaces. She introduced innovations, which included training students to interview elder family members and helping them bring these interviews into classrooms. Through this and other ethnographic teaching experiments students were encouraged to make explicit translations between the different domains and modes of their experience and to learn to orient to each in its own terms (Heath 1983).

Indigenous community schools, and indigenous language and culture programs in the schools, are located at a nexus between different communicative regimes. At that nexus many community members, as well as teachers, reflected similar concerns to those of their counterparts in Heath's study in their expectation that Apache language programs would foster success in school for Apache students by combating stigma, by helping students to know and feel proud of "who they are," and through benefits linked to speaking more than one language. In a sense, they were arguing for creating in the schools a translational space similar to the school–community work described in Heath's (1983) study.

On the other hand, the problem of what is recognized within the contextualizing practices of schools and culture centers as "Apache language" reinforces tacit assumptions and sets of political relationship that differ from those of extended familial environments as well as some forms of local leadership. So, as language and culture programs open up new possibilities for community members to participate in schools, they also bring communicative disjuncture between homes and schools into focus. In fact, on the Fort Apache reservation during my stay in the late 1990s, "traditional stories," or holy stories, were not stabilized as objects of cultural property, nor were they taught in most reservation schools. In the following chapter I show how religious leadership actively destabilizes traditional stories at junctures where they might be integrated into institutions of state. More specifically I focus upon community restrictions on traditional stories and "medicine man talk" (Samuels 2006) in school programs. So while the voices of Coyote and other deep ancestors serve as attractors for the folkloric project of documentation, as was the case in my own documentation of Coyote stories with John and Mary Altaha, they also provoke forms of push-back from religious leadership when they are included in cultural heritage projects in schools and culture centers.

Coyote-like stories continue to exert open-ended effects in the contemporary reservation community and in its articulation with broader social networks. I'll end this chapter with one such example. One of our consultants, Benjamin Benally, ran a division of the tribe's vocational skills center. During our stay he became involved in the Athabaskan languages conference, which is an annual meeting held at a different location each year and includes both linguists and members of indigenous communities. Reflecting the geographic distribution of Athabaskan languages and favorable terms of government support for indigenous language programs (see Meek 2010), the conference is often held in Canada. Our second year on the reservation Mr. Benally traveled there for the first time, along with a small delegation of educators and spokespersons that the tribe sent to the conference. Parallel sessions on linguistics and on community language efforts ran simultaneously. While linguists built professional ties with one another giving papers on pronoun obviation, evidentials, and on making the case for Dene-Yinesian historical involvements, parallel and overlapping networks were being formed among tribal members involved in community language programs. A week or so after he returned from the conference Mr. Benally told Tom Nevins and me a "story about stories" we all agreed was remarkable.

At the conference he was talking with some speakers of northern Athabaskan languages. He explained to them that he was from the south near the Mexican border and that he had come to the conference to see if it was true what he had been told: that there were people to the far north who spoke the same language as his people. They compared words for features of landscape, kin terms, and terms for everyday items and recognized much in common. One of the women said:

> Yeah, I heard about you guys. My dad told me a story about you. The way he tells it there was a big camp and they all had their dogs with them because

they used to help with carrying their things. One of the families had a dog that kept getting away and tearing things up in the camp of the *nant'an*, or leading person of the camp. The *nant'an* told the man whose dog it was to keep his dog under control or there would be trouble. The dog still kept getting away and tearing up the camp of the *nant'an*. So that man took his dog and his family and moved south, where they lived an easy life in the warm weather and got soft,

she said, teasing him at the end.

Benjamin recorded some of the words they had in common and brought them back with him to his office in Whiteriver. A day or so after he returned he was working in his yard in the neighborhood of Canyon Day when an uncle, who does not make it to the reservation's main town of Whiteriver very often, and who did not know about the language conference, said: "I haven't seen you for a couple of weeks. Where've you been?"[14] Benjamin said "I was visiting people to the north, in Canada. There are people there who speak our language." "Oh yeah," said his uncle, "I think I heard a story about them a long time ago from my grandfather . . . Something about a dog."

Notes

1 Goodwin published these stories in English translation. He had developed a shorthand for writing Apache, and worked with Neil Buck and others on translation. His original transcripts for these stories have been lost. Following Hymes (1981), I have converted the presentation format from Goodwin's paragraph to line and verse in order to provide visual expression for successive parallel sentences and for subdivisions in the telling. And, because Apache language does not afford indirect reported speech, I have converted a line in Goodwin from "One of them said he would try" to: "One of them said 'I will try.'" I have also replaced the word "shaman" in Goodwin's version with *diyiń*.

2 From Hoijer, Harry. 1938. *Chiricahua and Mescalero Apache Texts with Ethnological Notes by Morris Opler*. Chicago: University of Chicago Press. With kind permission from University of Chicago Press.

3 The term *ndah*, translated as 'enemy' or 'stranger,' appears in the early collections for a variety of strangers/enemies, including Tohono O'odham and Comanche. In the colonial encounter *ndah* began to be most frequently associated with *ndaa łighaí* 'White strangers,' and now *ndah* is taken to mean 'White person' as the unmarked default; other strangers are given more specific marked terms, e.g. *ndah diłhił* for 'Black stranger/person' or African American.

4 I have not modified Mr. Altaha's speech to conform with Standard American English because the variety of English John uses here reflects convergence with Apache grammatical patterns (Scollon and Scollon 1979). A pair of something, like shoes, corresponds to an Apache form class verb stem (Basso 1968) that is used to describe pairs and strings. Pairs are not treated as plural but are either used with dual verb forms or are unmarked for number. Mr. Altaha bends the formal resources of English closer to the provision made for pairs and duality in Apache with his consistent use of singular agreement forms with shoes.

5   Opler in his notes to the text identifies the agent making Coyote do and say these things as Child of Water/Tóbájiishchinéń, who appears in other Chiricahua and Mescalero stories as the one who made it possible for human beings to live on the surface of the earth. He is the younger brother of He Overcomes Evils/Nayenesghaní. In a manner that parallels White Mountain and Chiricahua relations to one another in the voicing of Coyote discussed earlier in the chapter, both describe the two brothers, but Chiricahua invest the role of focal enabling ancestor in the younger brother and depict the older brother as a coward, while White Mountain stories reverse those roles.
6   This connection is drawn most thoroughly by Anthony Webster in his work on Navajo poetry (2009).
7   However, many of the Goddard texts treat temporally deep ancestors like Coyote and are considered *godiyįh*, or holy, so care and restriction was applied to conditions of their circulation and performance. This is the topic of the following chapter.
8   I did not seek such contexts out, nor would we likely have been admitted to them as ethnographers, in part because reporting upon them would work against restrictions upon the circulation of "medicine man talk" asserted by Apache religious leadership (see next chapter and Samuels 2006).
9   I approached their home in this fashion in a return visit several years later so that John might sing over a family member undergoing health programs.
10 Mr. Altaha sat, along with other *diyiń*, on a cultural advisory board that was charged with oversight of the Apache language and culture programs in the schools. So it is likely that he expected that they would be able to influence the timing and manner in which the stories might have been included.
11 When used to refer to stories about contemporary people that circulate broadly, *ch'idii* is translated as "gossip."
12 Spitulnik (1997) develops this idea in her treatment of spoken uses of entextualized bits of media discourse in the everyday mediation of national belonging in Zambia. With *nágoldi'é* the form of imagined extended sociality is cast in a different idiom, temporality and with different operative agencies, but the principle by which extended relations are introduced into spoken interactions is the same.
13 Keane (2007) describes this difference as a difference in "semiotic ideology" which he introduces as an extension and complication of "language ideology" because it involves differences in objectification, subjects, objects, agency, different ways of rendering and reflecting upon language and upon selves, and different functions of speaking.
14 I did not witness this conversation, in which both speakers would have used Apache language. My story of Mr. Benally's story is an attempt to render what he recounted to me, which was in English.

References

Bakhtin, Mikhail (1981). *The Dialogic Imagination: Four Essays*. Caryl Emerson and Michael Holquist, trans., Michael Holquist, ed. Austin: University of Texas Press.

Basso, Keith. 1968. The Western Apache Classificatory Verb System: A Semantic Analysis. *Southwestern Journal of Anthropology* 24(3):252–256.

Basso, Keith. 1988. "Speaking with Names": Language and Landscape among the Western Apache. *Cultural Anthropology* 3(2):99–130.

Basso, Keith. 1996. *Wisdom Sits in Places: Language and Landscape among the Western Apache*. Albuquerque: University of New Mexico Press.

Basso, Keith and Nashley Tessay, Sr. 1994. Joseph Hoffman's "The Birth of He Triumphs over Evils": A Western Apache Origin Story. In *Coming To Light: Contemporary Translations of the Native Literatures of North America*. Brian Swann, ed., pp. 636–656. New York: Random House.

Bauman, Richard and Charles Briggs. 1990. Poetics and Performance as Critical Perspectives on Language and Social Life. *Annual Review of Anthropology* 19:59–88.

Bender, Margaret. 2002. *Signs of Cherokee Culture: Sekoyah's Syllabary in Eastern Cherokee Life*. Chapel Hill: University of North Carolina Press.

Deleuze, Giles and Felix Guattari. 1987. *A Thousand Plateaus. Vol. 2 Capitalism and Schizophrenia*. Minneapolis: University of Minnesota Press.

de Reuse, Willem. 2003. Evidentiality in Western Apache (Athabaskan). In *Studies in Evidentiality*. Alexandra Y. Aikenvald and R.M. Dixon, eds., pp. 79–100. Amsterdam: John Benjamins.

Gershon, Ilana. 2006. "When Culture Is Not a System: Why Samoan Cultural Brokers Cannot Do Their Job" *Ethnos* 71(4):533–558.

Goddard, Pliny Earle. 1920. White Mountain Apache Texts. *Anthropological Papers of the American Museum of Natural History* 24(4):369–527.

Goodwin, Grenville. 1994. *Myths and Tales of the White Mountain Apache*. Tucson: University of Arizona Press. (Original work published 1939.)

Hanks, William. 1986. *Intertexts: Writings on Language, Utterance and Context*. Lanham: Rowman & Littlefield.

Hanks, William. 1987. Discourse Genres in a Theory of Practice. *American Ethnologist* 14(4):668–692.

Hanks, William. 2010. *Converting Words: Maya in the Age of the Cross*. Berkeley: University of California Press.

Heath, Shirley Brice. 1982. What No Bedtime Story Means: Narrative Skills at Home and School. *Language in Society* 11(1):49–76.

Heath, Shirley Brice. 1983. *Ways with Words: Language, Life and Work in Classrooms and Communities*. Cambridge: Cambridge University Press.

Hinton, Leanne. 1994. *Flutes of Fire: Essays on California Indian Languages*. Berkeley: Heyday Books.

Hoijer, Harry. n.d. San Carlos Texts. Unpublished manuscript [except one narrative which is published in Basso and Tessay 1994] in the Hoijer Papers at the Library of the American Philosophical Society.

Hoijer, Harry. 1938. *Chiricahua and Mescalero Apache Texts with Ethnological Notes by Morris Opler*. Chicago: University of Chicago Press.

Hoijer, Harry. 1951. Cultural Implications of Some Navajo Linguistic Categories. *Language* 27(2):11–20.

Hymes, Dell H. 1972. Editorial Introduction. *Language in Society* 1(1):1–14.

Hymes, Dell H. 1981. *In Vain I Tried to Tell You: Essays in Native American Ethnopoetics*. Philadelphia: University of Pennsylvania Press.

Hymes, Dell H. 1994. Coyote, Master of Death, True to Life. In *Coming to Light: Contemporary Translations of the Native Literatures of North America*. Brian Swann, ed., pp. 293–306. New York: Random House.

Hymes, Dell H. 1996. *Ethnography, Linguistics, Narrative Inequality: Toward an Understanding of Voice*. London: Taylor & Francis.

Hymes, Dell and Louis Simpson. 1984. Bungling Host Benevolent Host: Louis Simpson's "Deer and Coyote." *American Indian Quarterly* 8(3):171–198.

Irvine, Judith and Susan Gal. 2000. Language Ideology and Linguistic Differentiation. In *Regimes of Language: Ideologies, Polities, and Identities*. Paul V. Kroskrity, ed., pp. 35–84. Santa Fe: School of American Research.

Keane, Webb. 1995. The Spoken House: Text, Act and Object in Eastern Indonesia. *American Ethnologist* 22(1):102–124.

Keane, Webb. 2007. *Christian Moderns: Freedom and Fetish in the Mission Encounter*. Berkeley: University of California Press.

Kroskrity, Paul V. 2000. Regimenting Languages: Language Ideological Perspectives. In *Regimes of Language: Ideologies, Polities, and Identities*. Paul V. Kroskrity, ed., pp. 1–34. Santa Fe: School of American Research.

Kroskrity, Paul V. 2012. Introduction. In *Telling Stories in the Face of Danger: Language Renewal in Native American Communities*. Paul V. Kroskrity, ed., pp. 152–183. Tulsa: University of Oklahoma Press.

Kuipers, Joel C. 1998. *Language, Identity and Marginality in Indonesia: The Changing Nature of Ritual Speech on the Island of Sumba*. New York: Cambridge University Press.

Latour, Bruno. 1993. *We Have Never Been Modern*. Cambridge, MA: Harvard University Press.

Lévi-Strauss, Claude. 1990. *The Naked Man. Mythologiques vol. 4*. Chicago: University of Chicago Press. (Original work published 1971, trans. 1981.)

Meek, Barbara. 2010. *We Are Our Language: An Ethnography of Language Revitalization in a Northern Athabascan Community*. Tucson: University of Arizona Press.

Merlan, Francesca and Alan Rumsey. 1991. *Ku Waru: Language and Segmentary Politics in the Western Nebilyer Valley, Papua New Guinea*. Cambridge: Cambridge University Press.

Morgan, Mindy J. 2009. *The Bearer of this Letter: Language Ideologies, Literacy Practices, and the Fort Belknap Indian Community*. Lincoln: University of Nebraska Press.

Nevins, M. Eleanor, 2010. The Bible in Two Keys: Traditionalism and Apache Evangelical Christianity on the Fort Apache Reservation. *Language and Communication* 30(1):19–32.

Nevins, M. Eleanor, Thomas J. Nevins, Paul Ethelbah, and Genevieve Ethelbah. 2004. "He Became an Eagle": A Contemporary Western Apache Oral Narrative. In *Voices from the Four Directions: Contemporary Translations of Native American Oral Literature*. Brian Swann, ed., pp. 283–303. Lincoln: University of Nebraska Press.

Nevins, M. Eleanor, Paul Ethelbah, and Genevieve Ethelbah. 2012. "Ndah Ch'ii'n": A Journey between Worlds. In *Inside Dazzling Mountains: Verbal Art of the American Southwest*. David Kozak, ed. Lincoln: University of Nebraska Press.

Nevins, Thomas and M. Eleanor Nevins. forthcoming. Speaking in the Mirror of the Other: Dialectics of Intersubjectivity and Temporality in Western Apache Metapragmatics. Special issue of *Language and Communication*, "Intersubjectivity: Cultural Extensions and Construals." Alan Rumsey and Eve Danziger, eds.

Opler, Morris. 1938. A Chiricahua Apache's Account of the Geronimo Campaign of 1886. Narrated by Samuel E. Kenoi. *New Mexico Historical Review* 13(4):360–386. http://etext.virginia.edu/toc/modeng/public/OplKeno.html (accessed November 6, 2012).

Opler, Morris. 1996. *An Apache Life-way*. Lincoln: University of Nebraska Press. (Original work published 1941.)

Ramsey, Jarold, ed. 1977. *Coyote Was Going There: Indian Literature of the Oregon Country*. Seattle: University of Washington Press.

Samuels, David. 2004. *Putting a Song on Top of It: Expression and Identity on the San Carlos Apache Reservation*. Tucson: University of Arizona Press.

Samuels, David. 2006. Bible Translation and Medicine Man Talk: Missionaries, Indexicality, and the "Language Expert" on the San Carlos Apache Reservation. *Language in Society* 35(4):529–557.

Sapir, Edward. 1909. *Takelma Texts*. Philadelphia: University of Pennsylvania.

Sapir, Edward. 1915. Abnormal Types of Speech in Nootka. *Geological Survey of Canada Memoir* 62.

Scollon, Ronald and Suzanne B. K. Scollon. 1979. *Linguistic Convergence: An Ethnography of Speaking at Fort Chipewyan*. Berkeley: University of California Press.

Silverstein, Michael. 1993. Metapragmatic Discourse and Metapragmatic Function. In *Reflexive Language: Reported Speech and Metapragmatics*. John A. Lucy, ed., pp. 33–58. Cambridge: Cambridge University Press.

Silverstein, Michael. 1996. The Secret Life of Texts. In *Natural Histories of Discourse*. Michael Silverstein and Greg Urban, eds., pp. 81–105. Chicago: University of Chicago Press.

Silverstein, Michael. 1998. Contemporary Transformations of Local Linguistic Communities. *Annual Review of Anthropology* 27:401–426.

Silverstein, Michael and Urban, Greg. 1996. The Natural History of Discourse. In *Natural Histories of Discourse*. Michael Silverstein and Greg Urban, eds., pp. 1–17. Chicago: University of Chicago Press.

Spitulnik, Debra. 1997. The Social Circulation of Media Discourse and the Mediation of Communities. *Journal of Linguistic Anthropology* 6:161–187.

Tedlock, Dennis. 1983. *The Spoken Word and the Work of Interpretation*. Philadelphia: University of Pennsylvania Press.

Tedlock, Dennis. 1999. *Finding the Center: The Art of the Zuni Storyteller*. Lincoln: University of Nebraska Press. (Original work published 1972.)

Thompson, Stith. 1966. *Tales of the North American Indians*. Bloomington: University of Indiana Press. (Original work published 1929.)

Toelken, J. Barre, and Tacheeni Scott. 1981. Poetic Retranslation and the "Pretty Languages" of Yellowman. In *Traditional American Indian Literatures: Texts and*

Interpretations. Karl Kroeber, ed., pp. 65–116. Lincoln: University of Nebraska Press.

Underhill, Ruth. 1985. *Papago Woman*. Long Grove: Waveland Press.

Vizenor, Gerald, ed. 1997. *Native American Literature: A Brief Introduction and Anthology*. Longman Literary Mosaic Series. Harlow: Longman.

Webster, Anthony K. 1999. Lisandro Mendez's "Coyote and Deer": On Reciprocity, Narrative Structures and Interaction. *American Indian Quarterly* 23(1):1–24.

Webster, Anthony K. 2009. *Explorations in Navajo Poetry and Poetics*. Albuquerque: University of New Mexico Press.

Weiner, James. 1991. *The Empty Place: Poetry, Space and Being among the Foi of Papua New Guinea*. Bloomington: Indiana University Press.

Woodbury, Anthony C. 1993. A Defense of the Proposition, When a Language Dies, a Culture Dies. *Proceedings of the First Annual Symposium about Language and Society – Austin (SALSA)*. Robin Queen and Rusty Barrett, eds. *Texas Linguistic Forum* 33:101–129.

7

"Some 'No No' and Some 'Yes'"
Silence, Agency, and Traditionalist Words

The snake song, where it starts up there by Alpine and clear down to Salt River too, you know. Every place they stop, it has the kind of song they sing down the line. It's real nice, but it's, kind of like a medicine world. So, in a way, for recording there are some "no no" and some "yes," you know, so. It's pretty hard to do. But there are some words that are used for a special prayer, you know, to heal a person. There are some words in there you don't say, you know, that are in the medicine world. It's like that. So that's why. (John Altaha)

It's better to know God. One time I didn't know Jesus. Lot of years I didn't know God, and then later on, today, I came to know him. I used to drink, I used to sell beer, I was a bootlegger. I thought I was doing good but it was bad. . . . But today I serve God. And the Lord is helping me with everything today, since I know him; that he is alive and works in mighty ways. Today he is the only one that's there. (Louise DeClay)

The two quotations that open this chapter come from recorded translation sessions conducted in the homes of John Altaha, a Traditionalist leader, or *diyiń*, and Louise DeClay, a lay leader of an Independent Apache Evangelical Christian Church. Although neither is directly addressing the topic of school language programs, both present arguments that are otherwise wielded in discussions about what should be included or excluded from such programs. For Traditionalists (most of whom also identify as Christian) there are some words you do not say outside of healing ceremonies; words that are associated with what John Altaha calls "the medicine world." Avoiding these words in one's speech across everyday contexts, including schools, is a reflection and enactment of the power associated with them (cf. Fleming 2011). Apache Evangelical Christians also argue that the schools should exclude words associated with Traditionalism but in their case this is because speaking them leads one down a path that they have chosen not to take, and that in their terms must be disavowed in order to, as Louise DeClay says above, "know Jesus." In order to be Christian in their terms it is necessary to see the written Bible as an exclusive (of Traditionalism) source of truth and to see Jesus of that Bible as: "the only one that's there today." In other speeches this same lay leader expounds on the theme "do not serve two masters," explaining that you cannot be truly Christian and also go to Traditionalist dances and ceremonies.

While the two groups disagree on the status of Traditionalist ceremony in relation to Christianity, they converge on the issue of school practice, both holding that words associated with Traditionalist ceremonies are not appropriate to the schools. Fort Apache is not unusual in this respect. It is not at all uncommon for heritage language program developers in indigenous communities to encounter restrictions posed by religious leadership upon what can and cannot be included in school programs. Curriculum developers working on indigenous language programs around the world have reported on this and some lament the silence of heritage language programs on traditional songs and stories, because this excludes from programs items that they identify with "culture" and "oral literature." Many curriculum planners complain that excluding traditional texts reduces the teaching of the language to prosaic matters, less likely to compete with English or the relevant colonial language for the attention of young people.

In this chapter I draw out an apparent paradox: that the silence of school programs on traditional stories and songs reflects neither the failure of such programs to be what they should be, nor an inevitability to their role as instruments of power that communities are resisting. Instead, the silence of school programs on traditional textual forms is a reflection of the fact that they provide opportunities for expressions of concern and control on the part of persons in a reservation community whose authority as speakers of the heritage language is drawn in other terms. Making room for push-back from alternate forms of authority is an affordance of the concept of "indigeneity" (see Chapter 2). Because it is difficult to maintain claims to authenticity without making room for elders and for speakers of an indigenous language amidst shifting fluency among young people, language programs contribute to the relative empowerment of alternate (with respect to the state) leadership in indigenous communities – just not always in terms anticipated in project planning or accounted for in program assessment.

On the Fort Apache reservation conflicting claims to Apache language arose along multiple axes among persons invested with authority to speak it across different public arenas, including schools, tribal council meetings, ceremonies, and churches. One axis of political tension can be traced between Apache language program developers in educational offices and various forms of religious leadership, including Traditionalists and Apache Evangelicals. Another axis of dispute concerned Traditionalist and Apache Evangelical religious leaders and their respective affiliates. As I noted in the second and third chapters, both sets of tensions can be important to political elections, and ramify via extended family, or "clan," politics among Traditionalists, and into skirmishes and fissures among extended families involved in different neighborhood churches among Evangelicals. And, as I hope to show, conflicts and arguments can be frustrating and disruptive but also work to establish relevance and concern for an indigenous language. After all, if it did not matter to people, no one would fight about it.

Language Programs and Religious Leaders

During my field term Traditionalist and Apache Independent Christian leaders (for different reasons) required Apache language programs to exclude language associated with Traditionalist ceremony. Traditionalists described such language as "sacred" and as belonging to the "medicine world" and therefore dangerous, especially for the uninitiated. Apache Independent Christians wanted it excluded as "medicine man talk" because they considered it sinful, and as potentially leading their children dangerously astray. Traditionalist and Apache Evangelical leadership exerted control through different channels. Traditionalist leaders, mostly *diyiń*, but also elder members of prominent Traditionalist families, exerted control in their capacity as cultural experts holding seats on committees and boards with supervisory powers. During my field term the relevant entity was the tribes' "cultural advisory board," which was an arm of Nohwike' Bágowa,[1] White Mountain Apache Tribe Culture Center Museum. Approval from this committee was required of projects and programs having to do with Apache culture and language. Apache Independent Christians exerted control through school boards, or through parents threatening to remove their children from Apache language and culture classes.

In this dynamic environment, determinations as to which forms of language were considered acceptable for programs and which were excluded as "sacred" or as "medicine man talk" were actively negotiated and subject to interventions from multiple interested parties. I worked on several languageprograms and found that the materials excluded from these programs included: Traditional cosmological stories (which could include Coyote stories, with exceptions), Traditionalist songs (both ceremonial and social songs), names of characters from Traditional stories and ceremonies, and certain individual words and idioms attributed with power, or *godiyįh*. One consequence of these kinds of exclusions has been discussed by David Samuels in his work on the neighboring San Carlos Apache reservation (2006). He noticed the prominence in Apache classes of Apache language versions of what were otherwise established as English language school songs and texts. These included songs like "Old McDonald Had a Farm" and "The Star Spangled Banner," translated into Apache and sung to the same melody. For stories teachers relied upon Mother Goose nursery tales like "Chicken Little" or Aesop fables like "The Boy Who Cried Wolf," translated into Apache. Program developers and teachers expressed ambivalence to Samuels about these songs and stories, and lamented the constraints imposed upon them by religious leaders and parents. One teacher said: "I hate those translated songs. But we have to deal with the parents." Samuels explains: "She had wanted to teach her children an Apache song, but some of the parents had been up in arms, because 'they think that's medicine man talk' " (Samuels 2006:536).

As discussed in Chapter 3, I worked on a media-focused language program run through the educational wing of the White Mountain Apache tribe's health authority. Our project director was a tribal member, a mother with young children, and held a graduate degree in social work. She grew up on the reservation and was credited with speaking the language fluently. Our Apache language expert was another tribal member, also a mother with young children who had acquired linguistic training through the Native American Language Development Institute. She taught Apache Language and Culture classes for an elementary school in the community of Cedar Creek on the reservation. She was also considered to be a fluent speaker. Even with fluent speakers working on the project, both with family histories on the reservation, it was difficult for us to anticipate the full range of materials that might be excluded as "sacred," or otherwise controversial.

The project included an Apache language alphabet with photos and sound files. Anticipating the concerns of religious leaders, we avoided terms from Traditionalist stories and songs, but also tried to create content that reflected settings in which students might encounter Apache language, or want to use it. We found, however, that we could not anticipate all the objections that might be raised about our materials on our own. For example, when we consulted with a member of the cultural advisory board, he identified several of our alphabet items as sacred and therefore off limits for language programs. These included two vocabulary words we had chosen to illustrate letters of the alphabet: *'aad*, or 'fog, mist,' and *tł'iish*, or 'snake.' We solved that problem by replacing *'aad* with *'aasitini*, meaning 'policeman,' to represent the "long a" and switched in *tł'oh*, 'rope/thread,' in place of *tł'iish* for the glottalized lateral affricate.

Silence, Omissions, and the Projected Demise of Languages

This sort of intervention and response is not limited to the Arizona Apache reservations but is encountered in other Native American language efforts as well. For example, in Morgan's treatment of Assiniboine language programs at Fort Belknap in Montana she notes:

> Certain subjects were not included in the lessons – paradoxically these were often topics about which students would like to know. Because the language is still used for religious purposes such as the Sun Dance singing and sweats, some young people expressed interest in learning vocabulary used in those particular ceremonies. This knowledge, however, is still considered esoteric and sacred and therefore was not included. (Morgan 2009:227)

Here Morgan contrasts the fact that students are interested in learning Assiniboine idioms proper to the Sun Dance ceremony with the constraints placed by religious leaders. Here language program planners complied with the restrictions placed upon them by religious leadership, but with some regrets. The exclusion of ceremonial language was a felt, and occasionally lamented, absence.

This sort of tension between language program developers and religious leaders has been observed in indigenous communities in the Pacific as well. For example, Florey (1993) worked on language documentation and maintenance in the village of Lohiatala, in Seram, Indonesia, whose members were undergoing generational shift from Alune, an Austronesian language of the Eastern Maluku branch, to a Malay, a language of wider regional circulation. She says:

> Another aspect that restricts access to knowledge . . . is the belief that the power of this knowledge is contained within the precise use of language. Consequently, misuse of language may have disastrous consequences for the individual or the community. (Florey 1993:302)

The language ideology reflected here has parallels in many Native American communities, including Fort Apache. This is part of the justification for why training as a *diyiń* and the circulation of traditionalist songs and stories are so carefully controlled. Florey identifies a consequence of this language ideology:

> [Fluent speakers'] role as possessors of sacred traditional knowledge requires them to limit its transmission, and to use Malay [not Alune] when imparting sacred knowledge in a mundane setting. (Florey 1993:304)

A parallel at Fort Apache for switching to a language of wider circulation in order to talk about sacred matters in a less sacred way is not found in school settings, where the topics are excluded, but in negotiations concerning publication of Traditional stories and songs. For example, several years prior to my field term, the cultural advisory board had approved republication of Grenville Goodwin's *White Mountain Apache Myths and Tales* with a foreword by tribal chairman Ronnie Lupe, and an introduction co-authored by two tribal members and two anthropologists (1994). Because the stories were presented primarily in English, they were not deemed to be *godiyįhgo*, so circulating them was determined to be permissible. The implication being that many of same stories told in Apache would be restricted.

In the same article Florey goes on further to charge that constraints placed on language use by religious leaders were working against language maintenance efforts and leading ultimately to the demise of Alune. She says: "In Lohiatala, it is precisely the domain of indigenous religion that, due to restrictions on the transmission of sacred knowledge ... is hastening the demise of Alune" (1993:304). Returning to Native American contexts, and Western Apache, David Samuels reflects upon the concerns of teachers in language programs:

> On one side, some Christians, many of them Pentecostal, argue that there is language that should not be preserved because of its inexorable links to devilish, un-Christian beliefs. On another side, some traditionalists argue that there is language too powerful to be entrusted to young speakers. The result, as one bilingual teacher explained it to me, is that the broad area of agreement about language learning for young speakers is narrowly delimited and inert. . . . If children want to use Apache language to order a cheeseburger at the vendor's stand, that's fine. But they should not learn anything that risks being construed as medicine man talk. And, as this teacher concluded, why would anyone want to learn that language? (Samuels 2006:551)

This quote makes it eloquently clear that at least some teachers perceive restrictions upon Traditionalist language in school language programs as harming language maintenance efforts. And at first glance it is easy to agree with them.

Having a Voice versus Silence – Heritage in Representative Democracy

Indigenous language programs occupy a political, contested space along several different social boundaries. The most salient boundary to outsiders is between an indigenous community and the surrounding, dominant polity. At this boundary, what is contested is couched in terms of who is included in and who is excluded from institutions like schools, governments, and professional offices through which the community is represented to wider polities. So the most readily reached for and most readily understood moral frame for community outsiders interested in language and cultural survival is that of inclusion and representation. The logic goes that to be treated equally with dominant languages, indigenous languages should be given the same institutional benefits of stabilization and reproduction through standardization, as is true for English, for example. The framing concern of heritage programs is to give indigenous languages a voice in the form of representation in quasi-national public institutions.

Silence and omission in the representational political framework is equivalent to disempowerment. And certainly, in the United States, in the context of public schools, concern about underrepresentation of Native languages in school programs is well justified. Where indigenous language programs exist at all, they tend to be allocated a minor slot in any student's total class time, typically one day per week. Available curricular materials are often lacking, and curricula development underfunded. For example, on the Fort Apache reservation, by comparison with the available materials for English, Apache language curricula tended to be piecemeal, sometimes handmade, and inconsistent across teachers and grades.

Because of the historical placement of indigenous communities with respect to colonialism, in many communities the speakers considered to be most fluent often do not hold university degrees, and tend to be hired on a different basis, and at lower status and pay than other teachers. This complicates issues of accreditation and funding for both personnel and programs in ways that do not apply to majority language programs. Also, because the audience for indigenous language media is circumscribed compared to English and other majority languages, there are fewer media sources in indigenous languages, and fewer supports for the production of indigenous media in a commercial driven marketplace. Therefore, across school programs and publication outlets that might support school programs, underrepresentation is a well-justified concern. It is often the concern of teachers and language planners, but it is not the only indigenous language concern voiced by differently positioned persons within Native American communities.

A Paradox – Silence and Indexing Power Elsewhere

Returning to Apache language programs on the Fort Apache reservation: amidst concern about underrepresentation and fluency loss among the young, religious leaders from Traditionalists to Evangelicals seem to be compounding the problem by requiring programs to be silent with respect to important cultural domains and practices. For some involved in language programs this community imposed silence seems self-defeating. However, it is worth considering silence on "Traditionalism" in school programs from the perspective of those families, elders, and religious leaders who have intervened in school programs to accomplish it. This requires that we treat silence as a kind of symbolic action. As Bauman notes:

> At issue is not simply the expression of symbolic meaning by means of a linguistic code, but the symbolism of the act of speaking or not speaking-itself: What does it mean to speak or be silent? . . . Such conceptions, like all patterns and functions of language, are cross-culturally variable – to be discovered, not simply assumed to be akin to the investigator's own. (Bauman 1983:16)

This is all the more salient when our subject matter concerns the articulation of indigenous communities within national polities. Here, ethnography is a means of attending to voices constituted via alternate terms and alternate forms of action, in dialogue with but not entirely contained by institutions of state.

Gal makes a complementary point about the relative meanings and political uses of silence:

> silence . . . in public life in the West . . . is taken to be a result of passivity and powerlessness . . . In a telling contrast, however, we have ethnographic reports of the paradoxical power of silence . . . silence can also be a strategic defense against the powerful, as when Western Apache men use it to baffle, disconcert and exclude white outsiders. (Gal 1991:175)

Gal's reference to Western Apache here is due to the fact that one of the earliest and best elaborated ethnographic treatments of Native American uses of silence is Keith Basso's "'To Give up on Words': Silence in Western Apache Culture" (1970). The study was conducted on the Fort Apache reservation.

In that article Basso focuses upon interpersonal interactions, but the meanings associated with silence are pertinent to our concerns. It is respectful and appropriate to be silent, or "give up on words," in the presence of persons whose familiarity is in question, whose social relation to you is uncertain, or for whom prohibitions on easy familiarity exist. Examples include kids returning home from long stints at boarding school, strangers, and, importantly, persons being sung over by a *diyiń* in a Traditionalist healing ceremony. Observing silence in these situations is often described as a display of respect, and failure to be silent is taken to indicate carelessness or disregard. That schools are required to maintain silence with regards to Traditionalism makes sense in relation to what Keith Basso describes as the Western Apache use of silence. Silence is used to show awareness of uncertainty, and the limits of one's knowledge and familiarity. Observing silence acknowledges the ambivalent power of others and is an expression of respect (Basso 1990:92–93).

This association between silence and respect is also at play in what other ethnographers of the Western Apache, most notably Grenville Goodwin, have described as avoidance relationships. These are most marked between in-laws of opposite sex, especially mother and son in-laws. And while the strictures of in-law avoidance are not observed today in the same way as in times past, some persons who hold this relation to one another are reluctant to talk to each other or about each other. More than once, following what I knew to be family visits, when I inquired after people who stood to my interlocutor as in-laws, the response was: "I don't know. We didn't talk," and for older persons: "We respect each other."

Another sort of speech avoidance surrounds *diyiń*, and language associated with Traditionalist ceremony and power in everyday life. For an ethnographer this is most evident when questions with consultants veer too close to matters associated with Traditionalist stories, songs, or ceremony, prompting a consultant to quip: "Why would you ask me that? Do you think I'm a medicine man?" And when I was working with consultants to translate Apache language recordings, people who otherwise readily enjoyed doing it were very reluctant to translate the speeches of *diyiń*, even when these were addressed to ostensibly prosaic matters. And consultants simply refused to translate or comment upon a *diyiń*'s songs, which they described as "prayers." So, a way of showing respect for *diyiń* is to be circumspect in speaking to them or about them and their field of knowledge. To talk about them would be considered careless and a display of disregard. So in a sense, religious leaders, when they require that the schools stay silent on matters of Traditionalist religion, are simply extending an avoidance relationship that is already in play in other domains of everyday life.

So I am proposing that in the context of schools, the marked silence concerning words, texts, and idioms associated with Traditionalist religion indicates their power; which is both ambivalent and consequential. The silence of the schools on Apache religious language locates the authority to define such domains away from the schools and distributes it to others in the reservation community. Schools do not simply ignore sacred language, or "medicine man talk," they are called upon to actively avoid it. In this way its presence elsewhere is felt by its absence from schools and from what is published for more general circulation by the culture center museum.[2] The ambivalence and power of Traditionalist religious languages is implicated in ongoing contests and conflicts between Apache Independent Christian and Traditionalist leadership, both of whom make extensive and innovative use of Apache language moral and religious rhetoric in public settings. This has the effect not of silencing Apache voices, but of locating power in Apache language rhetoric of both Traditionalists and Apache Independent Christians in contexts outside the schools and culture center.

While religious language is excluded, it is important that Apache language be included in the school curriculum. Measures to require every student to take Apache language classes and to pass a proficiency exam before graduating high school were passed by the tribal council. Speaking Apache is required of anyone running for tribal council or chairman. And many who sit on the tribal council are also religious leaders, or have close ties to religious leadership. So even while community members intercept language programs to require the exclusion of sacred language or "medicine man talk" this does not represent a blanket resistance to an imposed colonial form. Rather, it is part of a broader strategy to exert control and authority in engagements with government institutions. Indigenous language programs provide opportunities for this and also produce key symbolic means in the mediation of indigenous communities. My point is that they do not do this in isolation from other forms of authority in an indigenous community.

Power of Innovations in Religious Discourse

We have looked at institutions like schools and culture centers as sites of mediation at the boundary between indigenous communities like Fort Apache and surrounding national and international polities. Now let's turn our attention to another boundary with global resonance and reach within the Fort Apache community: the dynamic boundary between Apache Traditionalists and Apache Evangelical Christians. My purpose here is to illustrate the relevance of Apache language use in this domain, and the ongoing innovations in Apache language religious rhetoric implicated in the expression of these conflicting religious positions and commitments.

The Fort Apache reservation supports a proliferation of grassroots Apache Independent Christian Churches (AIC) some with neighborhood identifications like East Fork, Diamond Creek, Cedar Creek, and with the word "Independent" or "Miracle" in their names. As indicated above, there are also Traditionalists, including members of a pan-Apache rivalist movement, discussed in Chapter 5, called the "Holy Ground Movement." There are also Lutherans, Catholics, Assembly of God, and other extensions of Evangelical denominations. Less visible but still present are Mormons and members of the Native American Church. Religious identities such as "Christian" and "Traditionalist" crosscut participation in particular churches. Nearly everyone self-identifies as Christian, though not without contest from others. One of the most common themes in everyday gossiping and in political rhetoric is to question whether or not the object of one's gossip or one's political opponents are "really Christians."

Many Traditionalists attend ceremonies of the Holy Ground Movement, healing and coming of age rituals, as well as one of the Lutheran or Catholic mission churches. The Catholic missions on the reservation cultivate ties to Traditionalist ceremony, and have brought symbols associated with it, like prayers to the four directions, into sanctuary design and liturgy. While Traditionalist identities are internally fluid and inclusive, the boundaries between Traditionalists, the one hand, and AIC together with other Protestant Pentecostal Evangelical mission churches like Assembly of God, on the other, are drawn in sharply by the latter. AIC and Assembly of God congregation members find common cause in being avowedly non-Traditionalist. Refraining from participating in Traditionalist ceremonies is a primary criterion for being a "saved" member of an Apache Evangelical church. Many of my consultants described themselves as having changed church and ceremonial affiliations at different points and episodes in their lives. But at any given time, sustaining membership in an AIC church carried with it an implicitly anti-Traditionalist stance; and participating in Traditionalist ceremonies carried an implicit anti-AIC/Evangelical stance.

This is important because religious rhetoric and affiliation are prominent in political discourse on the reservation. The implicit boundary between Traditionalist and Apache Evangelical political positions is often at the center of ongoing political rivalries and debates. What is interesting from the standpoint of concerns for language maintenance is that in contrast with the Lutheran and Catholic missions (and in contrast with many of the personnel in the Bureau of Indian Affairs office), Apache language use is predominant within Traditionalist and Apache Independent Christian rhetoric. In many cases church and ceremonial exchanges at large AIC revival or Traditionalist exchanges overlap with and can flow directly into political elections. Between religious leadership, schools, and elected government officials, Apache language serves as both a symbol of an Apache nation and a means of differentiation with respect to that national order and with respect to one another.

In what follows I provide examples that illustrate that efforts by various parties to exclude speech associated with Traditionalist ceremony from schools does not hasten the demise of Apache, but in fact contributes to the constitutions of other domains of authority where Apache is spoken publicly and with ongoing relevance to contemporary Apache lives and Apache futures. In this, as in Apache strategies of differentiation treated in previous chapters, speakers establish power, relevance, and healing not by keeping to one side of an imagined boundary between Apache and English languages or between Apache and Western cultural forms, but by addressing and repositioning that boundary, figuring new truths that were already there, and claiming ongoing relevance for their voices.

Innovation and Relevance in Traditionalist Apache Language Rhetoric

Traditionalist religion can be thought of as an umbrella term for religious practices that depend on the ministry of religious specialists, or *diyiń*. *Diyiń* are spiritual leaders whose standing in the reservation community relies on individual reputations for piety and learning. Each *diyiń* is authorized to perform only those ceremonies that he or she has acquired through apprenticeship, which included properly executed exchanges, with other, usually older, more established *diyiń*. There is a wide variety of ceremonies addressed to different purposes. To have the intended effect, a ceremony, which may take hours to perform, must be executed with what other *diyiń* judge to be verbatim fidelity. The most potent language is the songs of ceremony. And for reasons that should be obvious those are not included in this book, or in this chapter. What I do treat here are speeches, or instances of *bá'hadziih*, 'speaking for someone,' given at large public ceremonial exchanges. I will also address translational practices surrounding ceremonies, in which relations between Traditionalism and Christianity, and Apache and English languages, figure importantly. I do this in order to convey something of the ongoing relevance of contemporary Traditionalism to *Ndee bik'ehgo yáti'*, or 'Apache language' as a matter of concern.

The most public manifestation of Traditionalist religion is a coming of age ceremony for girls called the *Na'í'ees*, known as the Sunrise Ceremony in English. The *Na'í'ees* involves elaborated gift, speech, and feast exchanges between two extended families, or clans: that of the girl undergoing the ceremony and that of a woman from an opposing clan chosen to be her godmother. The term *Na'í'ees* describes the focal event of the ceremony, when the godmother massages the girl, called the *Nab'í'eesń*, with her hands and her feet. Through the massage the girl is formed as a woman and for the span of the ceremony and four days after as the cosmological figure translated variously as "Changing Woman," "Painted Woman,"[3] and "Mary." Mary Altaha, during a translation session, described it this way:

> There again, when you say *Nab'í'ees*, you automatically know in your mind that the parents are going to get sponsors, and the sponsors are going to accept, and then all these dinner exchanges, and then crown dancing and all that. And then the final morning, you know, her godmother's going to put her down and massage her by hand and then by foot. And all that ritual, you know.
>
> The whole, it's a big ceremony, *Na'í'ees*. You just know all these things are going to happen. So, you can't just say: "she's going to be massaged," you know. . . . All these things go into, you know, that word.

Crowds for *Na'í'ees* run into the hundreds and the ceremony costs the families thousands of dollars. The ceremony proper proceeds according to a succession of songs, all memorized in Apache and consistent with song sequences recorded in the early contact period. A *diyiń* leads a group of singers, also called disciples, in performing the song sequence, which begins before sunrise and continues until just prior to lunch time, with dancing and with other ceremonial actions accompanying each song that may involve the participation of all present.

Contemporary Traditionalism locates the authority in the land, and in the precedents in particular places for the speech and other actions of elders and ancestors, that have enabled people to live. In oratory that accompanies the *Na'í'ees*, the land, and previous speech associated with it, continue to teach people how to speak and live well. Here is an excerpt from one such speech:

> *hayóó nádách'ikayóó 'ok'ąą siné',*
> wherever you go there's a prayer

kózhiné biyáti' si'ąąyóó, kózhiné' kóde, kózhinágo biyáti' si'ąą, áíyé
There its talk sits in place, there, right there, there its talk sits, and so

. . . dóniiná . . .
long ago

dáh ntł'éégo shidáł'iyátí' ni'
I used to hear good talk you know, [speech at that dance]

'akóó
and so,

náídíshdlá'
I started picking up some.

diyiń . . . dálíní
those medicine men that were living

'áík'éhgo yátí' 'asił'ą́ą́
according to that way, I am making my talk

báá dagone'níł silé' la
I really respect it

The speaker casts the talk of *diyiń* long ago, not in an inert past, but as an active agent extending to the present. Prayer, the still unfolding enabling acts of ancestors, their blessing, sits and talks in places (see also Basso 1996). The speaker models an orientation to ancestral voices as one of listening, of utilizing their precedent to form one's own actions, and respect.

The moral claims to land established through contemporary Traditionalism resonate with ongoing political claims to land, including reservation land. A little further in the same speech, the speaker says:

dohwaa 'indah k'ehgoyáłtí' 'áną́' da
not even one of them were talking like strangers/White people

ni' gozhǫ́ǫ́ní nohwaa dayóósbąá
the people that won these beautiful places for us

As in the previous excerpt, winning these places for the well-being of contemporary Apache people is based upon the agency of those who went before and whose way of speaking figures importantly as an enabling precedent through which the land around them was won. The speaker figures the winning of that land against countervailing efforts of others, *ndah*, or 'White people.' Another translation for *dohwaa 'indaa k'ehgoyáłtí' 'áną́' da* is: 'not one of them was speaking English.' In this and other ways, including work with anthropologists like Keith Basso on place names and narratives (1996), contemporary Traditionalists establish both historical and ongoing relevance for speaking in an Apache way, *Ndee bik'ehgo yáti'*.

Innovation and Relevance in Apache Independent Christian Rhetoric

Counterposed to Traditionalism in contemporary reservation politics (across several Apache reservations) is another significant religious movement: a proliferation of Independent Apache Christian Churches. Any neighborhood is likely to have several such churches, each accompanied by a ramada, or 'shade,' and cooking area, and handpainted signs. These are grassroots Protestant Pentecostal and charismatic Protestant churches. While church leadership is drawn from the local community, many also host non-Apache and non-Indian Evangelical Protestant preachers for tent revivals. One lay leader of the East Fork Independent Christian Church described her church in the following terms:

> There was another church by the shade, East Fork Riverside church.
> We used to go there in the evening.
>
> There were a lot of people used to come and make a lot of noise.
> And here I sure wanna go, just to go over there.
> So one night I went over there,
> And then I start attending every night over there.
>
> And I got saved in June.
> June, July . . . nine months, after that I was still there.
> April, May, June, and then to a year.
> In that month they came to my place when I wasn't home.
>
> And they built a shade too.
> So everyone started coming down here and going to church.
> And that's how we got started.
>
> And James and Bobby Goshenay, and Pete Susan got started building that shade.
> So that's how the church got started.
>
> When I wasn't home, I didn't know they were building the church.
> I was in Whiteriver.

I came home and it was all fixed up.
That's how we got started having church in there.
And they built the shade and they started church service right there.

And later on the church got division already across from Riverside church,
Riverside church, Independent church, and the House of God,
So it was division.
But today is still one, but with the different names.

And then Pete was here for years
And then I start knowing their kids
They bringing them here for years [from Canyon Day]

And a lot of more families start coming in here to the Independent church.
Some, a lot, left this church and went to another.
. . .
We invite a lot of people and they start coming down to our church in fellowship with us.
Now it's how many years, over 11 years now.

And then Pete Susan died.
The revival was here at that time and he died.
But he said to us ahead of time "whatever happens to me if I die, keep the church alive."

And we had a new pastor.
Her name was Theresa Henderson.
And she got married here in East Fork.
She was married to Clinto Rush
Those two run the church.

A lot of people from a Cibecue church come over here in fellowship with us.
We're happy for the people who come in fellowship with us . . .

This is Mrs. DeClay's oral English translation (roughly sentence by sentence) of a speech she first gave to me in Apache. I will turn to Apache language AIC rhetoric in passages from another speech presented below. This passage illustrates the importance of place and neighborhood to the beginnings, divisions, and proliferations of these churches. Pastors are presented as persons with prominent family names and histories of marriage and raising their families in particular reservation neighborhoods. Her account oscillates between division (which can be unpleasant and acrimonious) and conviviality and fellowship in visits and revival meetings with other churches. Here leadership is not based upon seminary training but upon "callings" which are felt by individual persons and recognized by others, who may intensify involvements with a prospective leading church member by building a church on her yard while she is away.

As is clear in Mrs. DeClay's speech, older churches fission readily into new branches, all the while maintaining connections with other independent churches on the reservation through revivals and invited visits. Apache Independent Christian discourse stresses personal salvation, healing, and reading the Bible. Apache Independent Christians orient to the notion of a written Bible as a text that circulates among other Protestant denominations. While there is a copy of the New Testament translated to written Apache, it is in limited circulation. Most AICs read the Bible in English language translation. However, the primary language used in church services and for Biblical exegesis generally is Apache. Among my consultants the terms *bá'hadziih*, 'speaking for someone,' was paired as a translational equivalent with "giving your testimony." And in testifying it was common to present reported speech, or "quotes," from an English language Bible within performances that were otherwise predominantly delivered using Apache language, and to contextualize these quotes with exegesis composed in terms of Apache language moral idioms.

AIC's members effectively claim for individual Christians access to the healing power otherwise associated in Traditionalist practice with *diyiń*. They do this while simultaneously asserting separation between themselves and Traditionalists. Some speakers, like Louise DeClay, are recognized as being especially good at making such translations. In the following passage she makes an allusion to Traditionalist ritual speech in order to pose equivalences between Apache Independent Christians and the healing power attributed to *diyiń*. But these equivalences are made to serve the project of conversion from Traditionalism to an exclusive Protestant Christianity as practiced within Apache Independent Churches. For example:

Nii'godzáń bikázhį Bik'ehgohidaań:
On the surface of the Earth, Jesus:

"I'm the light of the world" *nohwiłʼdii, 'áko*
"I'm the light of the world" he says to us, and so

"The light of the world,"
"The light of the world,"

nohwíbíghe' náńk'ai ditłʼé'íyóó díijįįgo,
if we are living in it today,

> 'Ánishok churchzhį nii'í.
> it's us Christian people on the church grounds.
>
> 'Ákóó nii' ko kedaáł'íyáti', áko
> And so, you're with them on the grounds here talking, and so
>
> Hayóó keł gózhǫ́ǫ́yóó
> Where you're with them, it's good,
>
> > ch'etł'éégo ch'ígo'aał, áko
> > people are smiling/shining, teaching/learning, and so.

Bik'ehgohidaań is a term used by both Traditionalists and AIC for God and Jesus in their respective orientations to Christianity. The surface of the Earth is a recognizable opening line to a number of Traditionalist ceremonies (see "prayer for life" in Basso and Anderson 1973). The image of light striking the surface of the Earth evokes a key moment in the *Na'í'ees* ceremony, and orientation to the rising sun at dawn is pervasive across many Traditionalist healing ceremonies and is also described as an ideal practice for everyday prayer. It is important to note that most church members, including the speaker in this passage, have experience with Traditionalist religion. Mrs. DeClay, when she says "the light of the world" in the context of the surface of the earth, evokes the power to heal associated with Traditionalist ceremonies. However, she follows this with a conditional statement: " 'The light of the world,' if we are living in it today, it's us Christian people on the church grounds." Mrs. DeClay claims that if healing is available today, its locus is with Christians, a religious affiliation she identified throughout her testimony with the Apache language term: *Ánishok*.

In the next passage Mrs. DeClay describes how a Christian person should try to appear to others, or the testimony they provide in their "walk," or their life lived in the open, in view of others. She says:

> Dohwah ch'init'įįgoda.
> Do not be seen to be gossiping.
>
> > "Áíń 'Ánishok highaał"
> > "This is a Christian person walking"
>
> > > daagodígo,
> > > is what they say about you
>
> 'Ákoo kikáázhį 'at'įį'ǫ́ǫ́.
> So it shows on us.

"Shaa'okąą nláá.
"Let her pray for me.

Áń baagodighį.
That person has the healing power.

Áń 'okąą hígháát."
That person, prayer is her walk,"

    dáyóódeé kichejibą' natsídíkęęz, 'áko.
    is what people think about you, and so.

Having the power to heal and walking with prayer are emphasized. This is of course an ideal reached for against unfolding personal and political disputes and gossip that often lead to fissuring of churches and to evaluative discussions concerning whether those who profess their Christianity loudest are "really Christian."

Rebekah Moody, in the years prior to my arrival, had attended the East Fork Miracle Church, where her late husband had been pastor. During that time she realized that by repeating a particular verse of the Bible she could receive the Holy Spirit and heal people by the laying on of hands. While a member of that church she did not participate in Traditionalist ceremonies. In the years just prior to his death, her husband had lost the church in a dispute with a faction of the congregation and had advised her to return to the Lutheran mission. When I was with her she attended church at the Lutheran mission every Sunday, and also participated in Traditionalist ceremonies. The Lutheran church does not recognize healing by laying on of hands, so she did not practice this in church. However, people did come to her with requests to be prayed over. One day early in our acquaintance my back had seized up on the morning of a big interfamily feast that Rebekah had hoped I would attend. When I called with the bad news, she instructed my husband to lay hands on my back where it hurt the most and put the phone to my ear. She prayed for me over the phone and my back relaxed by the end of her prayer. After the phone call I was able to move around, get up, and go to the feast.

Mrs. Moody's grandfather had been a *diyiń* and she had listened to his songs. She described the healing power that came through him, through other *diyiń* of her experience, and to her through the Bible and the Holy Spirit as "the same." While she no longer attended an AIC church, she discovered the ability to heal while attending one. She and Louise DeClay locate the power to heal otherwise claimed by *diyiń* in Christians. In Louise's testimony this is shown outwardly in smiling and in one's walk, which she said carried the image of "shining to the people."

So, the passage above, together with healing by laying on of hands, utilize marked Apache language religious idioms to establish equivalences between Traditionalist ceremony and sanctified speech of Christians; an equivalence that is obviated in Mrs. DeClay's account by divine historical progression and replacement of the former by the latter. As noted before, this use of Apache language to contextualize quotes from the Bible, and to claim the healing power associated with Traditional ceremony while also attempting to supplant it, is typical of AIC churches. It is also common for people to move across different religious affiliations over the course of their lives and to reinterpret the relationship between Christianity and Traditionalism as they do so.

I have argued elsewhere (Nevins 2010) that both Traditionalists and AIC might with justification be considered indigenous religious revival movements. Both emerged in the 1920s and 1930s as critical responses to the challenge posed to local Apache leadership by the Lutheran mission. In both cases, Traditionalist and AIC leadership utilized their experience with precedents in Apache moral discourse and their encounters with Christian missions and with the Bible to claim contemporary relevance for their voices. Both take as a given that the Bible is the word of God. Both claim the right to mediate relations to God and the Bible by drawing upon their own means of speech, and on precedents established in local political and religious rhetoric. However, they do so in competing, conflicting ways. In neither case do they confine their voices to one side of a boundary between Apache and White. Instead, they work at the boundary and reposition it in different ways, while still positioning their voices as indigenous, or Apache, voices.

The two groups disagree profoundly as to the status of Traditionalist stories, songs, and ceremonies. While AIC use Apache language idioms to recontextualize the written English language Bible within Apache rhetorical poetics, Traditionalists, on the other hand, read the Bible into Traditionalist ceremony, cosmological narratives, and song. Drawing upon some of the precedents set by Silas John Edwards, contemporary Traditionalists make their own realizations, discovering anew in moments of translations ways that their ceremonies have always been Christian. Some point to stories of a savior, *Nayenesganí* (He Overcomes Obstacles) born of a virgin, *Isdzan Nadleeshé* (Changing Woman/Painted Woman) and of human beings reestablishing themselves after a world flood (Basso and Tessay 1994). In this argument they have the cooperation of more ecumenical Christian churches. During my research term, Franciscan monks were often in attendance at public Traditionalist ceremonies. Culture centers connected *diyin* to more extensive global ecumenical religious networks.

The terms of translation are emergent and change with ongoing political dialogues. Silas John Edwards in the 1920s formalized a more widespread translational practice when he drew the following correspondences:

Isdzán Nadleeshé (White Painted Woman) for the Virgin Mary.
Bik'ehgohidaań (Because of Whom there Is Life) for God the Father.
Nayenezganí (He Overcomes Evils) for Jesus.

Other *diyiń* have recognized other correspondences. For example, Morris Gooday, commenting to us in an interview about a recording of a *Na'í'ees* he officiated, stated: "These songs tell about the creation of the world and everything that goes on in it. They are like the Bible, especially Genesis." He also described the movement of dancers in the *Na'í'ees* as reenacting the lapping and receding waves of the Genesis flood.

The translational pairing of *Nayenezganí* with Jesus is something that some Traditionalists make, but which is contested and denied by many Apache Independent Christians. However, the term *Bik'ehgohidaań* is paired with "God" across all denominations on the reservation of which I am aware. The Lutheran and Catholic ministers make use of the term, as do AIC and Traditionalists. Many people also use *Bik'ehgohidaań* as a translational equivalent with Jesus. In translation sessions with John and Mary Altaha, the translational pairings through which to describe the source of *Na'í'ees* songs and the source of Apache language emerges through dialogue in translation, emerging as a newly clarified relationship for Mary (PE is "John Altaha," GE is "Mary Altaha," and MN is "Marybeth Nevins" [me]).

PE: *Daits'é bahadot'ąą* . . . the first song they sang.

GE: They sang this song first

PE: yeah

GE: This is the first song they sang . . . although "they" isn't in there. I guess you could say "the first song that was sung."

MN: Okay, "that was sung"

PE: umhm, there you go.

MN: umm aa . . . like in English we'll just say that "they sang" or "they sang it" or "it was sung" but in Apache there are a lot of differences you make that maybe don't carry over much in English.

PE: yeah, right, yeah

MN: and so it's, ah, important when we get the final translation to make sure that we got that . . .

GE: oh yeah . . . to John: "*ánleí, bik'ehgo léni, daits'é nlį́,
Hán eílaí, dał'aha daakwi . . .
Bik'ehgohidaań 'eílai?*"

PE: *Bik'ehgohidań bizhaazhé nił nizané*

GE: *Dáńdi 'oyóó single world*

PE: *Éí, nat'ąą*

GE: I guess what I don't understand is; I was asking him: "who passed this down?"

MN: umm

GE: you know, several people, or one person? And he said "one." That would be, that would be the language that we were born with. He said "Jesus" passed that on to us. So I guess really the way we explain it, I guess, what we should be saying is: "you know, when Jesus gave us our language, that's how it was, and this was the first song he sang, instead of 'they' or 'it was sung.'" We don't have a word in there as to who did it but I guess that's the gist of it.

MN: umm ummm

In this passage, what began as a statement of action with an unspecified agent is progressively delimited through dialogue to a set of primordial relations between *Bik'ehgohidań* (God), *Bik'ehgohidań bizhaazhé* (God's child/Jesus), and what Mary Altaha describes as "our language," and also the first of many songs of the *Na'í'ees*. And this specification of ancestor, and child of ancestor, is explained to Mary Altaha via an idiom of leadership, *nat'ąą*. Less directly genealogical and not named here, but implied, is an action people undertake when they sing the songs of the *Na'í'ees*. The songs enact the singers' own child relation to *Isdzáń Nadleeshé*, 'Mary, Changing Woman, or White Painted Woman,' realized and remembered through singing.

Traditionalist practitioners who were not *diyiń* but who helped orient me by describing parts of the ceremony to me as it was unfolding often made recourse to similar translational equivalents. Some, as in the following passage, cast identities between Traditionalist and Christian cosmological figures as a state of affairs that was already there, and subject to new deferred realizations in translation:

Nłt'éé éí baanasísikęęz sígo
it's good, if you think about it

Okąa'íhí
the prayer

Dzáń Nádlééhé biháńt'íiní
Virgin Mary's power/yellow powder

Contemporary Traditionalists read the Bible into the cosmological figures and the textual forms of Traditional ceremony, songs, and sacred narratives. This is part of a larger translation strategy (Keane 2007; Nevins 2010) through which Traditionalists assert a contemporaneous relationship between Apache and Christian religions, an answer to the challenge of divine succession posed initially by the Lutheran mission, and today by AICs. In doing so they also lay claim to continuous, temporally deep relations to the surrounding landscape and to Apache language.

Keeping sacred language out of the schools is of a piece with keeping a listening, reciprocal relation with ancestral agents. To alienate ancestral speech from the flow of agency established through properly performed ceremonies, stories, and songs threatens to disrupt those ongoing temporal and moral relations. There is a striking parallel between the concerns of Traditionalists to restrict language involving ancestral agencies from school programs and the concerns of many Native Americans with respect to human remains from the relatively recent to the temporally deep human past on the land, which complicates orientations to the Native American Graves Protection and Repatriation Act. Their orientation to the ancestral past is not to "tradition" or to a particular cultural or ethnic identity, as these are understood by the secular state, but a listening orientation involving them in reciprocal moral relation with ancestral agencies embodied in land. Destructive analysis of human remains is akin to alienating the words of ancestors and suborning them to other purposes. The concern is with breaking the moral flow of remembering and of dialogic involvement of parents, grandparents, and temporally deep ancestors.

By contrast, AIC assert divisions between themselves and Traditionalists, and do make strategic breaks of moral involvement with temporally deep ancestors. However, they do not simply assimilate to an imposed Christianity. Instead they make use of aspects of Apache language moral rhetoric which remains unmarked for religious affiliation and loosely shared with Traditionalists. They look for and discover themselves in what was "already there" in the Bible, utilizing their own discursive means. Contemporary miracles place events parallel to events in the Bible, like burning bushes, on the local landscape. Temporally deep relations are drawn to an ancestral source (exclusive of Traditionalism) in the Bible, in the local Christianized landscape and through pilgrimage visits to "the Holy Land."

Below is the penultimate passage from the same testimony, or *bá'hadziih*, given by Louise DeClay, excerpted earlier. She addresses her testimony to the theme of "reading the Bible" In her emphasis on reading the Bible, she, like other AIC, positions herself in a network of similar grassroots and Pentecostal protestant churches extending beyond reservation boundaries. However, as noted above, one of the claims AIC make is access to the healing power otherwise (and for them, formerly) associated with *diyiń*. Therefore, much AIC discourse is polyvalent across these two domains.

For example, in this last passage the speaker draws upon understandings of healing and knowing familiar through Traditionalist ceremony to frame a practice of reading the Bible. Specifically, she encourages people to come to know their bodies through the Bible:

Bible bighe' 'ídaa 'ijaad 'igan ich'íí'QQ, góónla'.
In the Bible, it teaches you about your eyes, your ears, your hands.

'Ákóóya dágowá
And from here the whole [body]

béé k'ehdik'ikii, góónla, béézhí.
you can use it to ask about everything about it, use it.

Éí 'ákóóya bagoch'ik'éí góónla.
And from this in here, you find yourself in what it talks about.

Éíláawá, góónla
Everything [about yourself] is already in there.

Łiłdowá, dákíjáá 'enibíí,
It compares with everything, it even talks about your ears,

Dákíwoo 'enibíít'ah.
They even talk about your teeth.

Dákíkeegecho kígegan, dágowá
Even your big toe, your hand, everything

'At'ééhé dágoki-body, jaa sizį gobíít'ah.
It's there, about your whole body, knowledge about it, it says it.

'Ákóóye daagoz'áá Bible biye' íyah.
It's true too, it exists in the Bible

Háń 'ídats'ak le,
Whoever [hears my word], let him listen.

Háń 'ídahts'ak, the word of God,
Whoever listens to the word of God,

"Háń bijaa golįį ídíts'ak le" ndíigo
"Whosoever has ears, let him hear" it says

While the idea of reading the Bible in order to find your teeth, your ears, and your big toe sounds odd to many non-Apache (or nonindigenous) Evangelicals or Pentecostals, it makes sense in terms of notions of knowledge, the person, the body that characterize healing performed by *diyiń* within Traditionalist ceremonies.

Here the speaker sets up a framework in which Apache Christians should read the Bible for their own revelatory meaning. One should read the Bible in order to "find oneself," and finding points of reflexive complementarity between parts of one's body and parts of the Bible should shape the way one orients to the world through one's body. Here she casts the relationship between people and the Bible by using the reflexive pronoun *łił-* in *łiłdowá* 'it compares with everything.' Whereas in the first part of the testimony (not presented here) she establishes the relationship between biblical narratives and the thoughts of Apache Christians in a manner that draws upon some of the same interpretive practices applied to stories associated with the land (Basso 1996), here she establishes the relationship between what it says in the Bible and all the parts and aspects of a person's body. Again, the "comparison," or mutual reciprocal existence of the Bible and the body, creates a new state in which the Christian's body becomes what it becomes, and therefore perceives what it can perceive, by virtue of how it is shaped through the practice of reading the Bible.

Focus on the body as a way of knowing the world is noted in the literature on Apache and Navajo philosophy, narrative, and ceremonialism (Goodwin 1938, 1994; Nevins 2004:17–22, 30–32; Schwarz 1997, and, for other Amerindian societies, Vivieros de Castro 1996). Myths and some contemporary tales circulating on the reservation are full of incidents in which a person changes bodily form, becoming a *Gaan* (mountain spirit), a water spirit, a deer, an eagle, a snake, a soldier, a bootlegger, etcetera (Goodwin 1994; Hoijer 1938; Nevins et al. 2004). In the stories and in contemporary ceremonies, the steps of a ceremony reestablish or reorient the humanity of the person in part by reconstituting his or her body. The massage portion of the *Na'í'ees*, or girl's puberty ritual, is just such a moment. The girl's body has been "softened," and as her godmother massages her, her body (now becoming a woman) is formed. Ceremonies performed on recent returnees from the wars in Iraq and Afghanistan comprise another such example.

In the passage above, the speaker expresses a relationship between words, the body, and knowledge that would be foreign to most non-Apache Protestants but recognizable to Apache Christians. It sets a horizon of expectation that is different from that of more extended Protestant Evangelical networks and different from that of Traditionalists. This, and Traditionalist translation strategies discussed above, draw upon global discursive flows and upon established local precedents, and, through acts of recontextualization, pose interpretive possibilities for the reservation community that are not reducible to either.

Paradoxes of Voice and Recognition

Reservation public discourse is a contested field in which Apache language holds shifting values and is embodied in different discourse forms. Apache language was used during my field term and valued differently between extended family members in homes, between educators and students in language programs, among Traditionalists in ceremony, among Apache Evangelical Christians in testimony, and among those running for political office. A persistent paradox and challenge for representative democracies in accommodating the difference and diversity posed by indigenous communities is that "having a voice" in dominant institutions, by representing Apache language in schools, can also entail obscuring and even undermining other indigenous voices authorized in other terms. In some indigenous communities, requiring silence on matters of Traditional religion in schools locates the voicing of religious and cultural authority elsewhere in the community.

Therefore, what some language program developers view as a self-defeating conflict may actually work as a sort of sustaining dialectic between language programs and religious and political leadership on the reservation. In the best of circumstances language programs set the heritage language within terms of wider national and international recognition and, in so doing, set precedents religious leaders draw upon in making their own claims to nationally recognized indigenous identities. In turn, religious leaders, who are often the most valorized speakers of Apache language, provide a sort of target for fluent authoritative speech. They also exert control on language programs by placing constraints on language associated with religion, and by locating the power associated with religious language outside the schools in the contested ground between Traditionalists and Apache Independent Christians. I have tried to show that, at least in the case of the Fort Apache reservation, the contested domain of religious leadership is of vital relevance for continuing innovative use of the language.

I suggest that indigenous communities like Fort Apache share parallels of interaction with colonial processes, which is of course part of why so many indigenous communities are currently undergoing language shift. Their colonial histories, involving terms of difference in relation to an encompassing colonizing society, result in inevitable internal complexity of indigenous communities and translate today into parallel complexities of mediation within national and global social orders. The complex dialectic between language programs, religious leadership, and the continuing relevance of indigenous language use in the Fort Apache case instructs us to look for parallel complexities in indigenous communities elsewhere. Let me be clear that I am not arguing that school programs damage the fragile authority of religious leadership and that teachers and linguists should just leave indigenous communities alone. Indeed, by presenting a local indigenous language as a matter of concern, school and museum programs provide an opportunity for the ongoing enactment of the authority by local leadership. Part of that authority is, as Mr. Altaha states, to identify where "there are some 'no, no' and some 'yes.'"

I recently presented a paper on the complexity of community involvements in language programs to a conference audience that included Arizona language education policymakers. After my talk some commented that Fort Apache had a reputation for "factionalism." The same term has been used to describe most of the other indigenous groups of Arizona when plans and programs break down. While acknowledging that political disputes can seem discouraging, it is also true that becoming a focus of "factional" struggle can establish relevance for an indigenous language and encourage its continuing use in ways that tend to go unnoticed by language planners. Even those programs that went down in flames (as ours did, see Chapter 3) mobilize interest, leave new affiliations in their wake, and are followed by yet other attempts. After all, people fight over things that matter to them. The policy argument emerging from this book is not so much that language programs should be designed to deliberately stir up trouble, but that they should not be counted as failures when they do. If the dynamics at Fort Apache have parallels in indigenous communities elsewhere, this is an argument for broadening out forms of support and assessment criteria addressed to indigenous language programs to account for their historical placement and their complex role alongside other sites of discursive innovation in the complex mediation of indigenous communities.

Notes

1 This translates as "House of Our Footprints."
2 At the culture center, as in the schools, *diyiń* are invited to perform ceremonies, which can be as simple as offering a blessing or prayer, and to consult on matters as cultural experts. *Diyiń* are authorized through apprenticeship and training with senior *diyiń*, which is a

different network from that which animates the governing and representative functions of the culture center and schools, but with points of necessary overlap and intersection with them on matters of Apache language and culture.

3   As with the figure of Coyote discussed in Chapter 6, there are many other names for this personage, names that vary across situational use and with the histories of particular families and *diyiń*.

References

Basso, Keith. 1970. "To Give up on Words": Silence in Western Apache Culture. *Southwestern Journal of Anthropology*, 26(3):213–230.

Basso, Keith. 1990. *Western Apache Language and Culture: Essays in Linguistic Anthropology*. Albuquerque: University of New Mexico Press.

Basso, Keith. 1996. *Wisdom Sits in Places: Language and Landscape among the Western Apache*. Albuquerque: University of New Mexico Press.

Basso, Keith and Ned Anderson. 1973. A Western Apache Writing System. *Science* 180(4090):1013–1022.

Basso, Keith and Nashley Tessay, Sr. 1994. Joseph Hoffman's "The Birth of He Triumphs over Evils": A Western Apache Origin Story. In *Coming To Light: Contemporary Translations of the Native Literatures of North America*. Brian Swann, ed., pp. 636–656. New York: Random House.

Bauman, Richard. 1983. *Let Your Words Be Few: Symbolism of Speaking and Silence Among Seventeenth-Century Quakers*. Cambridge: Cambridge University Press.

Fleming, Luke. 2011. Enregistering Avoidance: Language Shift and Performativity of Indigeneity in the Northwest Amazon. Paper presented at the annual meetings of the American Anthropological Association. Montreal, November 18.

Florey, Margaret J. 1993. The Reinterpretation of Knowledge and Its Role in the Process of Language Obsolescence. *Oceanic Linguistics* 32(2):295–309.

Gal, Susan. 1991. Between Speech and Silence: The Problematics of Research on Language and Gender. In *Gender at the Crossroads of Knowledge: Feminist Anthropology in the Postmodern Era*. Micaela de Leonardo, ed., pp. 175–203. Berkeley: University of California Press.

Goodwin, Grenville. 1938. White Mountain Apache Religion. *American Anthropologist* 40(1):24–37.

Goodwin, Grenville. 1994. *Myths and Tales of the White Mountain Apache*. Tucson: University of Arizona Press. (Original work published 1939.)

Hoijer, Harry. 1938.*Chiricahua and Mescalero Apache Texts with Ethnological Notes by Morris Opler*. Chicago: University of Chicago Publications in Anthropology, Linguistic Series.

Keane, Webb. 2007. *Christian Moderns: Freedom and Fetish in the Mission Encounter*. Berkeley: University of California Press.

Morgan, Mindy J. 2009. *The Bearer of this Letter: Language Ideologies, Literacy Practices, and the Fort Belknap Indian Community*. Lincoln: University of Nebraska Press.

Nevins, M. Eleanor. 2010. The Bible in Two Keys: Traditionalism and Apache Evangelical Christianity on the Fort Apache Reservation. *Language and Communication* 30(1):19–32.

Nevins, M. Eleanor, Thomas J. Nevins, Paul Ethelbah, and Genevieve Ethelbah. 2004. "He Became an Eagle": A Contemporary Western Apache Oral Narrative. In *Voices from the Four Directions: Contemporary Translations of Native American Oral Literature*. Brian Swann, ed., pp. 283–303. Lincoln: University of Nebraska Press.

Nevins, Thomas J. 2004. World Made of Prayer: Alterity and the Dialectics of Encounter in the Invention of Contemporary Western Apache Culture. Dissertation, Anthropology Department, University of Virginia.

Samuels, David. 2006. Bible Translation and Medicine Man Talk: Missionaries, Indexicality, and the "Language Expert" on the San Carlos Apache Reservation. *Language in Society* 35(4):529–557.

Schwarz, Maureen Trudelle. 1997. *Molded in the Image of Changing Woman: Navajo Views on the Human Body and Personhood*. Tucson: University of Arizona Press.

Viveiros de Castro, Eduardo. 1996. Cosmological Deixis and Amerindian Perspectivism. *Journal of the Royal Anthropological Institute* 4:469–488.

8

Sustainability

Possible Socialities of Documentation and Maintenance

Tricksters roam the rearview mirror. (Vizenor and Lee 2003:69)

I'm giving a little bit of words. (Pete Moody, *bá'hadziih* at a dinner exchange)

My aim throughout this book has been to elucidate a particular axis of community articulation – one that bears upon the history of the Fort Apache reservation and the Americanist tradition in anthropology and linguistics: relations between university-accredited language experts and members of indigenous communities. I have presented an account from my experience on the Fort Apache reservation and contextualized that account within a history of documentary encounters there. At Fort Apache and in reservation communities elsewhere, indigenous languages have become boundary works through which university trained language experts and indigenous community members orient to one another and encompassing polities. Through the various chapters in this book I have demonstrated that encounters between university-accredited language experts and indigenous speakers who found their authority in other terms are often characterized by misrecognition, unintended consequences, and experiences of push-back from their opposite number. From the perspective of either party the effort to "save a language" can be a messy, or, as Sapir might have put it, a "leaky" process of creation and destruction.

Rather than being cause for alarm, my argument is that this messiness should interest us. It tells us that there is more to language shift, documentation, and maintenance than is apparent in the polemics of the language

Lessons from Fort Apache: Beyond Language Endangerment and Maintenance,
First Edition. M. Eleanor Nevins.
© 2013 John Wiley & Sons, Inc. Published 2013 by John Wiley & Sons, Inc.

endangerment literature. Exploring this messiness via ethnography offers to those concerned about language endangerment more than a critique of some of the blind spots of existing programs. What this sort of exploration offers is an expanded view of documentation and maintenance. We learn that these programs and efforts are something more than what their proponents claim them to be.

From Silas John Edwards' Holy Ground Movement to Lawrence Mithlo's attempt to alter what he described as *ndah*, or 'White' understandings of Apaches (Chapter 5), I have tried to reveal histories of documentation and maintenance as ambivalent and complex forms of civic engagement, regardless of whether they were understood as such by the researcher or documentarian. More recent local controversies surrounding language programs (Chapter 3), including interventions and limits placed upon programs by religious leadership (Chapter 7), direct our attention to the relevance of indigenous voices to the success and failure of programs, and should inform in a hopeful way how we think about the role of research in the political articulation of communities. Based upon the view this study affords, I sketch out a few propositions about what some have been proposing as a "symmetrical anthropology" (Latour 1993:103) and for what some from communities that have historically been assigned roles as the subjects of research have termed "decolonizing methodologies" (Smith 1999).

Perhaps obviously, it is neither politically sustainable nor accurate to proceed as if the community has the problem and the researcher has the answer to that problem. It is unfounded to even assume that they are concerned with the same sorts of things, even when they use the same terms, like "language loss," to talk about their concerns. To begin to address this I have made use of work in linguistic anthropology upon processes of entextualization (Bauman and Briggs 1990; Keane 1995, 2007; Mannheim and Tedlock 1995; Silverstein and Urban 1996). As the researcher is establishing her objects, community members carry on alongside her making their own, but in different ways and for different purposes. To quote Keane (2007:256), "what looks like discursive objectification can have sources other than just the disciplines, routines, and institutions associated with modernity." Attending to processes of entextualization outside documentary contexts in the nicknames, teasing, and wordplay that takes place among friends and family, in the oratory, narrative and song associated with ceremonial contexts, in the noted and recited words of respected elder family members – this provides a window on alternative ways of reflecting upon language and having a stake in it.

In previous chapters I have discussed stories, speeches, place names, all as examples of entextualization. I have tried to show how the attributed object-like quality of entexualized discourse allows what people identify as "the same" text to serve as a boundary object across contrasting regimes. This was the case for Lawrence Mithlo's account of "Old Apache Customs," explored in Chapter 5 (Hoijer 1938). Mithlo's oratory carries multiple frames at once. What for Hoijer stood as an item in a text collection documenting an Apache past was simultaneously constructed by Mithlo as persuasive speech directing his anthropological interlocutor to a new perspective upon their relation to one another. Different contextual frames can, as in this case, work against one another, destabilizing interpretive closure. Contrasting contextual meanings adhering to the same text tease at one another, turning documentary objects into Vizenor's "tricksters roaming the rearview mirror."

I draw upon Vizenor to suggest an alternate point of view from which to look at documentary objects. With "tricksters roam the rearview mirrors" he attributes to his imagined subject the shifting perspective of a traveler. Spotted through the rearview mirror as one goes along, the traveler's view of others she passes by is a partial one. Documented words, names, sentences, collected texts stand as remnants of past encounters, snapshots of others caught in the rearview mirror. The traveler may systematically assemble those texts that she has gathered, but the gap between the traveler's collection and the perspectives and positions of those speakers who presented them to her tugs at their meaning and calls out for an accounting. Person-relations, as partial involvements with others' perspectives, intrude on the documented text. Documented objects, in the traveler's line of hindsight, can become tricksters that tease at their attributed status in the record. As such, their meanings remain open ended and subject to reinterpretation and to new recognitions as they circulate to new contexts (also discussed by Moore 2006).

Contextualizing Documentation – the Tease of Texts across Multiple Regimes

Documentary field linguists are indeed travelers. They traverse long distances for little pay. Some battle local bureaucracies and prejudices in order to create new infrastructure in the form of dictionaries, school curricula, or voting ballots and may work in myriad other ways as political advocates for the communities they work with. While it is possible to read this book as a critique of documentation and maintenance, I do not see my argument as a critique. Instead, I invite readers to understand and support documentation and maintenance differently than the language endangerment literature would have us understand and support them. Where the endangerment literature describes language endangerment and documentation as opposed processes, a broader consideration of history and social context reveals endangerment and "saving" languages to be aspects of a continuous overarching process of negotiated political incorporation. From this standpoint, rather than saving and preserving something from the past, it is more accurate to describe documentation and maintenance as innovative social actions directly articulated with ethnonational forms of political recognition and participation, but also amenable to open-ended, underdetermined consequences and opportunities.

A central argument of this book is that the textual focus of documentation enables multiple possibilities at once. To illustrate what I mean by this I will treat local uses of a Western Apache–English language dictionary (Bray 1998), which was published by Bilingual Press and is in reasonably wide circulation on the reservation. Editor Dorothy Bray worked with a council of elders at Fort Apache to come up the dictionary entries. The names of contributors are acknowledged at the beginning of the book but do not appear with any of the dictionary entries. So in this respect the dictionary was similar to most dictionaries. Words appear as impersonal items, apparently common to Western Apache as quasi-national language.

Rebekah Moody's late husband, Neal Moody, was among those who participated in the dictionary project and his name appears in the credits. From listening to my host family read the dictionary and comment upon its entries, I learned that the dictionary project intersected in interesting ways with local naming practices. As several ethnographers and linguists have noted, coining new Apache language names and coming up with creative reinterpretations of old names is a highly valued verbal skill. Names coined and circulated are appreciated for their wit and aptness of fit to the place or situation to which they are applied (Basso 1996; de Reuse 2011; Nevins 2010; Samuels 2001; Webster 2000). Taking note of precedents in the community for creative acts of naming, it perhaps should not be unexpected that the body of entries in the dictionary comprises more than an inventory of conventional terms, but includes what others in the community recognize as signature creations reflecting the wit of noted contributors. Reading the dictionary in the Moody household, a repeated comment was that family members could recognize words that Neal Moody contributed because they remember these as terms he coined and as his favorite expressions used during his tenure as a minister for an Apache Independent Christian church. Similar repersonalizing practices applied to dictionaries have been attested in other indigenous communities as well (e.g. Morgan 2009).

On the one hand, the Western Apache–English dictionary sits on the shelf of the reference libraries of the world as a Western Apache addition to global multilingual resources. On the other hand, entries were actively personalized and attributed with the intent, sometimes described as the prayer, of the individual contributors. In this case, textual qualities, the objectification of speech through documentation, has left the use of those objects open ended and enabled new acts of creative recontextualization. As noted by Keane:

> [entextualized] speech – like the materiality of physical objects – leaves it open to appropriation in new contexts, its various properties shifting in their relative utility and significance, serving new purposes. The power of speech is not that it works, in Bakhtin's terms, as either utterance or text (1986:74), but that it can be both, as it plays its roles in different representational economies and gives rise to different modes of objectification. (Keane 2007:269)

Therefore, entextualization across two different regimes, in this case the signature neologisms of individual elders and reference-style dictionary entries, can be paired, and through pairing turned to multiple meanings and purposes. The dictionary becomes a means of bringing these two realms of meaning to bear upon one another in new ways. Even as texts are retuned and attributed with different meanings and purposes in a new context, they can also retain associations with prior contexts across different regimes. So the resonant authority and wit of particular elders teases at the dictionary entry in its appearance in schools and libraries for anyone who can recognize them; and the library or "reference" function of the dictionary entry teases at and amplifies the personal meaning attributed to their relative's words among the family of the contributors.

This demonstrates that researchers' or teachers' goals and meanings need not be the same as that of other stakeholders for their actions to complement and expand upon each other. What is at stake, what makes a language effort sustainable or not, does not depend upon perfectly matching a project to community norms (a moving, variable target in any case), but in building political negotiation into projects from the beginning and being mindful of difference in perspective between the various actors and stakeholders. For linguists this might mean scaling back their ontological claims and presenting what they identify as "language" as a reflection of their particular disciplinary interests and allowing for other definitions to stand as commensurable to their own and just as salient to the matter at hand. In practice the account presented in this book reflects what most documentary linguists and those who work in language maintenance are already doing when they work with communities. The implication is not that language workers should alter their practice, but that we need to change some of the ways they are understood by their disciplinary peers and supported by funding agencies. Accordingly, I have tried to show that sometimes apparently failed projects in fact contribute to the political sustainability of locally voiced concerns to "save our language" and the fact that indigenous language are very much of interest and at stake in community politics.

The Instability of Endangerment

While most of what I have discussed in this book supports an understanding of documentation and maintenance as open-ended deliberative practices, I do offer a critique of notions like "endangerment," "salvage," and "preservation." In the case of language endangerment as a cause articulated by linguists to justify the funding of language documentation, political sustainability problems can be exacerbated by the way that structural linguistics defines its object. For linguists the language defined or "discovered" through documentation presents itself to them already alienated from human action and intention, in this case already alienated from authorship and agency of exactly those people whom documentation and maintenance projects are ostensibly designed to benefit. We cannot assume that concern with an indigenous language presents itself in the same manner to members of indigenous communities. In critiquing endangerment I am not saying that there is no "danger" that neocolonialism and continuing political incorporation on unequal, coercive terms pose to the ability for indigenous speakers to form their communities as they choose. I also do not deny the poignancy of shifts away from an indigenous vernacular and alarm expressed by community members at what it lost to them by its dwindling viability among younger people. What I critique is the use of language endangerment in ways that trump the voices and political agency of members of affected communities by locating the authority to define the problem outside their reach. My critique is addressed to the rhetorical cover endangerment provides to neocolonial politics in the relation between scientific research and indigenous communities.

Language endangerment is a resource mobilization tactic and draws upon public familiarity with established "green politics" rhetoric of species endangerment and ecological crisis. As Latour (2004) points out, scientists play a special role in green politics. The statements of scientists have a different status than the statements of activists, advocates, and politicians. No matter how politically divided the internal world of scientific disciplines may be, when scientists are asked to speak as experts to the public, to represent "Science," they are presumed to speak from an ostensibly apolitical realm, a world of facts that are not subject to human agency. Scientists' words carry more unquestioned power than the words of politicians or activists because they speak for Nature. The special status of Science renders the public speech of scientists closed to debate and therefore impinges upon public life as a sort of deliberative black box.

Linguists assume a parallel role to that played by ecologists and population biologists with respect to language endangerment. Consistent with natural scientists, they render their object of analysis as if it belonged to an apolitical realm, separated from human agency. Documenting languages establishes grammars as facts that in comparison demonstrate the underlying equality to all languages, including politically stigmatized ones. In this way documentation contributes devices of political negotiation that can be useful to indigenous communities. And this is part of what motivates the study of "endangered languages" as socially relevant research. What is left unaccounted for, though, is the relevance of indigenous persons and voices to the state of indigenous languages.

The delimitation of linguistics to matters divorced from human intentional action was the subject of an anthropological critique of modern linguistics launched by Hymes forty years ago. Hymes noted how modern linguistics appears to succeed in having it both ways: to define an object denuded of human agency while also claiming to define something of great significance to human life:

> A major characteristic of modern linguistics has been that it takes structure as primary end in itself, and tends to deprecate use, while not relinquishing any of its claims to the great significance that is attached to language. (Contrast classical antiquity, where structure was a means to use, and the grammarian subordinate to the rhetor.) The result can sometimes seem a very happy one. On the one hand, by narrowing concern to independently and readily structurable data, one can enjoy the prestige of an advanced science; on the other hand, despite ignoring the social dimensions of use, one retains the prestige of dealing with something fundamental to human life. (Hymes 1972:56)

While the role of linguistics in language endangerment resembles the role of natural science in ecological endangerment, there is an important difference. Natural scientists speak for the nonhuman world that cannot, at least in conventional terms, speak for itself. Saving languages, however, is different because here scientists are not speaking for the viability of breeding populations or wetlands or global climate. Rather, in this case they are speaking on behalf of the speech of other human beings, for what some linguists have termed "vanishing voices" (Nettle and Romaine 2000).

This raises inevitable and uncomfortable questions. Do linguists rightfully claim the role of spokespersons for indigenous languages and voices? To the extent that language and language shift belong to the realm of human political agency, on what basis should scientists, as opposed to the bearers of indigenous languages, be accorded the authority to define them? For example, one of the people who I worked with in an educational office complained about the linguistic presentations at the Athabaskan language conference, saying that he found listening to White/*ndah* strangers use Apache and other Dine languages to claim authority for themselves made him uncomfortable, even angry. He felt as if these linguists were stealing something that did not rightfully belong to them. These questions and concerns may well be answerable, but they have only begun to be broached in the endangerment literature (Dobrin 2008, 2012; Rice 2011) and linger as unacknowledged disputes expressed through community responses to and interventions upon research and programs.

Therefore, I am critical of "language endangerment" rhetoric not because I want indigenous languages to fall by the wayside, or because I am opposed to language documentation and maintenance programs, but because the rush to save languages for science bears no safeguard for pluralism and it is applied to communities historically disempowered by histories of colonial domination. The urgency and implicit scientism of "endangerment" trumps deliberation with urgency.

We Have Never Saved Languages

The subtitle for this section is a playful allusion to a well-known treatise by Bruno Latour (1993). In making my own rather imprecise use of it I am not suggesting that there have been no language programs that can be counted as successes. What I am saying is that those programs that do flourish arrive at that status not through the narrow terms defined in the language endangerment literature, but through successful political negotiations garnering sustained participation and interest among community members. Therefore, we have never saved languages in the terms in which we thought we were saving them. And language has never been that isolated object denuded of human agency that we made of it. Language programs have succeeded not as forms of well-honed mechanical reproduction, but as political engagements. Therefore I draw an important distinction between the rhetoric of language endangerment and the practical workings of language documentation and maintenance programs within communities. To quote Latour:

> The moderns have always done the opposite of what they said: *this is what saves them!* There is not one thing that is not also an assembly. Not one matter of fact that does not drag behind it a long train of unexpected consequences that come to haunt the collective by obliging it to reshape itself. (Latour 2004:193)

Community-engaged researchers, then, confront a paradox made visible once we shift our gaze from grammars to the political sustainability of community-research relations. Projects often "fail," at least in terms of their stated goals and with respect to the internal accounting system of funders. But here I suggest that sometimes their failure as projects is actually what saves them as negotiated political engagements. Failed programs do not fail in a vacuum: one network has been intercepted by another and broken. Interventions and limits placed on programs, as described in Chapter 7, and controversy surrounding a program as described in Chapters 2 and 3, can paradoxically reflect sustainability, if we recognize the latter as the continuing viability and relevance of indigenous voices in defining what it means to know and speak the language in question. Attending to alternative authorizing networks (in this account extended families and religious leadership), and to the meanings and purposes attached to "saving language" among them, reveals programs that have suffered interceptions, limits, or failure to be more interesting and more hopeful than they might at first appear.

In the preceding chapters I have tried to peel back the historical curtain and show that objects of language documentation have never been reducible to isolated facts of grammar, but have always been refractions of the persons, utterances and political–ethical relations that brought them into being. I have placed documentation and maintenance alongside the "long train of unexpected consequences" that they unwittingly provoke. I point to breaking points, friction, and push-back, not in order to proclaim to linguists and teachers: "See! you were wrong after all," but because against the authority claims of linguistics as a science, the vulnerability to breakage and friction is precisely what saves documentation and maintenance as politically and ethically sustainable practices in the articulation of indigenous communities. Indigenous community members interceding and reworking the products of documentation to alternate purposes, circulating the texts and languages of colonial encounter to unexpected places (Deloria 2006) as in the dramatic case of Silas John Edwards and the Holy Ground Movement (Chapter 5), this is where the work of an indigenous collective continually reshaping itself occurs.

Telling a Better Story: Sustainability, Equivocation, and Reciprocity

A good deal of innovation is made possible by documentation, including much that those who document languages will inevitably remain unaware of. Many readers may object that I have not given due attention to what is now best practice in language documentation and maintenance: collaborative projects that involve coordinating researcher and community goals, that accord expert status to indigenous vernacular authorities and that provide access to formal university training for local language advocates (e.g. Field 2008; Hinton and Hale 2001; Thieberger 2012). The projects I worked on were collaborative in this way as well and still occasioned push-back and interception. My point is that the capacity for interception, the capacity to break scholarly networks, to say "no" to programs, while painful, is also necessary to their political and ethical sustainability. I argue that the messiness, controversy, and vulnerability to breakage attending the work of field linguists and indigenous language teachers in communities, is a hopeful sign of movement towards symmetry, or decolonization, in research relationships. What we need is to tell the story of engagement in language programs in ways that better recognize the success of apparent failures.

While the poetics of endangerment works against the political interests of indigenous persons in ways described in Chapter 2, if it is turned into a critique of that which caused the endangered state, and towards defining a sustainable alternative, those disadvantages can be obviated. Shifting our rhetoric from "saving" what is inevitably "endangered" to cultivating "sustainability" frames the purpose of indigenous language programs in terms that require the inclusion of indigenous agency, and suggests the health and well-being tropes evident in many community-generated programs.

Second, while communities should not be expected to grant linguists privileged authority to define indigenous languages, it is also neither necessary nor desirable that researchers simply adopt what they take to be the perspective of the people that they work with. Instead, what researchers might do is amend their claims about the ontological status of their objects of documentation. Rather than posing the artifacts of documentation as a straightforward account of the language in question, allow for documentation's equivocal status as boundary work with open-ended meanings and purpose. Rather than claiming to be able to save the language by documenting it, linguists might ask for permission to practice their craft for their own disciplinary purposes, and suggest ways that the products of that research might be useful or valued by community members. This gives the linguist a dual role: the center of her own research project and a consultant in contexts in which she is welcomed onto projects authored and controlled by community members. This is in fact what already happens in communities that have developed precedents for community-generated language projects.

And finally, if allowance is made for different objectives, the definition of research relationships must be moved from a poetics of contract around common objectives to that of reciprocity between persons whose objects are understood to be different, or equivocal. This is already a pervasive mode of action in the political articulation of Fort Apache and many other indigenous communities. Consider this short passage from a speech given by an Apache political leader "speaking for" his own family in the context of dinner exchanges leading in to a *Na'í'ees*, or 'Sunrise Dance,' a coming of age ceremony for girls.

Ai' deeyǫ́hago bich'ịsh'aah	I'm giving a little bit of words
Didáń deeyǫ́hago nohw'aah, datsį́ né'	We gave a little bit of food, as can be seen
'Okąąhí biłgo'adi'į́į́	We do it with prayer
(Pete Moody, *Nabíeesń bá'hadziih*)	

The speaker reflects upon what he is doing as offering up words and presenting them alongside a feast prepared by his own camp to a family different from his own. This moment of reflecting upon his own speech *deeyǫ́ha . . . bich'ịsh'aah* 'give a little bit [of talk] about it,' casts his act of speaking in terms analogous to the act of giving the prepared food *didáń deeyǫ́ha nohw'aah*, 'give a little bit of food.' Talk, like the feast, is rendered an object of reflection, a prepared offering extended from his person on behalf of his camp and offered for reception by the other assembled family camp. Alongside gifts of food, gifts of words are offered in reciprocal exchanges between families who otherwise stand to one another as different, or other. Could language expert and community participation be modeled on reciprocal "gifts of words"? Is this perhaps true in many cases already?

In the Sunrise Dance the two families highlight the difference in perspective between them, each orienting to their counterpart as "the other side," which is the same idiom used to refer to one's political opponents. Through gifts of food and words, cast within an overtly moral and temporalizing frame of "prayer," the families gradually come to establish the possibility of mutual commensurability. What is established through repeated gift and speech exchanges between the families is neither a contract nor a promise, nor a newly discovered transcendent "fact," but a new precedent for mutual recognition linked to other freshly realized precedents and suggestive of future possibilities.

I recognize in Pete Moody's "gift of words" an alternative way of thinking about what is already happening in many researcher–community engagements. Gift exchanges, and their negative counterparts in problems reflected upon as failed reciprocity (Nevins and Nevins 2012), proliferate at all levels of political life. An exchange of gifts is an exchange of implied futures. I suggest reciprocity as a frame for recasting language research and language programs in more politically sustainable, and therefore open-ended terms. Gifts of words can be offered in multiple ways, some of which may only become recognizable once a track record of mutual involvement has been established. As I try to show throughout the book, there is a sense in which this has already been the case in research and language program relations but not always recognized as such. And, as Lawrence Mithlo teaches us, attempted gifts of words and attempted exchange of perspectives can be recognized in new ways long after the fact in that "rearview mirror" which is the Americanist record of text collections.

Shifting the narrative – and the implied ethical frame – through which we understand indigenous language research from "saving endangered languages" to "sustainability" and "reciprocity" in community-research relations would not solve problems. But it would move us away from conferring upon the linguist a singular and untenable authority and towards a more open-ended set of possibilities. Controversies would still emerge around language programs. Projects will still be subject to breakage, interception, and renewal. But these would be understood as deliberative acts, not the failure of a system to function as it should. Our understanding of the actions of linguists and community members alike would be less gloomy, more democratic – and facts notwithstanding – more accurate.

References

Basso, Keith. 1996. *Wisdom Sits in Places: Language and Landscape among the Western Apache*. Albuquerque: University of New Mexico Press.

Bauman, Richard and Charles Briggs. 1990. Poetics and Performance as Critical Perspectives on Language and Social Life. *Annual Review of Anthropology* 19:59–88.

Bray, Dorothy, ed. 1998. *Western Apache–English Dictionary: A Community-Generated Bilingual Dictionary*. Tempe: Bilingual Press/Editorial Bilingue.

De Reuse, Willem. 2011. Han Athabascan and Western Apache Personal Names. Paper given at the Society for the Study of the Indigenous Languages of the Americas, Session on American Indian Personal Names. Pittsburg, PA.

Deloria, Phillip J. 2006. *Indians in Unexpected Places*. Lawrence: University of Kansas Press.

Dobrin, Lise. 2008. From Linguistic Elicitation to Eliciting the Linguist: Lessons in Community Empowerment from Melanesia. *Language* 84(2):300–324.

Dobrin, Lise. 2012. Reading the Encounter from between the Lines of the Text: Ethnopoetic Analysis as a Resource for Endangered Language Linguistics. *Anthropological Linguistics* 54(1).

Field, Les. 2008. *Abalone Tales: Collaborative Explorations of California Indian Sovereignty and Identity*. Durham: Duke University Press.
Hinton, Leanne and Kenneth Hale, eds. 2001. *The Green Book of Language Revitalization in Practice*. Bingley: Emerald Group.
Hoijer, Harry. 1938. *Chiricahua and Mescalero Apache Texts with Ethnological Notes by Morris Opler*. Chicago: University of Chicago Publications in Anthropology, Linguistic Series.
Hymes, Dell H. 1972. On Communicative Competence. In *Sociolinguistics*. J. B. Pride and Janet Holmes, eds., pp. 269–285. Harmondsworth: Penguin.
Keane, Webb. 1995. The Spoken House: Text, Act and Object in Eastern Indonesia. *American Ethnologist* 22(1):102–124.
Keane, Webb. 2007. *Christian Moderns: Freedom and Fetish in the Mission Encounter*. Berkeley: University of California Press.
Latour, Bruno. 1993. *We Have Never Been Modern*. Cambridge, MA: Harvard University Press.
Latour, Bruno. 2004. *Politics of Nature: How to Bring the Sciences into Democracy*. Cambridge, MA: Harvard University Press.
Mannheim, Bruce and Dennis Tedlock. 1995. Introduction. In *The Dialogic Emergence of Culture*. Dennis Tedlock and Bruce Mannheim, eds., pp. 1–32. Urbana: University of Illinois Press.
Morgan, Mindy J. 2009. *The Bearer of this Letter: Language Ideologies, Literacy Practices, and the Fort Belknap Indian Community*. Lincoln: University of Nebraska Press.
Moore, Robert, E. 2006. Disappearing, Inc.: Glimpsing the Sublime in the Politics of Access to Endangered Languages. *Language and Communication* 26:296–315.
Nettle, Daniel and Suzanne Romaine. 2000. *Vanishing Voices: The Extinction of the World's Languages*. Oxford: Oxford University Press.
Nevins, M. Eleanor and Thomas J. Nevins. 2012. "They Do Not Know How to Ask": Pedagogy, Storytelling and the Ironies of Languages Endangerment on the Fort Apache Reservation. In *Telling Stories in the Face of Danger*. Paul Kroskrity, ed., pp. 129–150. Norman: University of Oklahoma Press.
Nevins, Thomas J. 2010. Between Love and Culture: Misunderstanding, Textuality and the Dialectics of Ethnographic Knowledge. *Language and Communication* 30(1):58–68.
Rice, Keren. 2011. Documentary Linguistics and Community Relations. *Language Documentation and Conservation* 5:187–207.
Samuels, David. 2001. Indeterminacy and History in Britton Goode's Western Apache Placenames. *American Ethnologist* 28(2):277–302.
Silverstein, Michael and Urban, Greg. 1996. The Natural History of Discourse. In *Natural Histories of Discourse*. Michael Silverstein and Greg Urban, eds., pp. 1–17. Chicago: University of Chicago Press.
Smith, Linda Tuhiwai. 1999. *Decolonizing Methodologies: Research and Indigenous Peoples*. London: Zed Books.

Thieberger, Nicholas, ed. 2012. *The Oxford Handbook of Linguistic Fieldwork.* Oxford: Oxford University Press.

Vizenor, Gerald and Lee, Robert A. 2003. *Postindian Conversations.* Lincoln, NE: University of Nebraska Press.

Webster, Anthony. 2000. The Politics of Apache Place Names: Or Why "Dripping Springs" Does Not Equal "*Tónoogah.*" *Proceedings of the Seventh Annual Symposium about Language and Society – Austin (SALSA). Texas Linguistic Forum* 43:223–232.

Appendix A
Lawrence Mithlo (Hoijer Text 39: Old Apache Customs[1])

(39.1)
'Iłk'idą́, in"daaí 'it'ago hąhé łą́ daolaahát'édadą́,
Long ago, at a time long before there were many white men,

  "déí 'ił'ango 'ádaahooghéí díík'eh joogobago daahi"dáná'a.
  all of the different ones who are called Indians lived poorly, they say.

'Íyą̀ąda k'adi, Chidikáágo hooghéí 'ásht'į́.
But anyhow, I am one of those called Chiricahua.

Shin"déí, biłn"dénshłį́í,
My people, those people with whom I live,

  dásídá'át'égo 'iłk'idą́ daahi"dáná'aí baanałdaagosh"di.
  I shall tell you exactly how they are said to have lived long ago.

(39.2)
Daanahitsóyéí dáłeezhíighe'yá daahindáná'a.
Our grandfathers lived in the dirt, they say.

Dátł'ohná beekooghąshį́ dá'ádaa'ílaa.
Their houses were made only of grass.

Tł'oh bégoos'eelyá naasjé.
They lay on grass that had been spread out.

Ch'ide yá'édį.
There were no blankets.

Lessons from Fort Apache: Beyond Language Endangerment and Maintenance, First Edition. M. Eleanor Nevins.
© 2013 John Wiley & Sons, Inc. Published 2013 by John Wiley & Sons, Inc.

Beekooghaní yá'édį.
There were no tents.

Dooha'shį́ ła'jóláhát'éda.
None could be secured anywhere.

'Iban 'ádaat'éí gotł'aazhį k'édaadeesdizná'a.
Things like deerskin were wrapped about them, they say.

Naagołtįgo, tóí gok'izhį nkeedanlį́.
When it rained, the water flowed down upon them.

Zas naałtįgo, zasí gokázhį naadaałtį.
When it snowed, the snow fell on them.

Hago, dákǫǫná daagoch'ide.
In the winter, only the fire was their blanket.

(39.3)
'Ádą́, dák'aaná.
At that time, there were only arrows.

"Dé bik'a' k'aast'ą́.
The Indians' arrows were feathered.

'Áí k'aaí bilátahee tséí hiisk'aashgo k'ádaas'ą́.
Those arrows had sharpened stones set into their tips.

Daagok'a' dá'áíbee, naagojinłdzoo.
With just those arrows of theirs, they went to war.

Dá'áíbee, bįį, náa'tsíli, dáhaadí daajiyą́í, beenaadaajiłtsee.
With those only, deer, cattle, [and] anything that they ate, they killed.

(39.4)
Tsébeeshdiłtł'į́déí 'iłdǫ́ 'ijoo"deená'a.
The slingshot was also a help, they say.

Tséghe'si'ą́í 'iłdǫ́ 'ijoo"deená'a.
The stone axe was also a help, they say.

'Íláą́hdéí dáditsį́í dásíntł'izí 'i"daa beedaajóóshiizhná'a.
They fought the white man with spears which were [made of] very hard wood, they say.

(39.5)
K'adi díídíí dá'ákohégo ⁿdé bik'a'ná'a.
Now these were the only weapons of the Indians, they say.

'Iⁿdaanałʔí goostándiłtałí hah'áálgo, díík'ehnyá
You living as white men carrying six-shooters, from this could

ⁿdédáłeendasijaaí beenaał'a'áłádá.
by means of them to make slaves of a whole camp of Indians anywhere.

'Ágołdishⁿdí:
I say thus to them:

"*Naał'a'ánahałaaí nahí Chidikáágo hongéí doobaayándzįda.*
"We who are called Chiricahua are not ashamed that you made us slaves.

Han k'aa nahá'ágólaaná'ań 'áńá yaayáńzįhálí."
Perhaps whoever is said to have made arrows for us is ashamed.

Ákoo, dííjį, 'iⁿdaanałʔí 'iłtį 'ił'ango daadiłtałí
Then, today, you living as white men different kinds of guns

tsįníntsaazí bééshnt1'izí dá'áída díík'eh ghádaaniidágo nahá'ájílaa.
that pierce even big logs and hard metals, someone made for you.

'Ákoo, nahí Chidikáágo hongéí, k'aa nahá'ájílaaní 'it'ago
Then, we who are called Chiricahua, only arrows as before were made

biyeeshxahyá dooł'ináhá'ánáájídlaada."
nothing else did anyone make for us to use."

(39.6)
Góghégo ⁿdé gólįná'a.
The Indians lived a hard life, they say.

Díík'ehí yá'édįná'a.
Everything was lacking, they say.

Béésh yá'édįná'a.
There was no metal, they say.

Bee'itseełntsaaí yá'édįná'a.
There were no big axes, they say.

Bee'itseełbizą́ą́yéí yá'édįná'a.
There were no small axes, they say.

Dátsédeeⁿdíná gobeedaa'itseełná'a.
Only sharp stones were their axes, they say.

Dátsédeeⁿdíná daagobézhená'a.
Only sharp stones were their knives, they say.

Bįįda jiyałhéélgo, tséíbee ńdaajił'ahná'a.
When they killed a deer, they butchered it with stones, they say.

Tséí biyeeshxahyá, bééshdáha'deeⁿdíí gólįná'a.
Besides the stones, there was an even sharper knife, they say.

'Áí goghooíná'a.
That was their teeth, they say.

'Áí 'itsįį beedaajiłghałná'a.
They ate meat with them, they say.

(39.7)
Díídíí dá'ákohégo "Dé bibézhe gólįná'a.
These were the only knives the Indians had, they say.

'Áí nahí doobaayándzįda.
We are not ashamed of that.

Hań 'ághát'égo nahángóńhóń'ąná'ahálíń 'áńá yaodlodaná'ahálí.
Only he who is supposed to have made it so for us probably laughs at us.

(39.8)
'Iłk'idą́, dákǫǫda yá'édįná'a.
Long ago, even fire was lacking, they say.

Ditsį naaki łi' niiyá sitágo łi' bikáshį́ 'óó'ágo baa'nádaa'shdiłhisgo, beekǫǫ hanádaaji'áná'a.
Two sticks, one of which lay on the ground while the other stood erect and fire was made by twirling it repeatedly, they say.

Ditsį 'ałts'ǫǫ ségo daajiyaak'ashí dá'áí 'itsįįsbéézhí beehadaajiⁿdííáná'a.
A slender stick that had been pointed, they used it to take out boiled meat [from the pot] they say.

'Itsįį́ tsíghe'yá jiłt'eesgo 'iłdǫ́ dá'áłbee nábé'ijiyałtsiná'a.
With that also they turned over the meat they were broiling in the coals, they say.

Ditsį́ dáha'á'áłts_QQ_séí bighe' hadaa'jich'iishí dá'áí gobee'nł'dédíná'a.
Somewhat slender sticks in which they had made a hollow were used as spoons, they say.

Ditsįntsaazí 'idaas'áí nanshį́go ditsįdijoolí baadahnaas'áí
Ball shaped stick protuberances that lie on the side of large growing trees

   bighe' hadaa'jił'díí, dá'áí daago'ide'ná'a.
   they had hollowed them out inside, these were cups they say.

'Ikałí 'iłdǫ́ daago'ide'ná'a.
Their dishes were also [of] dried hide, they say.

Dákí gostł'ish 'isaa 'ádaajilaí beedaa'jiłbéézhná'a.
They cooked in clay pots which they had made themselves, they say.

(39.9)
Gahée yá'édįná'a.
Coffee was lacking, they say.

'Ádą́, 'ik'aneída, gołkąądeída, bihóóleída, díídíí díík'eh, yá'édįná'a.
At that time, even flour, sugar, and beans, all of these, were lacking, they say.

K'adi, dá'át'égo nahidáń gólį́í been"dá'ádą́í baanáágosh"di.
Now, I'll also tell what food there was upon which we lived at that time.

Díídíí:
These:

   'Inaada, goshk'an, nshch'į́, 'ighe'éłtsoi,
   Mescal, yucca fruit, piñons, acorns,

   gołchíde, chíłchį, hoshjishóhé, "dáazhin,
   prickly pears, sumac berries, cactus [sp.], spurge,

   tł'ahtso, tł'ohgahée, 'inaadą́ą́', dziłdaiskáné,
   dropseed, lip fern, corn, mountain plants,

   niigoyáhé, gahbi"dáa, naastáné, hanóósan,
   wild potatoes [sp.], wild potatoes [sp.], mesquite, stems of yucca,

   'iigaa'e, dzé, madááya, goł"diihi,
   flowers of tree yucca, chokecherries, pitahaya cactus, honey of the ground bee,

'ináshtł'izhee, tsiłⁿdáá'łtsoi bito'í, tsétkanee, digodé 'it'ąą,
honey [var.], honey of the bumble bee, mulberries, angle-pod,

deek'oshé dach'iizhé, diłtałé, diłtałétso, náa'tsíli,
salt, berries [sp], berries of the one seeded juniper, berries of the alligator bark juniper, wild cattle,

bįį, jilaahé, yóółⁿdáhé, dziłátaazhe,
mule deer, antelopes, white tailed deer, wild turkeys,

tsinaasdo'é, dáłdáné, ts'ijishgahe, chíshgagee,
doves, quail, squirrels, robins,

diłt'oshe, tsiidee, lóó'stso, dlǫ́í,
slate colored juncoes, song sparrows, wood rats, prairie dogs,

gah, góóchi dá'ákodeyáí, téjółgayé, tsaⁿdeezé,
rabbits, peccaries, burros, mules,

łį́, náa'tsílidiłhiłí, dibéhé dá'ákodeyáí, ts'isteeł.
horses, buffaloes, mountain sheep,[and] turtles.

'Ádíídíí díík'eh nahidáń.
All of these [were] our food.

'Áí nahí doobaayándzįda.
We are not ashamed of that.

Dá'ághát'égo, nahidáń nahá'ájílaaná'a.
In that way, they made our food for us, they say.

Jooba'éⁿdéłą́í yee'isdahóóka.
Many poor people lived by means of it.

(39.10)
'Ádą́ 'iłk'idą́, joogobago daajiⁿdáná'a.
At that time long ago, they lived poorly.

Ndah "déí 'isdzą́ą́yóí biche'shkéne gózhǫ́go yaahihⁿdíná'a.
But Apache women taught their children well, they say.

Biche'shkénei "dédaahaleeł ndah,
Even when their children became men,

keekéyóí 'isdzáńdaahaleeł ndah,
even when the young girls became women,

díík'eh bik'ehnaakaná'a.
all of them were obedient, they say.

(39.11)
"Shishke'é, doo'jódzįda.
"My child, one does not curse.

Doháń k'eshíⁿdiida.
One hates no one.

Doháń bich'įįlójigoda.
One behaves foolishly to no one.

Doháń baajadloda.
One laughs at no one.

Dohyáabaajó'įįlee'át'édań goshinsį.
One treats with respect those to whom one can do nothing.

Yóósń Tóbájiishchinéń bichįį'itédahdlii.
Pray to God [and] Child of the Water.

Áń dá'gobiłk'eh gok'ehgodaanⁿdá.
We live because of those two.

Niigosjáńí yáí 'ágoił'į."
They made the earth [and] the sky."

daayiiłⁿdíná'a.
they said to them, they say.

(39.12)
Jeekéyóí, 'itł'áyóí naadin 'anshdláánshį "dásá beenádaa'nat'įįł ndah,
Even when the boys [and] girls were twenty five and over,

bitaaí bimaí gózhǫgo daa'yéłts'ąná'a.
they listened well to their fathers [and] mothers.

'Iⁿdaanałį́í, dákogo:
You who are white people, then:

díídíí 'iłk'idą́ ⁿdé doo'ikóńzįdaí gólį̨́ ndah,
even though these ancient people knew nothing,

dá'át'égo koogha gótǫ́ǫ́yéí goos'ą́í bighe'yá
still, inside their poor camps,

dá'át'égo gózhǫ́go biche'shkéne yaahihⁿdíí,
still, they taught their children in a good way

nahí doobégonasįda.
you do not realize this.

Danghéí, chiⁿdáí, gok'azí, goosdoí, joobaí, díík'eh goniińłt'é ndah,
Though hardship, hunger, cold, heat, poverty all overmastered them,

Yóósń Tóbájiishchinéń goche'shkéneí beebich'į̨yájiłti.
they talked to their children about God [and] Child of the Water.

Bikooghą́í baajoogobááyéégo naagoos'ą́ ndah,
Though their camps were everywhere poor,

bighe'shį̨ saanzhóní hiⁿdínzhóní yeeyádaałti.
they inside of them spoke by means of good words [and] good thoughts.

Yeenaatsékees.
They thought by means of them.

Yee'aahihⁿdíná'a.
They taught by means of them.

'Ádíídíí díík'eh dááⁿdí.
All of this is true.

Dálóó'stso téjółgayé daahiiłghał nałdishⁿdíí dásí'ághát'égo dááⁿdí.
It is true just as that which I told you [about] our eating wood rats [and] burros is true.

Note

1 In Hoijer, Harry. 1938. *Chiricahua and Mescalero Apache Texts with Ethnological Notes by Morris Opler*. Chicago: University of Chicago Press. With kind permission from University of Chicago Press. An electronic edition of the corresponding Apache language text and linguistic and ethnological annotation is available at http://etext.lib.virginia.edu/apache/frames/A-E-Lch39.html (accessed November 8, 2012).

Appendix B
Eva Lupe on Her Early Life[1]

Díí ndaahíí hágot'éégo doníína
This White person, how it was long time ago.[2]

"Nágowagohíí baago shiłnágo" shiłndi, 'ákoo
"Tell me all about all it" she said to me, and so.

Shítaahí Russell Cruz hozee łéne.
My dad's name was Russell Cruz.

Áná shimaa adíí Amy Moody.
And my mom's name was Amy Moody.

Áná dónín báhá nidéédaiyóó shimaa adíí Amy Moody hozee.
That is, when she hadn't gotten married yet, her name was Amy Moody.

Shichosááńí Rachel Moody hozee.
My grandmother's name was Rachel Moody.

Áná shichostííńí Benjamin Moody.
And my grandfather was Benjamin Moody.

Kóó áíyé, shimaa adíí łaí shita adíí łiłdidaah ndíhí.
And so, when my dad and my mom got married.

Áíyé bigizhéyóó dohwada bínásht'ila.
From there, in between I don't know anything about it.

Lessons from Fort Apache: Beyond Language Endangerment and Maintenance,
First Edition. M. Eleanor Nevins.
© 2013 John Wiley & Sons, Inc. Published 2013 by John Wiley & Sons, Inc.

Łiłt'íísha nááné 'akóó díí naddhí biłnasht'í doę́ę́da ágot'ééną́.
I didn't even remember what was going on but I'm telling it to this white girl. <laughs>

Shiłdiigo dándí zhǫ́ łą́ą́go dohwaa binasht'ída.
She tells me to tell her all about it, but I don't know a lot about it.

Shitaa adíí 'ashiłdííyóó.
My dad told this to me.

June'í sixteen akónídaa ání ninteenthirty two shiłdíí.
My dad told me that I was born June 16, 1932.

Áná whiteriveryé BIAyéyóóhí august eight nineteenthirtytwo 'ashágo hózee.
At Whiteriver at the BIA my birthday is August 8, 1932.

Kóda áízhéyó zhoshį August ííbíyé nahíí.
That's all I use, the August day, for my birthday.

Naíí dohwaa.
The other one, not at all.

Shitaa adíí daníín hikááyí nłt'éégo ch'a'adí' łéne
My dad died when we were still young.

Tusconyóódi' łé, biná'igodiné'
He died in Tucson, they brought his body back.

Áíyé daaksíí year iíts'aa nágo shimaahí 'ásha'ánágoldó'
There are many years in between that and when my mom died after.

Gózhǫ́ ła' bishódóhaa nłt'éégo binádasht'íí dańdíhí
Some of them I just don't know it really good.

Da'ołtadyóó 'onékał łéne, ádách'itishé.'
We used to go to school when we were little.

Bus dohwaada.
There's no bus.

Daní' 'onékaa łehni'.
We used to walk.

Zhot'éé nagołt'įjh.
It would be really raining.

Ch'íh binádasiłdíígo onékaa łehni'.
We used to walk with a blanket draped over us.

Ná'íícho hat'í' 'ágodzééhí dohwaa bé dá'QQzida. <restrained crying>
We don't even know what "jacket" was

Áná zhǫt'éé dáńdí łehni', 'iłdó'
So we were just poor, also

Łą́ą́st'éégo schóólyóó dáni' onikéé łéne.
There were a lot of us at school, who used to walk.

Zas azhǫ́ chaa dágoyį nekáí łéne, 'akó.
When there was a lot of snow, we used to walk to school, and so.

'Akó 'á'iyé shą'
We used to be poor, it seems.

Dáńdí dágowé nłt'éégo, ná'ołtadyóó díijíí 'izhǫ́łt'éégo nhádá dogh'į́ ałdo' bish'ę.
Truly, if we had been going to school good, today we would be smart, you know.

Dánowá́ dohwada dá finish anołdził daada.
All of us didn't finish school then,

Shíiyóóhíí dáninth grade shisháaniyáá
I just only went to ninth grade

Dohwada at'éhé ná'į́įshisháa.
I didn't finish it

Kodííbi 'áshich'íshí íbiye'hóó,
When I was small

    zhQ t'édat'iyéhyóó łehni', nokée baa dowhaada łaí
    we used to be very poor, when we were little and we didn't have any shoes, and

    diyáágo zhó'dágową t'ééda'chQQ éízhQ.
    all our clothes were just ruined and wearing out.

Łeh náshijeí łehni' íí schoolyóó daa.
That's what we used to wear to school.

Diyáágé naketano ndah da'idééhgo. éí beena ółtag.
Those white people used to give just some clothes, and then, that's what we'd wear to school.

Dółghaiyé nóhwił nakih 'i shódohwaa hayóó hán init'įįh binída émá.
We used to ride, two at a time, on a donkey, nobody used to tease us for that.

Éíyóó o'ąígo,
And then, in the evening,

Lį'aalénaní' keegonaík'é łéne.
After it was over we used to walk home.

Ndííhí dohwaada dágogheé ani' 'ogołtad nt'éégo shį
We weren't lazy, it wasn't hard for us so we just walk home from school.

'Ákó ch'ischoolyóó níka
So we go to school

Dá'och'éda'o'aa.
So we could learn.

Áíyéhí nágowągo
And then, from there on?

Churchyóó nika łéne
We used to go to church

Kó áíyéyóóhíí tółgaiyé nádanobégo bikádanátsiłdíh'go.
We used to go to church on donkey, we have to put an old saddle on it,

Churchyóó nohwii nabikee. <laughs>
We used to ride the donkey to church.

K'ehgo'éí da'áí intiiń nibá'yóó tł'odasł'ǫ́ǫ́ ánádaitl'įįh ndí'.
We used to tie them by the roadside.

Dohwaa háńyaa naghaada łéne.
Back then, nobody would take donkeys if you left them tied up.

'Ákó áíyé 'ąął churchzhį.
So we would leave them there by the church.

Sht'éé nohił ánékéé łéne.
After church we used to ride the donkeys home.

Dágot'éhé nágołdéhé naíí.
We used to play all over the place

Appendix B: Eva Lupe on Her Early Life

Tółghaiyé nóhwił nakiih 'i shó dohwa hayóó hóń init'įįh binída émá
We used to ride donkeys and nobody used to tease us for it.

Dáłiłt'e ndah łéda déégo, nohwaa diyáá.
We used to play really good, that's what we did.

Áíyówoyóóhíí,
But from there,

> *zhitááh didáń didohwada dágową́*
> there was no food anywhere.

"Ration" hozee holį́į́ łéne, paper
There was something they called "ration," paper.

Nałt'aas sidaa foodstamp 'éígat'éé
Papers, there was a book like food stamps

Éí ałdo, bee didáń nách'isdiih éí
This, also, we used it to buy groceries there.

Łąąyóó zhałt'ó' keeye nałch'iłdii
If there were a lot of stamps you could buy shoes with them.

Dágową́, ration 'ágodzaa
All over, everyone had rations.

Binisht'į 'izhǫ́ ałkishchishé.
I remember, when I was little

Éí kodé Whiteriverzhį, about seven mileszhį
From here to Whiteriver it's about seven miles

Ndíího dáń'é 'ákó ani' keh.
We used to walk from here to Whiteriver.

Há'is'ą́ąyé sht'éé akódáne ch'náiłkee łéne.
Then at noontime we'd have to walk back.

Áná nohwiiyóó dagéé dátł'įį łéne.
And we used to live way up somewhere up there.

Peter Nash golį́ní bi'ishaahí shimáá 'adi' áíyé.
Where Peter Nash lives, that's where my mom used to live.

Golį́ní áná kįįh łá' á'á nt'įį łaíí
There was no house there like this one.

Dáh gogha bizhǫ́ bighé' nágo dą́'.
We used to live in the camp, tipi.

Golį́įgó 'iyáá kó dágowá
That's how we lived, here all around.

Nłt'éégo bansdéédaisk'įįns łé' tíní' dohwaa áń'įį'íí tł'į́įdééyé
We used to be kind to each other, we don't steal or anything.

Dohwaa hayóó háń hat'í bijaa nách'idé' neéną'
We were not supposed to take anybody's things, you know.

Dánohwiłdíígo nágoch'éyédast'í' łéne.
That's how they used to teach us.

'Ákó shádohwaa hayóó háń at'į́' bedat'į́h dah.
We never did steal anything from anybody

Biní' appleszhá dage ałiłt'įį anáyóóné.' <laughing>
Except we used to steal apples across the river.

Hástíínń fortytwo hozee bédant'į́į gołdé' binádá ła'ka łéne.
The old man, called "42," we used to steal his apples; and he used to run after us.

Áná zhédándí.
And that's what we used to do.

Áná didáńyóóhíí daadohwaada díh.
Since there was no food, at that time

  łádá ch'édokééł łéne,
  we used to ask for things.

Áń k'ad áń bi tłéédónkee 'óóndaah
We would be told to go over to this one or that one and ask for things, you know?

Éí bǫ́ǫn keeł hádá dageełyóó
Yeah, we used to go over there and ask for things

Kóda hánit'ée łich'odaah! <laughing>
We used to go over there fast as you can!

Tóó ndi' bikáńdah ch'idigo 'ałbįh nách'édédádání'.
They used to wake you and tell you to get some water.

'Ítsaa nakih jolé izáayoo.
Used to have two pails to carry kind of far.

Kó tóó díka'oníka łéne
That's we used to go get that, go get it

Ánáń k'adííyóóíí ii tóóną bich'é 'ádasts'aa de'.
Nowadays we have running water in the house.

Chagashé zhódaada digísé dágot'ééda dohwaadééda áíyé dágonííyá.
Nowadays the kids are lazy, when you ask them to do something, they won't do it.

Ánádo 'aníhííyóó nłt'éégo nádásizį́ łéne.
long time ago we used to work hard, but nowadays the kids are lazy.

Łádá ch'iłéé.
We used to make a lot of bread

Báń idé á'ách'iłé' 'ádé 'ákóó ch'iłdiiyóó 'ách'ilé' <laughs>
When they tell you to make bread, you used to do as you were told.

Ání zhǫ́dohwaa łi' chagashé báń áyíle' íínágozeeda.
Even little girls don't know how to make bread nowadays.

Báń nohí baadánt'óóngee éí zhébáń ádá'itłé' yédágonzį.
Only we older people know how to make bread.

'Ákó dádóółgaiyé dédáń nohwił nakííhye
We even used to run, the donkeys to get food.

Ta'noos gozééhi dédágo 'ádantł'é', łaí ch'įnk'ǫ́ǫzhé
Berries called "ta'noos," we used to go out and pick it up, and wild tomatoes.

Áná k'adyóó abiłdáńdíí iłdó' łáíí.
They're too lazy to pick them up nowadays, and.

Goshk'áń ndéé hozéé 'idágo 'áda'itł'égo tółgaiyé bén da'ideé.
We used to get those wild bananas and bring it back on a donkey.

Shįhla shįhgotsog ashinií shalaadaghą áí.
There was something yellow but I don't know what it was.

Anáą́ áí ah,
And then, from there,

Chích'il ndii bikagonáíka łéne.
We used to go hunt for acorn.

Shiwóóyósááń bikéédasidágo
I used to ride in back of my grandma

Gaagé Bit'ohé gozéé shiłjéí nádáíłt'áhyóó 'onáík'ahgo,
The place they call "crow's nest," that's the place where we used to get acorn,

Lakó shadakwii anidishikąął dédaghaał. <laughing>
I don't know how many days we used to spend a night there, hair getting dirty.

Éí onáíde k'ahde díí hikąął déé hozéé ńnii
We used to pick up what they call "cedar berries" too.

Nádáhitł'áh łéni, nłt'éé, gobiłdii.
My grandma used to boil it for us, it was good, that's how we ate it.

Bee shichósaań dégo nháná dohánáidaageego ndátł'ah.
My grandmother used to get it down off the tree for us to pick it up.

Izis bee nkehgo da'idé há'iłbé é'íshine ch'ikąą
We would fill 25 lb. flour sacks and my grandma would boil them,

   zhéłéne éí.
   that's what we used to do.

Éí "doléélá diłtałí" hozéehí, éí dáłikąązhį́ łéne
This that they call "cedar berries," it tastes just sugary.

'Ákóó łáń dííhíí shódóhwaa dá'binásht'íla.
There was alot, but I don't even remember.

Dadą́' shiłch'ííshn díídéégo,
When we were small,

Łééda kiłk'éés łé' na'éda Na'í'ees síkeego, <laughing>
We used to put on a Sunrise Dance,

'Át'ééhgo adíída dách'ilcháń dííhíí idágo déégo łá' dánánik'áh. <laughing>
We exchanged gifts like flowers, all kinds of different flowers.

Dá' binásht'į deeda áłdó.
Yeah, I still remember that too.

Appendix B: Eva Lupe on Her Early Life

Áná k'adyóhíí shííyóó sixtyfive shiłéégo gots'aa.
nowadays, with me, I'm sixty-five.

Kódíí ndahí West Virginiayé naghahídíí Nelson dííhíí dágots'į.
This White girl is from West Virginia, and they used to know Nelson.

'Ákóó shanádahí 'ak'ehgo
So she comes and visits me so that

   doníína hágo náshiní
   I'm telling her what was going on a long time ago.

   ba'shiłnágodí' aní'.
   I'm telling her about that

"Hago'í" 'átshiłdíí ndééhíí.
"How was it" she told me to talk about it, these Apache people.

Dohwaa dágowa dobínásht'ída.
I don't even remember everything.

Áí zhǫ́daa bínásht'í hagoshą' ládághą
I just don't remember for some reason.

Nahíkée dát'iní ńnaikaa násht'í'. \<laughs>
I remember that we didn't have any shoes.

Ni'á'ijah tóóyoo, 'onékah łéne
We used to go swimming in the water, that's where we used to go

Kóó, dáńdihíízhǫ́ ła'dohwaa binásht'ída.
And there's are many things that I don't remember.

Łą́ągozhǫ́ dágot'éhé nda'inąch'ikaye łéne, dáshit'íishina
We went around all over when we were small, we didn't have to wash dishes.

Ch'ikoo dágolį́į́ Eastfork isdzą́ bi'áshłíní, íbidah 'óoshtah biyé bíłnadágołsht'éé aní
So, I live at East Fork with ladies who I used to go to school with and play with.

Dáh biłkóó biłdaagonshłį́į́ áí.
They're still living with us.

Yané k'adyóó danéí, ánádágołdi'. \<laughing>
When we get together with them, we used to talk about those old days.

Bánádágołdígo hat'éé'oní baa dadloh náits'aago.
we used to talk about it and we used to laugh

Áná k'ádyóóhíí zhódáńdí nłt'éégo dágotł'íí gostok kóne nahátąą
And nowadays we just live good and stay here in a warm place.

Dáá kóne ndíí datóó nohwiłná'ádanoslį́
We even get running water in our house.

Doníínéyóóhí dohwa'ago'atééda ani'
A long time ago it wasn't like that.

Zhot'édaanłt'įįhyé náyindáh ashą' łát'įįdanokígo
We were just poor, and we didn't have nothing,

Nohínáłbił ndahdowhadah łéne, zhǫ́daant'įįda
We never did have any cars or nothing, just poor.

Leona white hozee njaa bitaa 'oné binałbił go
Just only Leona White, Leona's dad used to have a car

Łaíí Joe Quintero hozee.
And he was called "Jo Quintero."

Joe Quintero hastííń 'onáyóó gólį́ tódlį́yóó
Joe Quintero (old man) used to live across from where the spring water is coming out.[3]

Tsįnágháye góyé
He used to drive a wagon

'Oná'iłbą́ą́s 'ózhógozhǫ́ǫ́ éí Ch'ilwoozh dádakee áná Whiteriveryóó
He used to drive it and he used to go to Chilwoozh and Whiteriver.

'Ákó bit'áayą́ nádách'ed godíí łéne
He used to give us a ride.

Shichóstiiní Benjamin Moody hozee.
My grandfather was called Benjamin Moody.

'Ódáshízhǫ́tah iyáawąyóótah ashiłdíígo 'akó biła náshdashǫ́, storeíí
Every time when he wants to go to the store he used to tell me to go with him

Shichósaań díí izis at'éégo shaa iyé náitł'oh łéne.
when I go with him and my grandmother used to give me a lot of sacks

Anádán bídé'tłó BIAt'éda
To put food in them, it was BIA.

'och'é łaí díí łaíí díí shiłédíígo łi' 'ąą
She used she used to tell me "put one kind in here, another in there, stuff like that.

'Á'tą́ągo ní dohwayóó nádéję́ łéne dodáh
We used to get a lot of food.

Áíyóówóyóóhíí bikeé dikáhá nádaidéé łehni'
We used to get shoes too from those same people

   dǫǫzht'éé ádikeé.
   they weren't good but I had to wear them

Nchǫǫ 'égat'éé.
They weren't good.

Dohaa deez ndíhí dikée dadohwaada.
The shoes were not the right size.

Dohaa k'ehgot'éégo bikee dayóó ts'onts'a degá hágo bee ánóch'itaá be nách'oghah bee.
You don't have to be shy about it, you have to leave it on and then walk around with it.

Zhǫ tédant'íhyóó nagh'áh azhǫ́.
We were raised just poor.

Daáni' hége 'ágot'éégo, 'aní zhótaałt'éé dahósisįg 'íghee hágots'aá
When, just not too long ago, I noticed something about how it was.

Shichóstiiń 'ídashíízhǫ́ biłnáł'aázh biłna'ásht'i.
I was the only one that used to go with my grandfather

Tóółghayé bikáná sidaa nasheé shaí gołdoh Ch'ilwozh 'osaht'ash.
I used to ride a donkey and then he used to walk side by me to go to Whiteriver

'Ákóó di'áń naiłdiih hágo dágowa dabǫǫsįyé.
I know I was the one who used to go with him.

Shałdi nádałitsógí tóółghayé bikádaná.
Yeah, he used to tie those food together and put it on the donkey.

"Eva ałdo aíyé sht'égo" aíyé *'onáyi'ołdí'* <laughs>
"Eve, come along too" he used to put me on the donkey and head home.

Dákóó biłashdash.
Yeah the two of us used to come home together.

Dat'ishdí tł'égó shichóstiiní dohwada dobí ná'daghá
I used to be kind to my grandfather because he doesn't see.

Shimaa bikįh nadááhyóó.
When he used to come to my mom's house.

Bits'il got'áá nasgis łéne.
I used to wash his hair.

Hankerchief dách'ęę łéda nits'óo sé bátánasgis.
when he used to carry around the dirty handkerchief, I used to wash it for him too.

Soap bee batánísgis baa clean ánáslé godaá iłts'os.
I used to wash it using soap and then give it back to him.

Díįjįyóó yich'odahńdii' ashłįį́ nágonsee
Today I was thinking about how it was good that I did that for him.

*Dándii, kíł **gózhǫ́ǫ́**, baa **dózhǫ́**, 'abegoz **'ąh** ch'agé ch'**oghaał** gołda*
Truly, you should do good for people, grow with that, walk with that

"niłgózhǫ́" baa ch'adii 'ídágo.
so that "it's good with you" is what people say about you.

Doníina dołjį́įn,
Long time ago, those days.

łą́ni' bich'osdii na
I used to help a lot of people,

dágową
all of them

Notes

1 In this appendix I present the full version of what I present in Chapter 5 as excerpts of Rebekah Moody's account of her early life. Two matters need to be addressed. First, the

name of the speaker is presented here as "Eva Lupe," which is her actual name. I have opted to revert to it here while keeping the pseudonym in the chapter because the chapter excerpts stand in service of my argument, but the speech is presented in full here so that the excerpts might be placed within the whole of Mrs. Lupe's contextualizing rhetoric. And, from the beginning of her speech, Mrs. Lupe is concerned with grounding her account in the condition of having been asked by me, and placing herself in the line of persons that made her life possible and known to her. Prominent in the first passages are the names of her parents and grandparents. She recorded this with me for the express purpose of publishing it in a book, and to interfere with the names as she presented them would go against some of her purposes. Therefore, to maintain the integrity of her speech, I have opted, with her permission, to attribute it to her by name.

2   This is a long text that I have presented for the purpose of placing the excerpts used in Chapter 5 in the full rhetorical progression of Mrs. Lupe's speech. And I am confident that what I present here accomplishes that purpose. Here I recount the method according to which the speech as presented here was documented. Eva Lupe tape-recorded the speech with me in her home. Each passage, or line, was transcribed by me initially. Then with transcript in hand, I played back her speech, passage by passage, with Mrs. Lupe. She listened and translated each sentence into English, re-pronouncing each word to help me refine the transcription. Due to time limitations and because it is not crucial to my argument, I have opted to defer a careful morphophonemic analysis of the components of her speech to future work. Accordingly, when read by Athabaskan specialists my transcription is likely to suffer by comparison with the standards set, for example, by Hoijer (1938) and de Reuse (2006). For this, I beg the readers' patience.

3   The place is now called "Quintero Springs."

References

de Reuse, Willem. 2006. *A Practical Grammar of the San Carlos Apache Language*. With assistance from Phillip Goode. Lincom Studies in Native American Linguistics 51. Munich: Lincom Europa.

Hoijer, Harry. 1938. *Chiricahua and Mescalero Apache Texts with Ethnological Notes by Morris Opler*. Chicago: University of Chicago Publications in Anthropology, Linguistic Series.

Index

Note: page numbers in *italics* refer to figures; those in **bold** to tables.

Africa, 18
agency, 69, 73, 115, 122–5
  ancestor, 123, 124, 175, 177, 199, 208
  denuded, 221, 222
  diyiń, 123
  of families through time, 128
  indigenous, 224
  of traditional stories, 167, 174
Alchesay high school, 13
alcohol abuse, 47, 53
allotment system, 126
alphabet, Apache, 55, 189–90
Altaha, John, 158–9, 166, 167–74, 179, 186–7, 206–7
Altaha, Mary, 158–9, 166, 167–9, 174, 179, 198, 206–7
Alune, 190–1
American Indian movement, 165
Americanist tradition, 143–5, 165
ancestors
  agency extending from, 123, 124, 175, 177, 199, 208
  and coming of age ceremonies, 198–9
  respect for, 63
  and traditional stories, 169–70, 174, 175–6, 177, 179
  voices of, 116, 170, 179
ancestral actions, 115–16, 171, 174
Anishinaabe, 1
anthropologists, linguistic, 71–2, 83, 216
anthropology
  cultural, 52
  symmetrical, 162, 216
anti-immigrant political discourse, 16
Apache Independent Christians, 6–7, 27, 71, 218
  innovation and relevance in the rhetoric of, 200–11
  and school language programs, 186–8, 193, 195, 196–7
"Apache Wars," 23, 129, 132
Apache–English bilingualism, 50, 80, 99
  place-naming, 85, 89–90
Apache-English equality, 60–1
Apache-English inequality, 68–9
Apache-English slang, 27
Apache-English translations, 129–30, 133–42, 167, 168–9, 171–3, 229–48

Lessons from Fort Apache: Beyond Language Endangerment and Maintenance, First Edition. M. Eleanor Nevins.
© 2013 John Wiley & Sons, Inc. Published 2013 by John Wiley & Sons, Inc.

see also Western Apache–English
    language dictionary
archives, as boundary work, 142–3
Arizona, 16–17, 127, 132, 190, 212
Arizona Humanities Council, 12
    grant awards, 13
Asia, 18
Assembly of God, 196
assimilationist policies/ideologies, 4,
    20, 24–6, 49, 73, 120, 122,
    154, 165
Assiniboine language, 190
Athabaskan communities, 62, 64
Athabaskan language conference, 69,
    179–80, 222
audiences, active, 83
authenticity, claims to, 187
authority
    of elders, 48, 59, 67–8, 73
    and the land, 198
    of linguists, 221–2
    of scientists, 220–1
    and silence, 197
    to tackle language problems, 220
autonomy
    indigenous, 89
    individual, 62
avoidance relationships, 194–5

bá'hadziih (oratorical strategy, 'speak
    for them'), 6, 129, 133–43,
    197, 202, 208–9
Bakhtin, Mikhail, 219
Bakhtin circle, 114
Basso, Keith, 23, 24, 63, 68, 80, 81,
    85–90, 93, 97–9, 119, 132,
    175, 194, 200
Bauman, Richard, 105, 144, 193
Begay, Justinn, 56
Belacho, Duncan, 131
Benally, Benjamin, 69, 179–80
Bender, Margaret, 155
Bengay, 81–2, 90, 92, **94**, 95–6, 103
Bible, 7, 114–15, 119–21, 124, 166,
    187, 202, 204–10

knowledge of the body through,
    209–10
bígońłzih (awareness of others), 63
Bik'ehgohidaań (God), 120, 202, 203,
    206–7
bilingualism, 50, 80, 99
    cognitive benefits, 17
Birdwhistell, Ray, 132
Blommaert, Jan, 144
Bloomfield, Leonard, 79
boarding schools, 20–1, 49–50
Boas, Franz, 126–7, 144
body, knowing the, 209–10
boundary voices, 155–62, 164
boundary work, 215
    archives as, 142–3
    indigenous and national cultures,
        192, 193, 195–6
    language documentation as, 113–47,
        224
    texts as, 166–74
    and traditional narratives, 154–62
    Traditionalists and Apache
        Evangelical Christians, 196–8,
        202–11
Bourke, John G., 87–8
Bray, Dorothy, 218
bread-making, 64, 243
Briggs, Charles, 105, 144
Buck, Neil, 154
Bureau of American Ethnology,
    125–6, 127
businesses, tribal, 50
Bylas, Richard, 154, 157

Catholic missions, 132, 196–7, 206
Cedar Creek, 91, 189, 196
child-rearing, 138–41, 234–6, 242
children
    and language loss, 50
    removal of indigenous from the
        extended family, 20–1
    teasing of (socialization process),
        61–3
Chinatown, 92, **94**, 96

Chiricahua Apache, 23–4, 129–30, 132–3, 136, 140–1, 157–8, 229–36
  see also Mithlo, Lawrence
Chiricahua Apache language, 24
Chiricahua and Mescalero Apache Texts (Hoijer, 1938), 128, 129, 130–1, 141
Christian conversion, 123–4
Christianity, 7–8, 166, 186–7, 191
  muscular, 20
  and school language programs, 191, 200–5, 218
  see also Apache Independent Christians; Catholic missions; Lutherans
Cibecue, 168
civil rights movement, 165
clans, 8
  legends, 88
  names, 87–8, 96–7, 103, 107
  politics, 188
clothing, 239, 247
  camp-dresses, 100
Collard, Carl, 12–13
Collier, John, 126
Collier administration, 50
Collier reforms, 20
Collins, James, 21
colonial administration, 165
colonial agents, 122
colonial discourse, 23
colonial encounter, 4, 18, 19, 23, 24, 28, 39, 116, 119, 144, 153–4, 158
colonial histories, 23–4, 28, 211–12
colonial philology, 114–15
colonialism, 5, 18–21, 35, 39, 192
  and differentiation, 24–5
  and exploitation, 18–19
  and language endangerment, 18
  and modernity, 30
  non-plantation settlement, 19, 20
  settlement, 19, 22

coming of age ceremonies for girls (*Na'i'ees*), 12, 99, 123, 198–9, 203, 206–7, 210, 225
communicative competence, 49, 71
communities, 2–5, 7–10, 39–40
  as distinct ethnic entities, 29
  grounded in histories of colonial and postcolonial differentiation, 80
  imagined, 25–7, 104
  marginalization, 22
  place within the national/global social order, 192, 193, 195–6, 211–12
  as constituted through media discourse, 82, 84, 85, 89, 90, 102, 106
  as constituted through place-naming, 82, 85, 89, 90, 106, 107
  as constituted through storytelling, 165
  and the position of indigenous languages, 7, 37
community critiques, of language programs, 9, 40, 67–70
community definitions, 7–8, 37
  acts of, 5
community discourses, 4
community empowerment, 9
community factionalism, 49, 212
community leaders, 132–42, 154
  Traditionalist, 186–7
  see also diyiń
community mediation, 79, 115, 128
  and indigenous languages, 4, 12–40, 60
  and language documentation, 116, 129–30
  and national/global social orders, 212
  polysemic, 118–19
  and salvage documentation, 144
  and text collections, 129–30, 144, 165
  and traditional narratives, 167

community–researcher relationships
  changing, 51–3
  sustainability, 223
computers, 67–8
conflict/controversy
  within language advocacy, 48–9
  surrounding language projects, 12–15, 40
"conjunctural fields," 38–9
contextual variation, "erasure" of, 177
contextualization, 8, 38–9, 61, 131, 168–9, 177–8, 217–20
conversion
  Christian, 123–4
  radical, 167
  rhetoric, 133
Corn on the Cob, **95**, 95–7
cosmological narratives, 156–7, 159–62, 166–7, 169, 189, 205–7
Coyote stories, 6, 152, 154–60, 166–7, 169, 171–8, 179
  "Coyote and Mescal," 159, 167, 176
  "Coyote and the Creation," 156–7, 159–62, 169
  "Coyote and the Shoes," 158–9
  Coyote as "bungling host," 155–7, 159, 162
  "Coyote Reads the Letter as He Sits," 152, 154–5, 158
  Coyote's boundary voice, 155–62, 164
  cycle of, 164
  exposure to, 166–7
  and histories of differentiation, 162–4
  holy nature, 164
  "How Coyote Ruined It," 169, 171–4
  illusion of, 163
  repurposing speech, 175–8
Cruz, Russell, 237, 238
Culley, Marybeth, 54

cultural anthropology, 52
cultural centers, 36–7, 205
  see also museum culture centers
cultural experts, 168–9, 176–7
cultural knowledge, 1
cultural survival, relative nature, 4
culture, as bounded organic system with language, 79–80, 107–8
cycles, 164

dándi (speaking truly), 143
Dark Shadows, 92, **94**, 96, 103
DeClay, Louise, 186, 187, 201–5, 208–10
decolonizing methodologies, 216
decontextualization, 82, 101–2, 105
democracy
  liberal, 20, 21, 49
  representative, 192–3, 211
deprivation, 134–8, 140–2, 229–34, 236, 238–9, 241–7
Diamond Creek, 91, 196
dictionaries, Western Apache–English language, 218–19
difference, 72–3
  see also social difference, accommodation
differentiation, 39
  histories of, 22–5, 73, 118–19, 162–4
Dine language, 222
discourse genres, 82, 106, 107–8, 129–30, 143, 145
discursive action/regimes, multiple modes of, 8
disempowerment, 20, 192
diversity, as natural equilibrium, 35
diyiń, 113, 115–16, 119–20, 123, 128, 152, 154–5, 166–9, 186–8, 191, 194, 205–6
  equivalence with Apache Christian leaders, 202
  healing power, 204, 208, 210
  silence surrounding, 194–5, 197
"doing language," 9

dominant political discourse, 28
dominant political groups, and language shift, 20
DóósdQ'é, 88
Dorian, Nancy, 48, 49
Drake, Francis, 154
drug abuse, 47, 53

East Fork (*Hawóó be'ishęę'e*), 81, 91, 95–6, 167, 196, 245
East Fork Independent Christian Church, 200–1
East Fork Lutheran Mission, 113, 119, 120, 122–3, 132
East Fork Miracle Church, 204
ecology, global linguistic, 18–22
educators, privileging of, 59
Edwards, Silas John, 113–16, 119–22, 123, 127–8, 132, 143, 154, 155, 205–6, 216, 223
elders, 216
  challenges to the authority/legitimacy of, 48, 59, 67–8, 73
  and loss of language subtlety, 69–70
  respect for, 63, 66
  voices of, 116
Electronic Text Center, 130, 131
empowerment, indigenous, 21, 26, 40, 50
Endangered Language Fund, 32
England, Nora, 48
English language, 8
  Apache equality, 60–1
  Apache inequality, 68–9
  Apache versions of school songs and texts, 189
  indigenization, 107–8
  literacy, 120, 121–2
  mass media place names, 5, 79, 80–3, 89, 90, 91–107, **94–5**, 119
  see also Apache–English bilingualism
"English-Only" language movement, 16–17, 20, 25, 29, 120
"English-Only" legislation, 16–17

enslavement, 135–6, 231
entextualization, 175, 176, 216–17, 219
environmental prefixes, 136, 170
equality
  English-Apache, 60–1
  see also inequality
equivocation, 174–5
"erasure," of contextual variation, 177
ethnographic approach, 71–2
ethnology, salvage, 125–7
ethnopoetics, 165–6
evidential particles, 173–4, 177
expert indigenous language speakers, 116, *117*, 117–18, 192, 215
expertise, paradox of, 29, 31, 116
experts
  cultural, 168–9, 176–7
  "inside community member" language, 116, *117*, 117–18, 192, 215
  "outside linguistic experts," 36, 116–18, *117*
  see also linguists
exploitation colonies, 18–19
extended families, 7, 8, 13–14, 28, 37, 40, 60–1, 211
  dismantling of, 20–1
  and language loss, 53
  and language programs, 5
  pedagogies, 60, 61–8, 71, 72, 73, 119
  politics, 188
  positions of elders within, 48
  schools as threat to, 67–8
  strengthening of, 70–1
  and the Sunrise Dance, 225
  and traditional stories, 167–74
extended family-oriented language ideology, 58, 61–6, 67
extended sociality, 174–5

factionalism, 49, 212
family households, 36–7
  see also extended families

family sustenance, acts of, 139–40
Farrer, Claire, 99
Fatty, David, 131
fetishism, 123–4
Fishman, Joshua, 48
flood mythology, 205, 206
Florey, Margaret J., 190
Florida, 157
fluency, 192
  loss amongst young people, 14, 27, 63–5, 99, 187, 193
Fort Apache reservation, Arizona, 2, 3–4, 5, 9–10, 16, 40, 113, 122, 129, 132, 191–6, 211–12, 215, 218, 225
  as complexly mediated indigenous speech community, 27–8
  controversy and suspicion surrounding language projects, 15
  and difference, 23
  establishment, 120
  factionalism, 212
  language ideologies, 66–7
  language loss, 47–8, 66–7, 72
  place-naming, 5, 79, 80
  sacred language, 6–7, 188, 191–2
  traditional narratives, 166, 175, 177–8, 179
Fort Apache Scout (newspaper), 13, 53, 61
Fort Belknap, Montana, 190
Fort Sill, Oklahoma, 132

Gaan (mountain spirit), 210
Gal, Susan, 193–4
gaze, of the addressed other, 138
Genesis, 206
gentes, 87–8
Geronimo, 157
gift exchange, 225–6
Glaskin, Kate, 38
global linguistic ecology, 18–22
globalism, and language endangerment, 18

God, 119, 120, 121, 186, 203, 205, 206, 207, 235, 236
Goddard, Pliny Earle, 127, 154, 166
godiyįh, 189, 191
Gooday, Morris, 206
Goodwin, Grenville, 87–8, 152, 154–5, 157, 158, 191, 194
Goody, Linda, 53, 54
Goshenay, Bobby, 200
Goshenay, James, 200
Gossay, Amy, 64
gotaah (extended family compounds), 91
government
  national, 59
  tribal, 50–1, 58
government institutions, 27–8
gową (households), 91
grant-funded programs, 13, 50, 51, 59
green politics, 220
Griggs, Fiona, 100, 246
Guenther, Rev. Edgar, 119, 120

Handbook of North American Indian Languages (Boas, 1911), 126–7
Hanks, William, 145, 165, 176
Hans Rausing Endangered Languages Project, 32
Harding, Susan, 133
healing, by laying on hands, 204–5, 208, 210
Healthy Nations Ndee Benadesh: The People's Vision, 53–4
hearsay constructions, 171, 173, 174, 177
Heath, Shirley Brice, 153, 178
hegemony, Western, 83
Henderson, Theresa, 201
heteroglossia, 102
Hill, Jane, 48–9
Hoijer, Harry, 6, 23–4, 125, 127–32, 136, 141, 143, 154–7, 160–3, 166, 169, 217, 229–36

"Holy Ground Movement," 114, 116, 118–23, 127–8, 154, 196, 216, 223
Holy Spirit, 204
Hosay, Nick, 47, 55–6, 65, 69
human rights, 21–2
  see also civil rights movement
Hymes, Dell, 49, 71, 122, 128, 129, 144, 165–6, 221
Hymes, Virginia, 129
hypodermic model, 83

identity
  national, 84
  Native, 1, 79, 106
ideology see language ideologies
idolatry, 124
ignorance, 134, 140
imagined communities, and indigeneity, 25–7
immigrants, 16, 17
immigration law SB1070, 17
indigeneity, 8–9, 25–9, 36–7, 73, 80, 187
  and colonial encounters, 39
  and imagined communities, 25–7
  public discourse surrounding, 26
indigenous empowerment, 21, 26, 40, 50
indigenous rights, notion of, 21
inequality
  English-Apache, 68–9
  political, 22
infrastructure, 16, 22, 33, 217
in-law avoidance, 194
innovation
  power in religious discourse, 195–7
  in the rhetoric of Apache Independent Christians, 200–11
  in Traditionalist Apache language rhetoric, 197–200
"inside community members," 36
  as cultural experts, 168–9
  as language experts, 116, *117*, 117–18, 192, 215

institutions, 7–8, 37
integration, devices of, 25
Inter Tribal Council of Arizona, 17
intergenerational relationships, 63–8
Internet, 53, 54–5, 67
interpersonal subtleties of language, 69–70
intertextuality, 83–4, 164
Isdząn Nadleeshé (White Painted Woman), 205, 206, 207

Jesus, 120, 186, 187, 202, 203, 206, 207
job shortages, 50
jokes
  place-naming, 79, 80–2, 85, 90, 91–6, **94–5**, 99–101, 106, 107
  of traditional narratives, 168, 174
Jose, Clyne, 154
Journal of Linguistic Anthropology, 48
Jurassic Park, 81, 82, 90, 95, **95**, 96, 103

Kaut, Charles, 132
Keane, Webb, 123–4, 125, 167, 175, 176, 216, 219
Kenoi, Sam, 129, 130
KNNB (Apache radio station), 27
Knott's Landing, 92, 93, **94**, 96, 103
knowledge
  of the body, 209–10
  cultural, 1
  disavowal of personal, 173
Kroskrity, Paul V., 163

labor, 49
land, 198, 199, 208
  loss of in colonialism, 20
  policy, 126
language
  relationship with culture, 79–80, 107–8
  and religion, 115, 118–24

language advocacy, 2, 3, 7, 9, 28, 38
  conflict/controversy within, 48–9
  and state/national politics, 16
language development, 36
language documentation, 2–3, 5–7, 9, 18–22, 24–6, 36, 38–9, 79–80, 106, 108, 153
  Americanist text collections, 143–5, 165
  in an Apache history of plural mediation, 127–9
  as boundary work, 113–47, 224
  and community mediation, 116, 129–30
  contextualization of, 217–20
  equivocal status as boundary work, 224
  as inventive action, 29
  legitimacy claims, 125
  and the paradox of expertise, 31
  and the paradox of object(ives), 32–3
  possible socialities of, 215–26
  postcritical approach to, 35
  and sacred language, 190
  text collections, 125–45, 165
  and traditional narratives, 179
  see also salvage documentation
language endangerment, 1–2, 9, 26, 29, 36, 38–9, 73, 107, 114–15, 127–8, 130, 216–18, 224
  commonalities with language maintenance, 18–22
  conflict/controversy surrounding, 48–9
  global relevance, 4
  as impingement on established natural state, 34–5
  as improvement on assimilationist policies, 4
  instability of, 220–2
  and mass media use of world language, 83
  and the paradox of object(ives), 32–3
  relevance, 15–18
  salvage, 5, 24, 31
  temporal paradox of, 29–31
  and traditional narratives, 167
language extinction, 1
language heritage, relative nature, 4
language ideologies, 5, 61–7, 72, 107
  conflict of contrasting, 58, 66–7
  extended family-oriented, 58, 61–6, 67
  and sacred language, 191
  school-oriented, 58–61, 66–7
  and traditional stories, 176
language killings, 19–20
language loss, 4–5, 40, 47–74, 216
  and colonialism, 18, 19, 21
  and globalism, 18
  relative nature, 4
language maintenance, 2–3, 9, 15, 26, 36, 38–9, 49, 52, 60, 79, 107, 108
  and classrooms as translational places, 178
  commonalities with language endangerment, 18–22
  as improvement on assimilationist policies, 4
  and internal colonialism, 3
  as inventive action, 29
  involvement of extended families in, 70–1
  and the paradox of object(ives), 32–3
  possible socialities of, 215–26
  postcritical approach to, 35
  relative nature, 4
  relevance, 15–18
  and sacred language, 190, 191–2
  and the subsumation of indigenous languages, 5
  and traditional narratives, 167
  and the work of Keith Basso, 23
language preservation, 18, 59, 60, 218
  critique of, 220

language programs, 2, 5, 9, 36–8, 51–60, 211
  collaborative, 224
  controversy and suspicion surrounding, 12–15, 47–9, 51–61, 67–70
  as equivocal translational places, 178–80
  failed, 52–8, 70, 212, 223, 224
  grant funded, 13, 50, 51, 59
  as institutional loci of political integration, 72–3
  paradoxical nature, 28–34, 35–6, 67, 116
  and politics, 72–3, 222
  and religious leadership, 6–7, 186–93, 195
  see also Ndee Biyati' Apache Language Web Project; school language programs
language research, 36, 60
language revitalization, 2, 115
language rights, 1, 21–2, 26, 36, 165
language shift, 3, 5, 70, 98–9, 107, 127, 211–12, 215–16, 220, 221
  and colonialism, 18, 19–20
  and dominant political groups, 20
language socialization, 62–3
"language wars," 19–20
Latour, Bruno, 32, 34, 220, 222
leaders see community leaders
learning to listen, 61–6, 67
Lee, Robert, 215
Leningrad, 113
letter writing, 121
liberal democracy, 21
liberal democratic settler states, 20, 49
Liebe-Harkort, Marie-Louise, 80
Life Savers, 82, **94**, 96–7, 103
linguistic anthropologists, 71–2, 83, 216
linguistic markets, new, 22
linguists, 215, 219–20, 224
  authority of, 221–2
  dual roles of, 224

  as local language "experts," 59–60
  privileging of, 59–60, 221–2
literacy, 153
  English language, 120, 121–2
  extended family, 61
  indigenous engagements with, 152, 155
living histories, 113–16
local-global social field, 8
local meanings, 4, 22
local political discourse, 28–9
Lohiatala, 190–1
Lonesome Dove, 90, 91–2, **94**, 96, 103
Lowie, Robert, 126
Lupe, Eva, 237–48
Lutherans, 27, 113–14, 116, 119–24, 127–8, 154, 196, 197, 204–6, 208

macro-narratives, 34
  see also language endangerment
mainstream discursive norms, 80, 83
majoritarian language movements, 16–17, 20, 25, 29, 120
majoritarian norms, 16
Malay, 19, 190–1
Mary the Virgin, 206, 207
mass media
  hypodermic model, 83
  and place-naming, 5, 79, 80–3, 89, 90, 91–107, **94–5**, 119
  reception, 7–8
  and shared points of reference, 101–3
  titles, 103
Max Planck Institutes, 32
meaning
  encountering others across contrasting regimes of, 122–5
  local, 4, 22
"means of speech," 122, 128, 143
"measured verse," 165
media, indigenous, 192–3

media discourse, 80–4
  and place-naming, 5, 79, 80–3, 89, 90, 91–107, **94–5**
mediation, 34
  plural/complex, 27–9, 145
  political, 38–9
  see also community mediation
"medicine man talk," 179, 188–9, 195
"medicine world," 187, 188
Merlan, Francesca, 20, 21, 26
Mescalero Apache, 63, 99, 130, 163
Mescalero Apache reservation, 24, 122, 131, 132, 154
metapragmatic discourse, 102–3, 171, 174
Mexican immigrants
  immigration law SB1070, 17
  Spanish-speaking, 16
missionary movements, 113–16, 119–28, 132, 154, 204, 205, 208
Mithlo, Lawrence, 6, 23–4, 116, 125, 128–9, 131–45, 216–17, 226, 229–36
modernism, 34, 35
modernity, 30, 32, 34, 35, 73, 120
modernizing temporalities, 132
Moody, Amy, 237, 238
Moody, Benjamin, 50, 191, 237, 246, 247–8
Moody, Bernadette, 64
Moody, Darlene, 62
Moody, Levy, 65
Moody, Neal, 218
Moody, Pete, 215, 225
Moody, Rachel, 237
Moody, Rebekah, 6, 13–14, 61–2, 64–6, 100–1, 116, 125, 128, 131–5, 137–45, 204, 218
Moody, Robert, 47, 55, 56, 62, 64, 65, 69, 70
moral development, 63, 66
Morgan, Mindy J., 155, 190
Mormons, 196
movies, 103–4

Mufwene, Salikoko S., 18–20
multiculturalism, 73
multiethnic models, 73
museum culture centers, 167, 169, 176–8, 188, 195, 212
Museum of Natural History, 127

nágoldi'é (telling a perceptual surround again), 170, 175
Na'í'ees (coming of age ceremonies for girls), 12, 99, 123, 198–9, 203, 206–7, 210, 225
Nakaiyén ('Mexican Clan'), 16
names
  clan, 87–8, 96–7, 103, 107
  see also place-naming
narratives
  macro-narratives, 34
  oral, 129–31, 133–43
  traditional, 152–80, 189, 191, 205, 207–8
  and clan names, 88
  cosmological, 156–7, 159–62, 166–7, 169, 189, 205–7
  and place-naming, 86, 87, 96, 97–9
  and Traditionalist ceremonies, 167, 170
Nash, Patricia, 54
national government, tribal relations with, 59
national identity, 84
national/global social order, place of indigenous communities within, 7, 37, 59, 82, 84–5, 89–90, 102, 106–7, 165, 192–3, 195–6, 211–12
nationalism, 30
nationalists, 38, 58
nation-state, 22, 29, 32, 35, 73, 106, 108
Native American Church, 196
Native American Graves Protection and Repatriation Act, 168, 208

Native American Language Development Institute, 189
Native American Literature, 166
Native identities, 1, 79, 106
nature/culture hybrids, 34–5
Navajo, 127, 129, 210
Nayenezganí (Jesus), 120, 205, 206
Ndah bik'ehgo (White way of doing things), 67, 68–9, 80
Ndah bik'ehgo yatí' (White (strange) ways of speaking), 23, 63, 68
ndah (White), 14, 23, 24, 37, 38, 73, 80, 101, 121, 129, 130, 133–42, 155, 157–8, 162, 199, 216, 222
ndee (Apache), 24, 38, 73, 80, 121, 129, 158, 162
Ndee bik'ehgo (Apache way of doing things), 66–7, 80
Ndee Bik'ehgo Biyatí' (Apache language), 15, 58
Ndee Bik'ehgo yatí' (Apache ways of speaking), 23, 37, 68, 198, 200
Ndee Biyati' Apache Language Web Project, 13–15, 53–7, 59, 70, 131
Nevins, Thomas, 52, 54, 131, 132, 158, 179
New Deal era, 126
New Mexico, 127, 132
New Testament, 202
Nohwike' Bágowa, White Mountain Apache Tribe Culture Center Museum, 188
norms
  mainstream discursive, 80, 83
  majoritarian, 16
"not listening," 63–6
not-self, 158–9, 162

object(ives), paradox of, 29, 32–4, 116
Oklahoma, 127, 157
"Old Apache Customs" (Hoijer), 128, 133–41, 144, 217, 229–36
Oliver, Bessie, 100

One Step Beyond, **94**, 95
Opler, Morris, 24, 130, 132, 141, 154, 163, 164
"oral literatures," 163, 165
  exclusion from school language programs, 187
  reframing as poetry, 165–6
oral narratives, 129–31, 133–43
oratory, 133–45, 217
Other
  awareness of, 61–6, 69, 158
  encountering across contrasting regimes of meaning, 122–5
  gaze of the addressed, 138
  marking out, 133–4
Otherness
  generativity across boundaries, 38–9
  of the researcher, 128
"outside linguistic experts," 36, 116–18, *117*
  see also linguists
Over the Rainbow, 92, **94**, 96, 97, 103, 105

paganism, 123–4
Paiute, 15
paradoxes, 28–34, 35–6, 193–5, 223
  of expertise, 29, 31, 116
  of object(ives), 29, 32–4, 116
  temporal, 29–31, 116
  of voice and recognition, 211–12
participation
  in family life, 63, 64–6, 70
  political, 106
  and traditional stories, 175
past, Apache, 115–16, 133–43
  active, 199
  agency of, 123
  ancestral, 208
  disrupted and superseded by a modern present, 116, 120, 144
  moral alignment with, 138
  purified, 155
pastors, 201

pedagogical contexts, 59–69, 71, 72
  extended family, 60, 61–8, 71, 72, 73, 119
  school, 60, 61, 66–7, 69, 72–3
Pentecostal Christians, 191, 196, 200, 208, 210
perspective
  differences of, 133–43
  exchanges of, 143, 145
philology, 113, 114, 115, 119–20
philosophy, 1
Pinetop-Lakeside, 104–5
place-naming, 79–108, **94–5**
  Apache English bilingual, 85, 89–90
  Apache language, 85, 86–9, 96–8
  associated with narratives, 86, 87, 96, 97–9
  as borderline genre, 89, 107
  commonalities between English and Apache language, 96–8
  describing physical attributes of a place, 86–7, 93–5, 96–7
  English language mass media, 5, 79, 80–3, 89, 90, 91–107, **94–5**, 119
  established/traditional places, 90–1, 97–8, 100–1
  names applied to people and used as interpretive frames, 87–9, 97–8
  newly built housing developments, 80–1, 85, 90, 91–3, 95–101, 107
  place name genre expectations, 103–5
  speaking with names, 87
  and traditional stories, 170
poetics, of stories, 174–5
poetry, reframing "oral literatures" as, 165–6
points of reference, shared, 101–3
political asymmetry, 71–2
political discourse
  anti-immigrant, 16
  dominant, 28
  local, 28–9
political integration, 22–5

political mediation, 38–9
political participation, 106
political relations, 27, 222
  and boundary work between Traditionalists and Apache Evangelical Christians, 196–7
  extended family, 188
  green, 220
  and language ideology, 58
  state/national, 16
political tension, 188
poor, the, 21
  see also poverty
"portraits of 'the Whiteman'," 80, 99–100
postcritical approach, 34–6
poverty, 134–8, 140–2, 229–34, 236, 238–9, 241–7
  see also poor, the
Powell, John Wesley, 125–6
power
  healing, 204
  of innovations in religious discourse, 195–7
  and recontextualization, 105–6
  of sacred language, 188–92
  and silence, 193–5, 197
Pratt, Richard Henry, 20
prayer, Apache, 141–2, 199, 204
Price, Anna, 154
prison camps, 157
prisoners of war, 131, 132, 157–8
proposition 203 ("Unz initiative"), 16
Protestantism, 20, 123–4, 196, 200, 202, 208, 210
public, alternative, 106–7
public discourse
  reservation, 211
  surrounding indigeneity, 26
punning, 81, 90
"purification," 32, 34

quasi-national entities, 26–7, 31, 79, 108, 118–19, 218
Quintero, Joe, 246

radical conversion, 167
radio, 100, 101–2
Radio Zambia, 102
Rainbow City, 92, **94**, 96–7, 105
rations, 241
reading, 152, 155
realization, deferred, 174
reciprocity, 225–6
recontextualization, 8, 39, 49, 84, 102, 120, 132, 219
   institutional, 60
   and place names, 82, 97, 105–6
   and power, 105–6
   and traditional narratives, 167, 176–7
religion
   fetishistic, 123–4
   and language, 115, 118–24
   see also specific faiths
religious discourse, power of innovations in, 195–7
religious leadership, 179, 205
   Apache Christian, 200–5, 218
   and language programs, 6–7, 186–93, 195, 211–12, 216
representative democracy, 192–3, 211
research diplomacy, 165–6
research relationship, 224–6
   reconfiguring of, 129
researcher–community relationships
   changing, 51–3
   sustainability, 223
researchers
   Otherness of, 128
   position of moral involvement, 131, 136–45
residential schools, repression of Native languages in, 126
resource extraction, 18
rhetoric, 133–42, 144–5
   Apache Independent Christian, 200–11
   Traditionalist, 197–200

rights
   civil, 165
   human, 21–2
   indigenous, 21
   language, 1, 21–2, 26, 36, 165
Riley, Thomas, 154
ritual speech, 175–6
Rush, Clinto, 201

sacred language, 6–7, 188–92, 195, 197, 208–9
Saint John's residential school, 49–50
salvage documentation, 114, 125–8, 144
   critique of, 220
   temporal argument of, 125–7
salvage ethnology, 125–7
Samuels, David, 80, 85, 89, 90, 93, 99, 189, 191–2
San Carlos Apache reservation, 16, 23, 27, 50, 127, 129, 189
   and the Holy Ground Movement, 122
   and place-naming, 89, 93
   and traditional narratives, 154–5, 157
   and written language, 121
Sapir, Edward, 127, 215
Saussure, Ferdinand de, 114
saving languages, 35–6, 218, 221–3, 224, 226
SB1070, 17
SB2281, 16–17
school language programs, 5, 9, 25, 36–7, 40
   alternatives to, 70–3
   ambivalence towards/criticisms of, 47–9, 52, 54–8, 60–1, 67–70
   and the empowerment of alternate leadership, 187
   and the Independent Apache Evangelical Christian Church, 186–7
   materials, 54–6, 189–90

religious restrictions on school
    programs, 6–7
silence on traditional stories and
    songs, 187, 189–93, 195, 208,
    211–12
  and Traditionalists, 186–92
  and underrepresentation, 192–3
school-oriented language ideology,
    58–61, 66–7
schools, 7–8, 238–40
  communicative disjuncture with
    communities, 178–9
  as communicative interface with
    communities, 153
  local cultural experts in, 168–9
  and the Ndee Biyati' Apache
    Language project, 13
  pedagogy, 60, 61, 66–7, 69, 72–3
  power inequalities with families,
    68
  and proposition 203, 16
  and SB2281, 16–17
  social context, 49
  and traditional narratives, 167,
    168–9, 176–9
  as translational places, 178–80
  see also boarding schools; residential
    schools, repression of Native
    languages in
"Science," 220–1
scientists, authority of, 220–1
Scollon, Ron, 129
Scollon, Suzanne, 129
self
  confrontation with the not-self,
    158–9, 162
  from the other's point of view,
    134–8, 143
"shifters," strategically deployable, 35
Shoshone, 15
silence, 187, 189–95, 197, 208,
    211–12
  and authority, 197
  as expression of respect, 194
  as strategic defence against the
    powerful, 193–4
Silverstein, Michael, 72, 102, 175
Smith, Charles, 130, 156, 169
Smurfville, 81, **95**, 96, 103
snake song, 186
social context, 49
social difference, accommodation, 21
social embeddedness of language, 49
social order, 79
  national/global, place of indigenous
    communities within, 7, 37, 59,
    82, 84–5, 89–90, 102, 106–7,
    165, 192–3, 195–6, 211–12
sociality, extended, 174–5
socialization
  and language programs, 5
  teasing as, 61–3
social-scientific reflexivity, 72
sociocultural order, and traditional
    narratives, 153–4
sociopolitical order, 4
songs, Traditionalist, 186, 189, 191,
    198, 205–6, 207–8
Southern Athabaskan communities, 64
Spanish, 129
speech
  "means of speech," 122, 128, 143
  repurposed, 175–8
  ritual, 175–6
spiritual leaders *see diyiń*
Spitulnik, Debra, 83–4, 101–3
stigmatization, 178
  of indigenous culture, 20
  of indigenous language, 20, 26
storytelling, 152–80
  and cycles, 164
  distinct print literary market, 165
  ethnopoetics, 165–6
  as extended sociality, 174–5
  object-like nature, 175, 176
  poetics of, 174–5
  and research diplomacy, 165–6
  as threshold genre, 176

storytelling (cont'd)
  and Traditionalist ceremonies, 167, 170
  see also Coyote stories; narratives; Traditionalist ceremonies, and traditional stories
Strathern, Marilyn, 22, 143
structural linguistics, 114
Sun Dance ceremony, 190
Sunrise Dance (coming of age ceremonies), 12, 225, 244
Susan, Pete, 200, 201
sustainability, 215–26
Swahili, 19
symmetrical anthropology, 162, 216

teasing (socialization process), 61–3
technocratic expertise, 33, 34–5, 73, 80, 108, 118
technology, threat of, 67–8
Tedlock, Dennis, 165
television shows, 100, 101, 103–4
temporal frames, 173
temporalities, 128
  extended, 174
  modernizing, 132
  paradox of temporality, 29–31, 116
  and political relations, 116–18, 128
  writing at the boundary of dueling, 119–22
Terralingua, 32
Thieberger, Nicholas, 118
"thing-y," 175
tipi, 242
Tithla, Bane, 154
Tolowa, 21
toponyms, 87–8
Torres, Horace, 130
Town Bemba, 19
trading posts, 154–5
tradition, notion of, 30, 143–4
traditional narratives/stories, 152–80, 189, 191, 205, 207–8
  and clan names, 88
  cosmological, 156–7, 159–62, 166–7, 169, 189, 205–7
  and place-naming, 86, 87, 96, 97–9
  and Traditionalist ceremonies, 167, 170
Traditionalist ceremonies, 187–90, 194, 203–5, 210–11
  and traditional stories, 167, 170
  see also Na'i'ees (coming of age ceremonies for girls); Sun Dance ceremony; Sunrise Dance (coming of age ceremonies)
Traditionalist leaders, 186–7
  see also diyin
Traditionalist songs, 186, 189, 191, 198, 205–6, 207–8
Traditionalists, 6–7, 27, 113–14, 115–16, 119–24, 127–8
  and Apache Evangelical Christians, 196–8
  innovation and relevance in Apache language rhetoric, 197–200
  and school language programs, 186–93, 195, 211
translanguage, 145
translation, politics of, 106
translation pairs, 89
tribal councils, 50–1, 57
tribal government, 50–1, 58
Tséé Hadigaiyé (Line of White Rocks Extends Up and Out), 86, 87
Turkey Creek, 127
Tuzhį' Yaahighaiyé (Whiteness Spreads Out Descending to Water), 86
Two Steps Beyond, **94**, 95

underrepresentation, and school language programs, 192–3
United Nations Declaration on the Rights of Indigenous Peoples, 21–2
United Nations Educational, Scientific and Cultural Organization (UNESCO), 1, 32

United Nations Universal Declaration
    of Human Rights, 21
Urban, Greg, 175

Valor, Palmer, 154
value systems, 1
verb stems
  dual, 136
  singular, 136
video-making, 53–4
Vizenor, Gerald, 1, 2, 9, 26, 31, 79,
    106, 145, 215, 217
voices
  alternative, 144–5
  of ancestors, 116, 170, 179
  boundary, 155–62, 164
  dead/dying, 115
  of elders, 116
  relevant, 115, 116
  vanishing, 221
Voloshinov, V.N., 113, 114, 115, 132

Wagner, Roy, 79
Warm Springs reservation, 166
Washoe, 15
Weiner, James F., 38
Western Apache–English language
    dictionary, 218–19
Western hegemony, 83
White *see ndaa* (White)

White majoritarian norms, 16
White Mountain Apache, 3–4, 127
White Mountain Apache Lands, 3–4
White Mountain Apache Reservation,
    3, 49, 51–8, 60
  and place-naming, 83, 86–7, 89–90,
    93, 102, 107
  and traditional narratives, 154,
    157–8, 166
  and traditional texts and religious
    leadership, 189
Whiteriver, 81, 91–3, 105, 180, 200,
    238, 241, 246–7
wordplay, 96–7, 100–1
world languages, dominance of, 83
worldview, 1
writing, 113, 120–1, *121*
  "experts" on, 59
  letters, 121
  as symbol of temporal rupture, 120

young people
  issues of, 47, 53–4
  and language loss, 47–8, 50, 51, 57,
    63–6, 69, 99
  loss of fluency amongst, 14, 27,
    63–5, 99, 187, 193
  and traditional narratives, 168

Zambia, 83–4, 101–2

www.ingramcontent.com/pod-product-compliance
Lightning Source LLC
Chambersburg PA
CBHW060311240426
43661CB00059B/2726